FASCINATING RHYTHM

BATHING IN THE SUNSHINE

(The Sunshine of My Baby's Smile)

Lawrence Wright

PRINTED IN ENGLAND

FASCINATING RHYTHM

Peter Cliffe

Foreword by Brian Rust

EGON PUBLISHERS LTD

First Published in 1990 by
Egon Publishers Ltd
Royston Road, Baldock, Hertfordshire SG7 6NW
England

ISBN 0 905858 49 2

Designed, typeset and printed by
Streetsprinters
Royston Road, Baldock, Hertfordshire SG7 6NW
England

IVOR NOVELLO.

AUTHOR'S AND PUBLISHER'S NOTE
Because of the age of the photographs used herein as
illustrations, none less than 50 years old, and many much
older, it has proved impossible to ascertain original
ownership. We offer our sincere apologies if any copyright
has been unwittingly infringed.

CONTENTS

DEDICATION

TO MARIE
whose unfailing encouragement made it possible,
I dedicate this book with love and gratitude.

Foreword

The heyday of popular dance music in America and Europe was loosely the two decades separating the end of World War One and the beginning of World War Two. The band leaders, and often the musicians, became household names – almost household gods – and their appearances on stage, radio and records spread their art among people who could never hear them in their West End hotel ballrooms, supper clubs and nightspots.

Their story is as fascinating as that of any fiction; as a keen admirer of their music from the ripe old age of five, I would go further and say without exaggeration that no fiction, however well-written, has ever held my attention as has the true-story account of the beginning, the growth and (alas) decline and fall of the dance bands of those years.

This book tells that story, in detail and with valuable attention to accuracy, something for which Peter Cliffe is well-known among those interested in all forms of twentieth century popular music. He is not content to list catalogues of hard facts, but surrounds the telling of them with rivettingly readable prose. If you wish to know when this leader was born, or that member of his band moved to some other band, you will find it here. Nor are the composers of dance music omitted; Mr Cliffe gives them the same treatment (and I know of nowhere else I can find such detail). Also, he quotes details of the recordings that merit this attention.

Peter Cliffe has done me the honour of asking for a Foreword to his fascinating work, and thus I was privileged to read it through in manuscript. It might be assumed that after so many years as a record collector, I would find little I did not know. On the contrary, I found much that was new . . . about this fascinating rhythm that caught the hearts and feet of millions in those strange days between the wars.

Brian Rust

Acknowledgments

Many people helped generously with the preparation of this all too inadequate review of the popular music heard between two World Wars. It is no more than simple courtesy to place on record their kindness.

Brian Rust, who rarely has much free time at his disposal, answered so many questions I feel a valued friendship must have been sorely tried at times. Without his encylopaedic memory and selfless co-operation, this book would have been the poorer. He has contributed a Foreword and read the manuscript, offering suggestions, making contributions, and providing additional information. I must emphasise, however, that should any errors have crept in, the blame is solely mine.

I wish to thank Chris Hayes for information on Lawrence Wright and Sam Browne; and Lawrette Williams (*née* Wright) for additional information on her father; Clara de Groot for her hospitality and much help with the section on her father, David de Groot; Maisie Stewart for writing to me about her father, Archibald Joyce; Cavan O'Connor for telling me about himself and Maurice Elwin; Anne Ziegler and the late Webster Booth for a charming and informative letter; Peter Tanner for biographical details of Chick Bullock; Duncan Campbell of Lindy's for greatly increasing my knowledge of Layton and Johnstone; Joyce Stone for lending me *Lew Stone – A Career in Music*, and for some delightful telephone conversations.

In addition, I owe debts of gratitude to Joe Daniels for the loan of a magnificent photograph; to Tiny Winters and Anne Lenner for their friendly and helpful letters; Judy Shirley for help by telephone; Roy Faiers for explaining who actually composed *Old Father Thames*; to Malcolm Knapp and Alan Redmond for gifts of invaluable old magazines and newspapers; and to John Street of Egon Publishers for his personal interest and help with this book.

My gratitude to my wife is boundless. Without Marie's tolerance of my collectomania and hours spent at the typewriter, no book would have been possible.

Finally, I hope all who dip into these pages will experience something of the pleasure I derived from delving into a musical past that did so much to brighten the uncertain years of the Twenties and Thirties.

Peter Cliffe
Hitchin: July, 1990

Chapter One

1920–21

'Ain't We Got Fun?'

On January 1, 1920, the *Evening Standard* informed its readers that the New Year had been hailed in London 'with a rattle of jazz drums and a frenzy of syncopation.' The newspaper thus set the scene for a colourful decade sometimes styled the Jazz Age, because many people thought that jazz and syncopated dance music were the same thing.

It was the kind of comment which later amused or irritated people who realised that jazz was played by Louis Armstrong, Bix Beiderbecke, Johnny Dodds, Mezz Mezzrow, Jelly Roll Morton and King Oliver, and not by America's Club Royal Orchestra, Art Hickman, Roger Wolfe Kahn and Waring's Pennsylvanians, or our own Bert Ambrose, Jack Hylton and Savoy Orpheans.

One could hardly blame the general public for such confusion. The instrumentation was similar; a steady, pulsating beat drove a good dance band as surely as one playing jazz; and there was some interchange of tunes. But the treatment differed, and nobody hearing a record by King Oliver's Creole Jazz Band was likely to mistake it for one by the Benson Orchestra of Chicago. It wasn't what they did, it was the way that they did it!

But dance music in the Twenties was always jazz to the popular press, and record companies hardly helped matters. The 'Queen's' Dance Orchestra was labelled Jack Hylton's Jazz Band by Zonophone in 1921, even when it played waltzes; and the Original Dixieland Jazz Band, one of the few examples of the genuine article to enter the His Master's Voice catalogue, went into the Dance section.

At this time, hardly any true jazz records were available, because the leading record manufacturers didn't regard them as a commercial proposition. They were undoubtedly right. Most buyers wanted their dance music to be lively, and were quite happy to hear some hot licks from trumpet or saxophone, but collective improvisation was different. It was too loud, and where was the tune? All American companies recorded jazz, but it was never produced in large quantities, and thus, such records now command high prices and are treasured by collectors.

1920 was not really a turning point in popular music, for all the changes which took place. That occurred between 1910 and 1913, when ragtime reached its peak, delivering a jolting set-back to the stately waltzes, schottisches and quadrilles of a more decorous age. It was popular ragtime, of course, served up by Tin Pan Alley, and not the exquisitely fashioned piano rags of Scott Joplin, Louis Chauvin and others, with which few people were familiar. The big record companies had shunned them too!

Ragtime inspired such delightful songs as Irving Berlin's *Alexander's Ragtime Band*, and many very bad ones, before it was swept away by the Great War; but it had been featured in some popular New York and London revues, thus making a lasting impression.

Wartime songs were often maudlin or jingoistic. Afterwards, people wanted no reminders of carnage and austerity. Musical taste was ripe for change, and the fox-trot became the catalyst.

The fox-trot followed hard on the heels of ragtime, and in America was publicised by Vernon and Irene Castle, a husband-and-wife dancing partnership who demonstrated it in 1914. The same year it was danced in London, but there was no stampede to the 400 Club in Bond Street, to hear it played by violinist-bandleader Stroud Haxton. It took the theatre to introduce the fox-trot to a wider audience.

Irene Castle gave up her dancing career in 1917 after her husband Vernon (whose real surname was Blythe) died in an aeroplane accident.

That happened the following April, when *The Passing Show of 1915* opened at the Palace Theatre, a high-spot of this famous revue being *Ballin' the Jack*, by the talented black composer Chris Smith. As duetted by Elsie Janis and Basil Hallam (who recorded the song for HMV), it brought the house down. Before long, the fox-trot became all the rage, and it held its own for about 40 years.

Over in America, KDKA of East Pittsburgh, Pennsylvania, was the first radio station to broadcast regularly, beginning in November, 1920. It could be picked up by British crystal sets. By 1924 the States had 1105 stations on the air, many only short-lived. Britain's more cautious approach avoided the same chaos, but progress here was rapid. In June, 1920, Dame Nellie Melba made an historic, half-hour broadcast of songs from Marconi's Writtle studio.

Irene opened in April at the Empire Theatre, with 24-year-old Edith Day, fresh from her success at the Vanderbilt Theatre in New York. She captured everyone's heart with *Alice Blue Gown*, Joseph McCarthy's intelligent and amusing lyric well-matched by Harry Tierney's lilting waltz melody. It lingered on into the early years of World War Two, and was heard again in the mid-seventies.

Tierney was born in Perth Amboy, New Jersey, on May 21, 1894, studied at New York's Virgil Conservatorium of Music, and became a concert pianist for ten years. He dabbled in ragtime composition, creating *Checker Board Rag, Fleur-de-Lys Rag* and *Black Canary Rag* in 1911, and *The Tierney Rag* in 1913, but *Irene* was his first full score. He died in 1945, the year in which *Irene* was revived at His Majesty's Theatre. It was again revived at the Adelphi in 1976.

Alice Blue Gown was much recorded, and the version by Joseph C. Smith's Orchestra appeared on HMV. Smith, an American violinist whose sweet but sometimes quite peppy dance band was formed during the war, recorded for Victor, much of whose catalogue was issued here by the Gramophone Company under a special agreement. He came to London in 1925, dropped out of sight not long afterwards, and died in 1969.

Back in 1918, McCarthy wrote the lyric for a song which was still popular here in 1920. The melody of *I'm Always Chasing Rainbows* was filched from Chopin's Fantasie Impromptu in C Sharp Minor and credited to Harry Carroll. The classics were often mined by song composers, few of whom had the grace to admit the source of their tunes.

Carroll, who was born in Atlantic City, New Jersey, on November 28, 1892, received no musical training. He wrote a number of individual songs, but also composed for Shubert musicals and the Ziegfeld Follies.

I'm Always Chasing Rainbows was recorded by the Mayfair Dance Orchestra towards the close of its long existence. Assembled from session musicians, it was simply a 'house' ensemble for HMV, committing to wax a host of long-forgotten tunes from 1912 to 1922.

In 1920 it also recorded Haven Gillespie's *I'm Getting Tired of Playing Second Fiddle*, from *The Whirligig*, a Palace Theatre revue of 1919 in which it was sung by Anita Elson. A fox-trot, it was recorded on a 12-inch disc, a practice soon to cease, few later dance tunes exceeding two and a half minutes' duration.

Although the fox-trot soon led the way, waltzes remained very popular. They were particularly favoured by the earlier style of dance orchestra, about to lose ground to the brass and saxophone dominated bands, but still much in demand for Hunt Balls, 'coming out' dances and other Society functions.

Pre-eminent among them was Joyce's Orchestra, directed by Archibald Joyce, who was well-named the English Waltz King, as anyone hearing such ecstatic melodies as *The Passing of Salome, Dreaming, A Thousand Kisses* and *Love and Life in Holland* would really agree.

Born in Paddington on May 25, 1873, Joyce began as a pianist at the Oxford Music Hall in the heyday of Marie Lloyd and Dan Leno. Somehow he found the money to assemble a large dance orchestra and never looked back. In 1912 he made a batch of records for HMV, but late in 1920 he began to appear on the newly introduced Aeolian Vocalion label.

The Vocalion recordings by Joyce included two fox-trots, one by a composer then little known. *Swanee*, first heard in 1918, with a lyric by Irving Caesar, was George Gershwin's first successful song and composed for Al Jolson. *You'd be Surprised* came from Irving Berlin, whose career had begun in 1907, when he wrote a lyric for *Marie from Sunny Italy* to a tune by Nick Nicholson, pianist at Pelham's Cafe in New York's Chinatown. In America, *You'd be Surprised* was considered rather daring, quite surprising when one considers that Berlin was never one to sully his reputation with risqué material.

The Vocalion label was discontinued in 1927, but Joyce was still composing early in the Forties. He died in his 90th year on March 21, 1963, some of his sparkling melodies surviving as old-time dance music.

Early in the Twenties it was light orchestras and 'house' bands which recorded most of the waltzes here. Mary Earl's *Beautiful Ohio*, composed in 1918, but still going strong two years later, appeared on HMV by de Groot and the Piccadilly Orchestra, a very popular little salon-type ensemble at the Piccadilly Hotel Grill; and on Winner by the Bohemian Band, a studio aggregation also known as the Royal Court Orchestra.

Mary Earl was actually Robert A. Keizer, who also called himself Kathleen A. Roberts and Bob King. Born in 1861, he became a successful songwriter in 1903, and continued to compose, sometimes in co-operation with others, until his death in 1932.

Sol P. Levy's *That Naughty Waltz* had a lyric added later by Erwin Stanley. Its chirpy little melody appeared on Zonophone, played by the Black Diamonds, the label's 'house' military-style band.

But in Britain, the man who made more money out of waltzes than anyone else was Lawrence Wright. Born in Leicester on February 15, 1888, the son of a violin teacher, he became known as 'The Daddy of Tin Pan Alley'. At eighteen he sold song sheets from a market stall, but discovered he too had the gift of writing music which people enjoyed.

In 1912 he moved to London, establishing his own publishing house in Denmark Street, and poured out songs, originally

For twenty years de Groot provided exquisitely performed light orchestral music in the Piccadilly restaurant and grill.

Lawrence Wright: From a market stall in Leicester to 'The Daddy of Tin Pan Alley'.

under his real name, but later using various others. He
selected good lyricists, turning particularly to Edgar Leslie
and Archie Gottler.

Throughout the Twenties, Wright created hit after hit,
aided by a very real understanding of publicity; and during
the Thirties he remained popular. In addition, he produced
On With the Show at Blackpool from 1925 to 1956. He died
there on May 19th, 1964.

For *Wyoming*, published in 1919, Wright called himself
Gene Williams. His lyricist was Gene McCarthy, possibly
also an assumed name. This well-loved waltz was recorded
by the Mayfair Dance Orchestra.

Delilah, another waltz, was recorded by Winner's Bohemian
Band. On this occasion, Wright became Horatio Nicholls, the
name with which he was most associated. It was derived from
his brother Horace, and his mother's maiden name Nicholls.
First published in 1917, and lingering on, *Delilah* had no
lyric.

Edison Bell launched The Winner in 1912, aiming at the
popular market. For many years it depicted a racehorse
passing the grandstand, the jockey clutching a record in
either hand. The definite article was dropped early in the
Twenties and the label underwent various colour changes,
the horse and jockey motif finally disappearing. When F. S.
Tull, the Receiver, put Edison Bell up for auction in January,
1933, Decca became the new owners, discarding Winner two
years later.

By 1920, what is now regarded as the typical configuration
of an early Twenties dance band, namely, small brass and
reed sections, probably a violin, a banjo, and usually a brass
bass to hold the beat steady, had come into being. Two
particularly innovative leaders were attracting considerable
interest on the Pacific Coast; one already at the zenith of his
popularity, the other on the brink of international fame. They
were Art Hickman and Paul Whiteman.

Hickman had been fronting Californian bands since 1913,
and was a pioneer of the hotter style of dance music. He was
not a jazz musician, although a Columbia publicity blurb of
February, 1920, would have us believe otherwise, but he did
record such bona fide jazz compositions as W. C. Handy's
Hesitating Blues. Long established in San Francisco, he
moved to Los Angeles in 1921, having been invited to open
the Coconut Grove Restaurant in the prestigious Ambassador
Hotel.

His was typical of a then somewhat frantic style, probably rooted in ragtime, and suffering from a common disadvantage of the time. Columbia might boast: 'Without being able to read a note of music – indeed, all of Hickman's nine musicians play entirely by ear – Hickman has a keener sense of counter melody, tempo and rhythm than many a conservatory graduate.' That also held true of any proficient New Orleans or Chicago jazz unit, but jazz musicians began to recognise the limitations imposed by an inability to read music – and jazz moved on.

Announcement
Exclusive Columbia Records
Art Hickman's Orchestra

WIZARDS of Jazz are Art Hickman's orchestra from the St. Francis Hotel, San Francisco, who have recently shown li'l old New York and the rest of the U. S. more about Jazz gyrations than even that home of the Jazz ever imagined.

Through special exclusive arrangements the Columbia Company brought Art Hickman and his sybarites of super-syncopation from the Pacific Coast to make a series of records.

Jazz is a chemical compound of Art Hickman. Without being able to read a note of music—indeed all of Hickman's nine musicians play entirely by ear—Hickman has a keener sense of counter melody, tempo and rhythm, than many a conservatory graduate.

The exclusive Columbia records of Art Hickman's orchestra announced in this supplement are the most wonderful examples of genuinely instinctive, foot stimulating, blood exhilarating, dance *making* Jazz records ever offered to the public. The first note plunges you into an hilarious abandon from which there is no rescue 'til the record stops.

Taken from a Columbia (New York) records supplement of February, 1920, the florid prose being typical of its time.

So indeed did dance music. Other pace-setters, notably Paul Specht, Isham Jones and Paul Whiteman, were coming to the fore, and they knew the value of disciplined performance and good arrangements.

But Hickman's contribution to dance music was significant, and his records are of great interest, particularly when he used a string bass where a brass one was more usual. Unfortunately, he soon became a spent force, retiring before the Twenties were out. He died at San Francisco in 1930, long remembered for his composition *Rose Room*.

Art Hickman's star might wane, but Paul Whiteman's was in the ascendancy. With thinning hair, tiny moustache, moon face and considerable bulk – he eventually reached 20 stone – he made an imposing figure, his ideas being of the same stature. He gave dance music discipline and polish, demanding and getting respect for his men wherever he played.

His title King of Jazz was absurd, for he was no jazzman, but he did employ such jazz giants as Bix Beiderbecke and Frankie Trumbauer late in the Twenties, paying them well and giving them a measure of security. A good-natured, generous man, he was 'Pops' to those who joined his bands.

Paul Whiteman was born in Denver, Colorado, on March 28, 1890, the son of a music teacher. As a young man he played violin for the Denver Symphony Orchestra, and when he moved to California he joined the San Francisco Symphony Orchestra. On the West Coast he discovered ragtime, finding it raucous but exciting.

When America went to war in 1917, Whiteman joined the Navy and directed a large band. In 1919 he formed a small dance combo, gradually establishing himself in San Francisco, but became dissatisfied with a purely local reputation and decided to move east.

By the summer of 1920 he was at the Palais Royal on Broadway, but soon transferred to the new Ambassador Hotel in Atlantic City, New Jersey. There he came to the attention of the Victor Talking Machine Company of Camden, and was asked to make some records.

His first two, made in August, were *The Japanese Sandman*, a charming novelty by Raymond B. Egan and Richard A. Whiting, and *Whispering*, which required the combined efforts of Richard Coburn, Vincent Rose, and John and Malvin Schonberger. Easily recognisable fox-trots, they were entirely instrumental, the day of the vocalist having yet to dawn.

Victor and HMV coupled these recordings, and sales came close to two million copies. The playing was zestful, with a piquant touch of ragtime, and the music well arranged, thus arousing intense interest.

The arranger was Ferde Grofé, who had spent ten years playing viola for the Los Angeles Symphony Orchestra before joining Whiteman in 1919. Born Ferdinand Rudolph von Grofé in New York on March 27, 1892, he became Whiteman's regular pianist and arranger, also finding time to compose suites and concert music.

Paul Whiteman in November, 1920, becoming a big man in every way.

It was Paul Whiteman who premiered Grofé's *Grand Canyon Suite* at Chicago in November, 1931, launching a work which has deservedly become a classic. Grofé, still active in 1950, wrote the incidental music for the film *Rocketship X-M*, starring Lloyd Bridges. He died at Santa Monica, California, in 1972.

Whiteman's dance and show band gradually became bigger; his influence on our own Jack Hylton was profound. His best-selling records gave the new style of dance music a terrific boost and, with others eager to take up the challenge, an era of wonderful entertainment was assured.

* * *

Tin Pan Alley could be singularly insensitive at times. When Enrico Caruso died in August, 1921, George Walter Brown, George A. Little and Jack Stanley wrote *They Needed a Songbird in Heaven, So God Took Caruso Away*, hardly a tasteful tribute to the greatest operatic tenor of all time.

Better taste was revealed when *Sally* came to the Winter Garden Theatre in September, 1921, with a score by Jerome Kern, and 23-year old Dorothy Dickson in her first leading role. B. G. 'Buddy' de Sylva wrote a lyric for *Look for the Silver Lining*, one of the best songs in the show.

Sally was a pleasant but quite conventional musical comedy, whereas a novel and daring stage experiment began in June, when *The Co-optimists* opened at the Royalty Theatre. The traditional venue of a pierrot troupe had long been the seaside; it required great courage to bring such entertainment before a sophisticated West End audience. But the cheery informality of *The Co-optimists* paid off, and in various editions brightened the London scene for ten years.

Its success owed much to Melville Gideon, the singer and pianist, who provided more than a hundred of his own songs, but genial Davy Burnaby made a splendid compère, others in a changing but always superb company including Laddie Cliff, Phyllis Monkman, Betty Chester, Elsa Macfarlane, Austin Melford and Stanley Holloway.

The Co-optimists had an early hit with *Coal-Black Mammy*, written by Laddie Cliff and composed by Ivy St. Helier, a popular actress and singer. Born Ivy Aitchison, she took her stage name from her birthplace in Jersey. As a fox-trot, her song was the first recording made by the New York Havana Band, directed by Bert L. Ralton.

Dorothy Dickson, the former dancer from Kansas City, Missouri, who made her London debut in June, 1921, and stayed to become the leading lady of many West End productions.

Stanley Holloway, stage and screen star, renowned for his humorous monologues.

Ralton was with Art Hickman until 1919, leaving to front his own band. Whether he played in Cuba is uncertain, but in 1921 he came to London, securing a Columbia recording contract, and installed a small band at the Savoy Hotel. Ralton played clarinet, and soprano and alto saxophone; his violinist was Cyril Ramon Newton, and his pianist John Firman (brother of Bert and Sidney) who later directed 'house' music for Zonophone.

In 1920, the Queen's Hall Roof, a Society venue with a floor show patronised by the Prince of Wales, opened in Langham Place. The 'Queen's' Dance Orchestra, a seven man unit, began to record for HMV the following year. There was no official leader, that honour (unpaid) being conferred upon the pianist, as only he could arrange their music.

Conceivably, the other players failed to appreciate the significance of such a move, but Jack Hylton undoubtedly understood. When 'directed by Jack Hylton' appeared on record labels the public accepted him as a bandleader and he was shrewd enough to capitalise on it. At the end of 1922, Hylton formed his own band, and his meteoric career began.

Until then his life had followed a rather erratic pattern, always on the fringes of show business. At fifteen he conducted the orchestra for a touring pantomime, and just before the outbreak of war was organist in a Stoke Newington cinema. The end of hostilities found him in France as assistant pianist for a concert party entertaining troops at Wimereux Casino. He once partnered Tommy Handley, touring the Halls as Hilton and Handley; then calling himself Jackson Hilton.

Born at Great Lever, near Bury, on July 2, 1892, he was the son of George Hilton, an innkeeper. In 1922 he married Florence Ennis Parkinson who, as Ennis Parkes, was a talented soubrette, singer and song composer, originally from the Isle of Man. The marriage ended in 1931, and she died on October 21, 1957. Hylton directed some of Britain's finest showbands until April, 1940, going on to become an equally famous impresario – his last show was *Camelot*. He died on January 29, 1965.

The 'Queen's' was a bright little band, which made some attractive records in 1921. Two were waltzes with simple, pretty tunes that anyone could whistle on the way to work. *Sweet and Low*, published in 1919, was created by J. Stanley Royce and Charles L. Johnson; *Silver Star* was composed by Horatio Nicholls, with a Worton David lyric.

Jack Hylton: from Singing Mill Boy *to* Camelot.

There were no vocals. Those wishing to hear the words could buy Robert Woodville's versions on Zonophone. He probably reminded them of Peter Dawson, being indeed the famous Australian bass-baritone using one of his many aliases.

Hubert Worton David first wrote lyrics for Wright during the war. Born in Leeds, he studied at Hampstead Conservatoire. As lyricist he called himself either Worton David or Hubert W. David, and he also wrote musical accompaniment for early silent films. At one time a musical adviser to Fox Films, he founded Wordav Orchestral Services in the Strand.

Waltzes made easy listening, but a good fox-trot brought out the best in a band. The 'Queen's' recorded *Mon Homme*, by Maurice Yvain, a Frenchman whose work became well-known over here. The tune appeared on Zonophone, credited to Jack Hylton's Jazz Band.

Mon Homme was enjoyable, but *The Bullfrog Patrol* sheer magic, as played by the 'Queen's'. An unusual tune by Jerome Kern, it was performed with tremendous verve, the clarinet of Ed Jenkins soaring over the ensemble. Today this remarkable record is exceptionally difficult to find.

Edmond T. 'Ed' Jenkins later went to Paris, like other black musicians, dying rather mysteriously in 1926 at the age of 32. He may have been mugged. One wonders why Hylton let him go; a player of that calibre would have been an asset to his new band.

An explanation of the relationship of Zonophone to HMV

Nothing severely functional about the gramophone in January, 1921, when this advertisement appeared.

may prove helpful to those unacquainted with record manufacturing history. In 1903 the Gramophone Company bought
out a rival, the International Zonophone Company, then
producing celebrity records. It became the lower-priced
subsidiary of HMV, sometimes featuring the same artists but
often the most peculiar novelty items. Zonophone lasted
until the end of 1932, being then merged with Regal to create
Regal-Zonophone.

Lawrence Wright had several song successes in 1921. For
Only, a fox-trot, he was again Gene Williams, and using a
Gene McCarthy lyric. On Columbia it was played by the
Century Dance Orchestra, purely studio-assembled, but a
vocalist was employed, which was in itself most unusual then,
and moreover he was named, although for many years the
only references to band singers on a label were 'Vocal
Refrain', 'Vocal', or even 'V.R.'.

Fred Douglas, who sang *Only*, disguised as Stewart Morton,
appeared under a variety of names and made scores of
records. The writer thinks he was Buck Douglas with Big Bill
Campbell's Rocky Mountain Rhythm during the early Fifties.

Imagination (Gene Williams) and *Blue Bird* (Horatio
Nicholls) were waltzes, recorded for Zonophone by the Black
Diamonds Band. Its name of unknown origin, it first began to
record in 1906, going out when Zonophone did. Over the
years it played ragtime, excerpts from opera and musical
comedy, light orchestral novelties and marches. Early in the
Twenties it went in for song hits, lacking the parade ground
stiffness which dogged the Coldstream Guards Band on
HMV.

The Black Diamonds provided a sprightly version of
Avalon in 1921, a distinctive song which got its creators, Al
Jolson and Vincent Rose, into serious trouble. When its
unmistakable strains were first heard, Giacomo Puccini sued,
claiming the chorus to have been lifted from *E lucevan le
Stelle* in *Tosca*. He was awarded substantial damages for
infringement of copyright.

Thoughts, originally published in 1917, may have been the
only waltz composed by Kenneth J. Alford. As played by the
Black Diamonds it seemed undistinguished. Stirring marches
were Alford's true métier. Born in 1881, Major Frederick
Joseph Ricketts used his mother's maiden name. Between
1912 and 1942 he wrote a succession of now classical
marches, equal to anything by Sousa. He retired from the
Royal Marines in 1944 and died in May, 1945.

In January, 1921, a C. B. Cochran revue, *The League of Notions*, became the first production at the New Oxford Theatre, a lavish remodelling of the old Oxford Music Hall. The Trix Sisters (Helen and Josephine) were in the cast and the score was by Augustus Barratt. Obviously poking fun at the recently constituted League of Nations, it ran for a year but only made a small profit.

Barratt's rather old-fashioned *League of Notions Waltz* was of little interest to the dance bands, although Joyce's Orchestra recorded it in traditional style for Vocalion.

It was 'jazz' the public wanted in 1921, preferably full of novelty effects. People must have liked *Railroad Blues*, as played by Joseph Samuels' Jazz Band, which certainly did not play jazz. Actuelle credited it to the Synco Jazz Band, but it was merely a fox-trot, given tongue-in-cheek treatment by a quintet which included Samuels on clarinet and Ephraim Hannaford on trombone.

Charles Luckeyeth 'Luckey' Roberts composed *Railroad Blues* as a piano piece in 1920. Born at Philadelphia in 1890, he wrote many piano rags, as well as complete scores for revues and musicals, from late Edwardian times to about the end of the Forties. At one time he directed his own Society dance orchestra, eventually becoming the proprietor of a night club.

Actuelle, owned by Pathé Frères Pathéphone Ltd., issued some interesting if minor records from September, 1921, to December, 1928. It boasted a showy label with a pinkish-cream, octagonal centre, surrounded by an ornate gold border and surmounted by Pathé's red cockerel. Regrettably, the sound quality of Actuelle did not match its appearance.

Edison Bell's Blue Amberol cylinders, once among the élite, were still valiantly struggling on, although fighting a losing battle. Among their many dance tunes was *I Found a Rose in the Devil's Garden*, an oddly-named fox-trot by Willie Raskin and Fred Fisher, played by Harry Raderman's so-called Jazz Orchestra. A trombonist who later joined Ted Lewis, Raderman also recorded the tune on disc for Winner. It was a good, brisk performance, but Winner's acoustical sound quality was never of the best.

Composer Fred Fisher (originally Fischer) was born in Cologne on September 30, 1875. In 1905 he wrote *Ev'ry Little Helps*, with George Whiting, and had a big hit in 1913 with Alfred Bryan, the catchy *Peg o' My Heart*. When *Siam* (lyric by Howard Johnson), was published in 1915, the sheet music cover still spelled his name in the German manner. A highly-regarded Tin Pan Alley tunesmith, he died on January 14, 1942.

Fisher also composed *Wimmin*, for which entertainer Eddie Cantor wrote the lyric. In December, 1921, it was recorded for Victor by the Club Royal Orchestra, resident at a New York night club, where this first-class band had been installed by Paul Whiteman, under the direction of saxophonist Clyde Doerr. It was there from the autumn of 1921 to the summer of 1922, the banjoist for a time being Harry Reser.

Whiteman was still at the Ambassador and recording frequently for Victor. *Ty-Tee* was a fox-trot by Irving Bibo; and *April Showers* one by Louis Silvers (1889-1954), with an (unheard) lyric by Buddy de Sylva. The latter song was in the New York production *Bombo*, at Al Jolson's 59th Street Theatre, starring Jolson himself. Sigmund Romberg also wrote music for *Bombo*.

George Gard 'Buddy' or 'B. G.' de Sylva was born on January 27, 1895, in New York, but educated at the University of Southern California. A remarkably successful librettist and lyricist, his first contributions to the stage were three songs for Jolson's very popular *Sinbad*, at New York's Winter Garden Theatre in 1918. In the latter part of the Twenties he became well-known in Britain for his fruitful partnership with Lew Brown and Ray Henderson. He died in Los Angeles on July 11, 1950.

The Benson Orchestra of Chicago has so far been unfairly neglected by those who transfer old records onto long-players. It was managed by Edgar A. Benson and directed initially by Roy Bargy, who left late in 1922, and then by Don Bestor, both men being pianists. It was Bestor who brought saxophonist Frankie Trumbauer into the band.

Despite his personal popularity, Al Jolson hated audiences to applaud anyone else in his shows.

Among its 1921 records for Victor was *Ain't We Got Fun?* by Raymond B. Egan, Gus Kahn and Richard A. Whiting, often quoted as expressing better than any other song the philosophical sentiments of the early Twenties.

The Benson Orchestra recorded from September, 1920, to May, 1925, by which time, like other bands, it had a vocalist. Some of its records, issued by HMV, show it to be well above average and using imaginative arrangements.

Incredibly prolific and versatile, Gus Kahn was born at Koblenz on November 6, 1886, but left Germany with his parents to settle in Chicago. Among his earliest songs was

Everybody Rag with Me (1914), composed by Grace LeBoy, a pianist employed by music publishers Jerome H. Remick, who became Mrs. Kahn. Other early Kahn hits were *Sunshine and Roses* (1913), *Memories* (1915) and *Pretty Baby* (1916), all with music by Egbert van Alstyne.

Kahn provided lyrics for several Broadway productions, notably *Kitty's Kisses* (1926), in collaboration with Con Conrad; Eddie Cantor's *Whoopee* (1928), for which he and Walter Donaldson wrote *I'd Rather be Lonely than Happy with Somebody Else*, sung by Ruth Etting; and *Show Girl* (1929), a major success for Ruby Keeler. For *Show Girl*, Kahn joined the Gershwins to create *Liza*, which became a smash-hit record for Al Jolson.

In 1933 the Kahns went to Hollywood, where Gus supplied lyrics for RKO's *Flying Down to Rio*. He was associated with many other films, his last being MGM's *Ziegfeld Girl*, released in 1941. His last song appeared that year too, the lovely *Day Dreaming* being his only collaboration with Jerome Kern. He died in Beverly Hills on October 8, 1941.

Richard Whiting, composer of *Ain't We Got Fun?* was born at Peoria, Illinois, on November 12, 1891, and had his first hit in 1915, *It's Tulip Time in Holland*, with a lyric by Dave Radford. He had a much bigger one in 1918 with *Till We Meet Again*, a waltz for which Raymond B. Egan was lyricist. Whiting eventually went to Hollywood, where he composed for movies, writing *Louise* for Maurice Chevalier. He died in Beverly Hills on February 10, 1938. His daughter Margaret became a very popular singer.

Not everyone could afford to buy new records by the leading manufacturers at a time when unemployment exceeded two millions, and well-ploughed second-hand ones had little appeal. To cater for those with slender means, the Crystalate Gramophone Record Manufacturing Company launched its tiny Mimosa discs in 1921, initially with a 5½-inch diameter, although a half-inch was added later.

Of dubious sound quality, they lasted until 1928, offering abbreviated performances by artists who were usually anonymous. Probably few people cared who was on them, anyway. They wore the records out or broke them, and then threw them away. One can still find beautifully preserved records from the Twenties: they are unlikely to be Mimosas.

Chapter Two

1922–23

'Yes! We Have No Bananas'

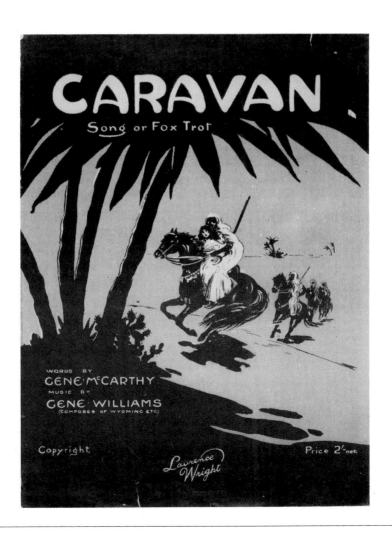

By 1922, British record buyers had a wider choice of dance music, although it was still only a trickle preceding a future flood. HMV supplements offered enticing fare by Ben Selvin, Joseph C. Smith, the Benson Orchestra, the Club Royal Orchestra, Paul Whiteman, and a Whiteman unit called the Virginians. All appeared originally on Victor.

Columbia imported some interesting music from New York, played by Ray Miller, Eddie Elkins, Paul Specht and Ted Lewis, although the last of these was more showman than bandleader, enquiring 'Is everybody happy?' and flourishing a hard-used topper, as well as giving forth with hammy vocals and excruciating clarinet solos of the gaspipe variety.

Domestic dance records remained sparse. Bert Ralton's New York Havana Band made about two dozen sides for Columbia, and the 'Queen's' Dance Orchestra twice that number for HMV or Zonophone, while Winner issued a few each by the resident orchestras at Blackpool's Tower Ballroom and the Hurlingham Club. But that was about all there was on offer.

One could buy 'house' band records, of course, but the faithful Mayfair Dance Orchestra disappeared in August, 1922. Imperial had Derrick's Band, of minor interest, but Winner's Bohemian Band and Zonophone's Black Diamonds were hardly dance units in the accepted sense.

Throughout the Twenties the dance bands had competition from Hawaiian-style music (occasionally authentic), which had become popular during the war and was still much in evidence. A steel guitarist named Frank Ferera made an enormous number of such records, sometimes partnered by Helen Louise, his generously proportioned but technically proficient guitarist wife. Born in Honolulu on June 12, 1882, of Portuguese descent, Ferera popped up on all kinds of record labels over the years, but eventually committed suicide.

Louise and Ferera had quite a varied repertoire, and not all their recordings were uncompromisingly commercial. *Waiu Luliluli*, which appeared on HMV, was also known as *Milk Shake Rag*, a fascinating fusion of two quite distinctive styles of music.

'House' bands contributed many soothing melodies in the Hawaiian manner, as adapted for North American tastes; usually gentle-paced fox-trots or waltzes by composers more familiar with Yellow Cabs and the New York Subway than the swaying palms and silver sands of Waikiki.

Best-known and most prolific was Victor's Hilo Hawaiian

Orchestra, directed by Nathaniel Shilkret or his assistant, Leonard Joy. It recorded in New York from 1924 to 1931, finishing shortly before tropical moons and hula skirts gave way to purple sage and lonesome cowboys.

In 1922 one could choose from Hawaiian guitar solos and duets; trios often including a xylophone; and various other combinations. Even the 'Queen's' dipped a toe into blue Pacific waters and recorded Rollo de Freyne's waltz *Hawaiian Eyes*.

The British Broadcasting Company was formed in October, its famous London station, 2LO, being located at Marconi House in the Strand. But nothing good is ever free, and November saw the introduction of the wireless licence, costing ten shillings (50p), quite steep, considering the wages of the time.

Theatre managers regarded 'wireless' with dislike, fearing a sharp reduction in box-office receipts, but good stage musicals still attracted large audiences. *The Lady of the Rose* came to Daly's Theatre in February, with 32-year old Phyllis Dare in the lead. She and her elder sister Zena had once appeared on literally hundreds of picture postcards.

The score for *The Lady of the Rose* was by Jean Gilbert, who listed *The Girl in the Taxi* (1912) and *The Cinema Star* (1914) among earlier successes, and was back in 1925 with *Katja the Dancer*. His music had a European lilt, and the waltz from *The Lady of the Rose* was recorded for HMV by the 'Queen's' Dance Orchestra.

Gilbert, whose real name was Max Winterfeld, was born in Hamburg on February 11, 1879. At one time Musical Director of Berlin's famous Apollo Theatre, he eventually went to Buenos Aires, dying there on January 4, 1943.

Revues, having helped to brighten the grim wartime years, remained popular. *A to Z* opened in October, 1921, and had a long run. Jack Buchanan, Gertrude Lawrence (in her first leading role) and the Trix Sisters headed the cast, Helen Trix, a stylish pianist, contributing to the musical numbers.

Jack Buchanan's two best songs long outlived the show. *And Her Mother Came Too* was by Dion Titheradge and Ivor Novello; *Limehouse Blues* by Douglas Furber and Philip Braham. Both were recorded by the 'Queen's' in 1922.

Furber, a distinguished lyricist and librettist, was a Londoner, born on May 13, 1885. During the war he had acted in West End revues, but found time to write lyrics for such famous ballad composers as Dorothy Forster and

At the end of World War One, Jack Buchanan was in a Concert Party at Wimereux, entertaining the troops. Jack Hylton was relief pianist.

Alice Delysia's maiden name was Lapize. In World War Two, then in her fifties, she toured the Middle East and North Africa with E.N.S.A.

Melville Gideon, urbane New Yorker who made his home in London. On records his American accent was hardly detectable.

A. Emmett Adams. *Limehouse Blues* was in no sense a blues as the American negro understands the term.

Its composer, another Londoner, made notable contributions to revues and musical plays. Philip 'Pa' Braham was born on June 18, 1881, and went to Charterhouse and Clare College, Cambridge, where he obtained a B.A. His first stage composition was accepted in 1913. He died on May 2, 1934.

In March, 1922, the revue *Mayfair and Montmartre* came to the New Oxford Theatre, starring Alice Delysia, then 37. She sang a Maurice Yvain number called *J'en ai Marre – I'm Fed Up* – with a lyric by Albert Willemetz and Georges Arnould. An English translation was provided by Adrian Ross, a brilliant lyricist and scholar. The lively tune was recorded by both Bert Ralton and the 'Queen's'.

However, *And Her Mother Came Too* and *J'en ai Marre* were also recorded by Derrick's Band, directed by alto saxophonist Jack Derrick. From October, 1922 to June, 1923, it was a 'house' band of Imperial, a label launched by Crystalate in 1920, at first quite showy in rich blue and gold. Imperial lasted until 1934, when Rex took over. Derrick eventually got the sack, apparently because he was an alcoholic.

The Co-optimists left the Royalty Theatre in 1922 to take up residence at the Palace, long famous for its revues. Melville Gideon composed a delightful hit called *If Winter Comes*, for which Clifford Grey wrote the lyric. Apart from the 'Queen's' version, Gideon recorded it himself for Zonophone, to his own piano accompaniment. The song was inspired by A.S.M. Hutchinson's phenomenally successful novel of that title, published in 1921 and filmed the following year.

Melville Joseph Gideon, a New Yorker, was born on May 21, 1884, and made his debut at the age of 12, playing solo piano in Carnegie Hall with the New York Philharmonic Orchestra. He obviously became enamoured of ragtime, for he came to London in 1912 as pianist for the American Ragtime Octet, a vocal group which included Nat D. Ayer, who also decided to make his home in London.

In addition to his songs for *The Co-optimists*, Gideon contributed to revues and became a bandleader briefly in the early Thirties. Always a heavy gambler, he was declared bankrupt in 1913 and again in 1923. A genuine Anglophile, he died on November 11, 1933.

Nat D. Ayer's career to some extent paralleled that of Gideon. His fox-trot *Shufflin' Along*, recorded by the 'Queen's'

in 1922, came from *Snap*, a revue at the Vaudeville Theatre, and had a lyric by Ralph Stanley.

Equally famous as song composer and entertainer, Ayer was probably English. He was born in 1887 and attended Haverford College in America, composing his first successful music in 1909, in collaboration with John W. Bratton, of *Teddy Bears' Picnic* fame.

Ayer will always be remembered for *If You Were the Only Girl in the World*, with its Clifford Grey lyric. It was first heard in 1916, duetted by Violet Loraine and George Robey in *The Bing Boys are Here*, at the Alhambra. Like Gideon, little is known of Ayer's private life. He died on September 19, 1952.

Shufflin' Along was also recorded for HMV by Ennis Parkes, who composed a pretty song in 1922, writing her own gently ironic lyric. *Evergreen Eve* was recorded by the 'Queen's' with a vocal by Peter Dawson who, rather surprisingly, received no label credit.

Left – *Nat D. Ayer composed* If You Were the Only Girl in the World, *but was he American or English?*

Above – *Peter Dawson was one of the most popular artistes in the HMV catalogue, but when he recorded* Evergreen Eve *with the 'Queen's' Dance Orchestra, his name was left off the label.*

Jack Raine played trumpet for Jack Hylton from December, 1922, to December, 1936, save for a short while in 1936 with Mrs Jack Hylton's Band, while Jack was in America.

The 'Queen's' Dance Orchestra last recorded for HMV in November, and soon afterwards Jack Hylton formed his own band, including Jack Raine, a fine trumpet player; Noel 'Chappie' d'Amato, playing alto saxophone and later singing with the band; and Alfred Gill, a violinist who, as Alfredo, became a well-known bandleader himself a little later on.

Hylton's first HMV record was *I Ain't Nobody's Darling*, by Elmer Hughes and Robert (Keizer) King. As he was already on his way up, and destined to lead one of the world's most exciting showbands, the title was hardly appropriate and certainly not prophetic. The vocalist was again Peter Dawson.

Apart from *J'en ai Marre*, Maurice Yvain had other song successes in 1922. *Ça, c'est une Chose*, was recorded for HMV in salon orchestral style by de Groot and the Piccadilly Orchestra; and *Ta Bouche* for Columbia by Bert Ralton. Yvain must be regarded as one of the few Continental composers to catch the spirit of American-style dance music, theirs usually being quite different, and more suitable for light orchestras.

Ralton's New York Havana Band also recorded Fred Fisher's *In My Tippy Canoe*, a waltz which Winner featured too, played by the Tower Ballroom Blackpool Orchestra, directed by J. Woof Gaggs. The latter orchestra also recorded *Catalina*, a fox-trot by Byron Gay, an often tasteful (occasionally dreadful) American composer of whom little is known.

J. Woof Gaggs was probably the Tower's Musical Director. His orchestra made a few sides for Winner in 1920 and 1922; more were made in 1924, by which time Arthur Davis had taken over. Winner must have liked Blackpool, recording the Blackpool Syncopators in 1923 and the Blackpool Winter Gardens Orchestra in 1924.

Provincial bands seem to have lacked the attraction of those in London for most record buyers, and Winner's worthy ventures must have been poorly received, judging by the few sides issued. The position changed somewhat in the Thirties, when Bertini's Tower Blackpool Band and Billy Merrin's Commanders, of Nottingham, became quite popular and made many records.

The Black Diamonds Band recorded more dance music for Zonophone in 1922, some of it by Lawrence Wright under his various aliases. *Golden Dreamboat* and *Rainbow* were Horatio Nicholls waltzes, but the fox-trot *Caravan* was credited to Gene Williams. *Caravan* was also recorded by Stuart Vaughan,

an obscure baritone who had a brief flirtation with Zonophone. His version illustrated the unintentional hilarity of
the lyric.

Gene McCarthy was apparently unaware that a caravan in
this context meant a desert convoy and not the abode of a
Saharan gypsy. Probably few people spotted the gaffe, or
cared if they did, popular songs rarely being subjected to
analysis.

Stuart Vaughan joined the Black Diamonds to add his
vocal to Jay Eltinge's waltz *Drifting on a Dream*. The day of
the band singer was drawing near; but the era when mediocre
vocalists would reduce the role of bands to mere accompanists
lay far in the future. It began around the start of the Second
World War, by which time the golden age of dance music was
over anyway.

In 1922, Ted Lewis and his Band recorded *Georgette*, a fox-
trot by Lew Brown and Ray Henderson. Despite his clowning
propensities, Lewis occasionally made some interesting
records for Columbia, but all too frequently his clarinet or his
singing – it is debatable which was worse – marred an
otherwise enjoyable performance.

Born in Circleville, Ohio, on June 6, 1892, Lewis organised
his first band in 1919, and at one time employed the famous
jazz cornetist Francis 'Muggsy' Spanier. He made London
appearances in 1925 and 1930, and died in New York on
August 25, 1971.

It was not until 1925 that Buddy de Sylva joined Brown
and Ray Henderson to form a remarkable partnership.
Brown, lyricist, librettist and play producer, was born in
Odessa on December 10, 1893, but educated in New York.
After many Broadway successes, he started to write for the
films in 1929, when the craze for short musicals began. He
died in New York on February 5, 1958.

Henderson, a composer with an instinctive understanding
of what made a sure-fire winner, came like the famous lyricist
Jack Yellen from Buffalo, New York, where he was born on
December 1, 1896. A former choirboy, he attended the
Chicago Conservatory of Music, became a song plugger, and
in 1925 began to compose scores for musical plays. When the
three men went their separate ways in 1930, he became a film
producer. He died at Greenwich, Connecticut, on December
31, 1970.

In May, 1921, Sissle and Blake's all-black revue *Shuffle
Along* opened at New York's 63rd Street Theatre and had a

very long run. Starring Florence Mills and Noble Sissle, the show scored a big hit with *I'm Just Wild About Harry*. All the music for *Shuffle Along* was by Eubie Blake.

Blake's death on February 12, 1983, five days after his hundredth birthday, severed one of the few remaining links with the ragtime era. In 1914, as J. Hubert Blake, he had composed *Fizz Water*, one of the hits of the time. Born in Baltimore, he was a fine pianist and a gifted composer. In an active old age he used to lecture on the music of his youth, having a fondness for that of Leslie Stuart.

Noble Sissle, his equally talented partner, was born in Indianapolis on August 10, 1889, and visited London several times. In 1926 he sang there with Blake at the piano; in 1928 his accompanist was Harry Revel. He brought his Sizzling Syncopators over in both 1929 and 1930, appearing briefly at Ciro's on the second occasion. Sissle died on December 17, 1975.

Shuffle Along stayed in New York, but *I'm Just Wild About Harry*, as a one-step, was recorded in 1922 by the Royal Court Orchestra for Winner.

Although he recorded frequently for Columbia early in the Twenties, little is known about Ray Miller. Often based in New York, his orchestra at one period included Spanier and Trumbauer. The band sometimes played jazz, but most records were of routine dance tunes, competently performed, such as Ted Koehler and Frank Magine's fox-trot *Venetian Love Boat*, made in 1922 by Miller's Black and White Melody Boys, who at one time featured the veteran New Orleans trombonist Tom Brown.

Some of the records by Paul Whiteman in his formative years still retain their arresting quality. Outstanding in 1922 was de Sylva and Gershwin's *I'll Build a Stairway to Paradise*, with its ecstatic muted-cornet solo by Tommy Gott. This novel and beautiful arrangement revealed Grofé at his best.

But Whiteman's star trumpeter was Henry Busse, who helped him form his first band. Born in 1894, a former German acrobat, rotund of body and gutteral of speech, he was the highest paid musician, and all were paid well.

Typical of Busse's muted-trumpet style was *Hot Lips*, which he supposedly helped Henry Lange and Lou Davis to write. Long an audience favourite, it became his signature tune when he formed his own band in 1928. Busse was still fronting a band in April, 1955, when he died suddenly from a heart-attack in Memphis, Tennessee.

Although Prohibition had begun on January 16, 1920, and

was fairly vigorously enforced, big money was being made by bringing in illicit 'hooch' by sea. Edgar Leslie and Walter Donaldson ironically saluted the blockade runners with a pretty song called *On the 'Gin 'Gin, 'Ginny Shore*, a play on both gin (much in demand by bootleggers) and Virginia, a coastal State. The point was somewhat lost in Whiteman's non-vocal recording.

Another Donaldson hit was *Carolina in the Morning*, with a lyric by Gus Kahn, who must have collaborated with nearly every song composer. Whiteman's version was again instrumental only, but in England it was recorded (for HMV) by the Australian comedian Albert Whelan, renowned for his tuneful whistling.

Walter Donaldson, who wrote so many enjoyable songs, was born in Brooklyn on February 15, 1893. He scored a hit in 1915 with *Just Try to Picture Me Down Home in Tennessee*, with a Billy Jerome lyric; and he caught the restless mood of returning soldiers in 1919 with *How Ya Gonna Keep 'em Down on the Farm, After They've Seen Paree?* for which Sam Lewis and Joe Young wrote the verse. He was immensely active throughout the Twenties and Thirties.

Although in the early Forties Donaldson worked with Harold Adamson, Peter de Rose and Mitchell Parish, his health began to fail. He died in Santa Monica, California, on July 15, 1947.

An outstanding song of the early Twenties was *The Sheik of Araby*, inspired by Edith Maude Hull's daring novel *The Sheik*, and Rudolph Valentino's screen portrayal of the importunate desert lover.

Ted Snyder wrote the music for this sultry ballad; and the lyric, by Harry B. Smith and Francis Wheeler, must have elevated a few eyebrows when first encountered:

I'm the Sheik of Araby, your love belongs to me.
At night, when you're asleep, into your tent I'll creep.

This naughty fox-trot was much recorded on both sides of the Atlantic. In 1921, Clyde Doerr's Club Royal Orchestra did so for Victor, and Ray Miller's Black and White Melody Boys for Columbia. In the Spring of 1922, the Black Diamonds Band and the Regal Dance Orchestra recorded it for Zonophone and Regal respectively.

The studio-assembled Regal Dance Orchestra was one of several units directed by Albert W. Ketèlbey, then Director of Light Music for the Columbia Graphophone Company in London. He had already composed such distinctive light

Top – *Albert Whelan, Australian comedian and tuneful whistler. The Three Trees was among his popular sketches, heard on the radio as late as the early post-war period.*

Bottom – *Rudolph Valentino detested* The Sheik *and admitted he was uncertain how to play the part.*

orchestral pieces as *The Phantom Melody*, *In a Monastery Garden* and *In a Persian Market*, with many more to come.

In 1922, plum label HMV records cost 4s 0d (20p) for a 10-inch disc, and 6s 0d (30p) for a 12-inch one. This was far too expensive for many people. The Aeolian Company launched a 5½-inch (later six-inch) Little Marvel record to compete with Crystalate's Mimosa, costing only sixpence each (2½p) at Woolworths. Well-known artists may have recorded for it, but their names were never disclosed and reproduction was poor.

* * *

Theatregoers who liked a good revue had a treat when *Brighter London* came to the Hippodrome in March, 1923. Not only could they applaud old favourites like Billy Merson and Lupino Lane, but also revel in the exciting music of Paul Whiteman. Such was the impression Whiteman made on Jack Hylton, the latter was determined to create a showband as versatile and impressive in this country.

The Whiteman band visited the HMV studios, recording Irving Berlin's *Tell Me with a Melody*. Whiteman got on well with Herman Finck, a distinguished composer-conductor, who wrote much of the music for *Brighter London* and directed the theatre orchestra.

Finck, a genial soul, perhaps rather too fond of his own jokes, took Whiteman and his players to the Savage Club, a gesture greatly appreciated. Before returning home, the Whiteman 'boys' presented Finck with a loving cup on which all their names had been engraved.

Other pioneer American bandleaders came forward as the 'Dancing Twenties' gathered momentum. Among the most successful was Ben Selvin, who made several thousand records, under all kinds of pseudonyms. In 1923, he was resident at the Moulin Rouge, a New York night club. Towards the end of the year he recorded *You're in Kentucky, Sure as You're Born*, a fox-trot by George A. Little, Larry Shay and Haven Gillespie. It was issued here by Vocalion.

A New Yorker, born in 1898 and trained, like many future bandleaders, as a violinist, Benjamin Selvin became famous for his treatment of waltzes, but he could handle a fox-trot with the best. He sometimes used such star session musicians as the Dorsey Brothers, Jack Teagarden, Adrian Rollini and Benny Goodman. In the late Twenties he provided stylish

accompaniment for the young New York singer Annette Hanshaw. He disbanded in 1934, becoming an artists' manager, and died in the city of his birth on July 29, 1980.

Paul Specht, another violinist, formed his first band in 1919 and remained active throughout the Twenties. Little seems to be known about him personally. In the Spring of 1923 he brought a band to Lyons' Corner House in Coventry Street; his Kittens were at the Kit-Cat Club in 1925. The following year, Paul Specht's Canadian Club Orchestra appeared at this famous night-spot, directed by Orville Johnson; Specht himself came to London again in that Spring.

Among the records which Specht made for Columbia in 1923 was a lingering little serenade by two young Canadians. *The World is Waiting for the Sunrise* was created in 1919 for the Pierrot Players, a Canadian theatrical group, probably similar to a concert party.

Eugene Lockhart wrote the lyric, but Specht's version was non-vocal. As Gene Lockhart, he later became a character actor with a whole string of film successes, while Ernest J. Seitz, who composed the almost caressing melody, was to

Above – The Paul Whiteman Band on June 1, 1923. Left to right: Hal McLean, Tommy Gott, Hal MacDonald, Hal Byers, Harry Reser, Henry Busse, Sammy Lewis, Jack Barsby, Ross Gorman, Ferde Grofe and Paul Whiteman.

Below – Paul Specht, famous bandleader of the Twenties, who came to London in 1923.

distinguish himself as a concert pianist and symphony orchestra conductor.

Paul Specht's fox-trot version appeared in the Spring. In November he saluted Joe McCarthy and Harry Tierney, still going strong after their runaway success with *Irene. Take, Oh, Take Those Lips Away*, another fox-trot, was typical Specht, peppy enough but steering well clear of jazz. He was then resident at the Hotel Alamac in New York.

The California Ramblers, who undoubtedly were jazz-influenced, came together in the east and never went near the West Coast. The band was formed in 1921 and lasted until 1929, clinging throughout to an almost unchanging style. Directed by Ed Kirkeby, its alumni in a constantly changing line-up included Red Nichols, Adrian Rollini, the ubiquitous Dorseys, and (for an Eastern States tour) Roy Fox.

The Ramblers recorded profusely for Columbia, but like other bands appeared elsewhere too, suitably disguised. Both the Ramblers and Fred Rich were issued here on Imperial as the Golden Gate Dance Orchestra; and Columbia sometimes called the former the Hannan Dance Band on British releases, although there was a short-lived 'house' band with that name too.

Under their own name, the California Ramblers recorded *Kaintucky* for Columbia in 1923. This was a fox-trot by a man who was not only a front-line bandleader but a prolific song composer, the highly accomplished, although not particularly well-liked Isham Jones.

With his severe expression and austere personality, Jones seemed a most unlikely individual to compose sentimental ballads, yet he came up with some outstanding hits, for which his lyricist was the dependable Gus Kahn.

Born in Coalton, Ohio, on January 31, 1894, Isham Jones fronted his first band while Britain was at war, and climbed rapidly to the top. In 1936 he decided to disband, but within a year was back in business, continuing to direct bands of above average interest until the early Forties.

Jones, who played tenor saxophone and piano, was undoubtedly a disciplinarian. He had quickly discovered, as Glenn Miller, Benny Goodman, Tommy Dorsey and our own Jack Hylton would later, that a tightly controlled band is most likely to survive in an intensely competitive environment.

Nevertheless, Isham Jones had his players' respect, even if he stood no nonsense. This was a smooth and thoroughly relaxed band, and it could generate a gentle swing in contrast to many others which simply played the tune. Jones' theme song was *You're Just a Dream Come True*, and one such dream may have been realised in 1925, when the Isham Jones band began to play at London's Kit-Cat Club.

When Jones disbanded in 1936, one of his sidemen took over, wasting no time in putting his own ideas across to the public. Woody Herman began well with his Band that Plays the Blues. One of the most gifted and genuinely loved of all the great bandleaders, Herman later dispensed swing of an almost searing heat, with 'Herds' whose prowess is now legendary. The writer has personal recollections of the Herman brand of magic. Woody died on October 28, 1987.

Isham Jones lived to see many of the big swing bands come and go too, dying in Hollywood on October 19, 1956. His was no transitory fame; today his records are eagerly sought out by discerning collectors.

Back in 1923, Kahn and Jones achieved a singular success with *Swingin' Down the Lane*, a much-recorded fox-trot. Among the bands committing it to wax was the Great White Way Orchestra, one of Victor's most interesting 'house' bands, directed from the piano by Hugo Frey.

Swingin' Down the Lane has long been regarded as one of Isham Jones' best tunes, whereas *Barney Google*, also recorded by the Great White Way Orchestra, was just a fleeting novelty. The lad with 'the great big googley eyes' was created by lyricist Billy Rose, abetted by Con Conrad. Born in New York on June 18, 1891, Conrad contributed songs to several Broadway shows, the best-known being *Mercenary Mary*. He died on September 29, 1938.

Most bands were required to record such comedy songs, but the players' opinion of them was probably unprintable. An imaginative fox-trot was another matter, and Hugo Frey's boys treated *Beside a Babbling Brook* with the respect it deserved. This was not the song much later made famous by Donald Peers, but a zippy little number by Gus Kahn and Walter Donaldson.

One of the most interesting bands to emerge in America at this period was Waring's Pennsylvanians, whose dogged struggle to achieve recognition ended when their first recording became a rip-roaring success. The song was *Sleep*, and it was never intended originally for the popular market, nor was it issued under the composer's real name.

A slow, haunting melody, played as a waltz by the Pennsylvanians, it came from *Visions of Sleep*, a serious piano composition by the blind, 68-year-old organist Adam Geibel. Born in Neuenheim on September 15, 1855, he had arrived in the States as a child of seven.

Waring's sensitive arrangement was made with the composer's permission, but as Geibel was unwilling to be associated with dance music, it was credited to 'Earl Lebieg'. *Sleep* was recorded for Victor in October, 1923, gently, almost dreamily, ending with a reverently intoned vocal by members of the band. Even today it attracts attention when first heard; then it proved a sensation.

Fred Waring was born on June 9, 1900, in Tyrone, Pennsylvania, of a musical family. He was playing local gigs as a semi-pro while at Penn State University, and left without graduating to form Waring's Banjo Band, which began to tour. It made little impact until it reached Detroit. There its fortunes began to improve, the name was changed, and *Sleep* made it famous.

In later years it was his Glee Club, not his orchestra, by then reduced to a supporting role, which ensured the lasting popularity of Fred Waring, long after the 'dance band days' had ended forever. This intuitive and determined showman devoted much of his time in early years to the performance of trivia, although even then he was a fanatical perfectionist.

But Waring knew what he was about, aiming squarely at a lucrative sector of the music market with unerring judgement. His records were of great appeal (like those of Johnny Hamp) to the campus set. During the Thirties the band became a little more sophisticated, altering with the times, the brass frequently displaying a punch and precision worthy of better music than it usually performed.

Another piano piece not originally intended for dancing was *Chanson*, composed by Rudolf Friml in 1923, which soon became a fox-trot, re-named *Chansonette*. It was briefly popular, but achieved a more lasting success when it reverted to its original title and was converted into a light orchestral composition. It underwent a further transformation in 1937, becoming *The Donkey Serenade* with the aid of Herbert Stothart, Bob Wright and Chet Forrest. As such, it was sung in MGM's *The Firefly* by the tenor Allan Jones, who recorded it for Victor with outstanding success.

Charles Rudolf Friml's career has been well-documented. Born in Prague on December 7, 1881, he studied at the local Conservatory of Music, and went to America in 1903 as accompanist to the Polish violinist Jan Kubelik, an association lasting five years.

After his success with the original *Firefly* in 1912, Friml wrote the music for a series of operettas, many undistinguished, but his sparkling melodies for *Rose-Marie* and *The Vagabond King* keep his memory evergreen. He died in Hollywood on November 12, 1972.

Two recordings of *Chansonette* made in 1923 are of passing interest. That by Joseph Samuels and his Orchestra was pleasantly brisk, but lent no support to his jazz pretensions. It appeared here on Imperial, credited to the Lucky Strike Dance Orchestra.

A British version was issued on Zonophone by Marius B. Winter's Dance Band, one of the earliest records it made. After that, Winter dropped out of the record supplements for five years, by which time he was at the Hotel Cecil. This rather obscure bandleader played frequently in Europe.

Marius Bernard Winter, a drummer, was born at Streatham in 1898, and formed a band after his war service. On March 26, 1923, his was the first band to broadcast over 2LO, his sole claim to fame. Winter recorded spasmodically here from 1923 to 1931; and from 1924 onwards could often be heard over Radio Paris.

Marius B. Winter: In March, 1923, his was the first band heard over 2LO.

Although dance music soon became one of the most consistently popular forms of wireless entertainment, the BBC always seemed reluctant to acknowledge the fact. The Year Books (sometimes called Hand Books), which began in 1928, only made brief mention of dance music and 'variety', preferring to enlarge upon more cultural aspects of entertainment. For this attitude, the Calvinistic influence of Sir John Reith was undoubtedly responsible.

Nevertheless, the cream of the London bands, and many of the better provincial ones, began to broadcast frequently, often being relayed from hotels, restaurants and night clubs. The first broadcast from a dance floor took place at the Carlton Hotel on May 24, 1923.

Aware of press hostility (newspaper proprietors feared a diminution of sales as a direct result of newscasts), the BBC launched its own magazine. The *Radio Times* first appeared on September 28, 1923, costing twopence. Here again, prejudice against dance music was discernible. It listed music to be performed by light orchestras, but never that of the bands.

The Savoy Havana Band (as the New York Havana Band had been renamed early in 1922), was one of the earliest to broadcast, but Bert Ralton was still restless. He decided to

Reginald Batten: Violinist who began to direct the Savoy Havana Band in the autumn of 1923.

William Debroy Somers directed the Savoy Orpheans from 1923 to 1926, when he formed his own band. During the Thirties he provided music for Continental commercial radio.

try Australia, sailing in October, and most of the band went with him, although Ramon Newton stayed behind. A new band with the same name was promptly assembled by Wilfred de Mornys, with violinist Reginald Batten as leader. Newton joined it as second violinist.

The new players included Jimmy Wornell on trumpet; the American Van Phillips, doubling clarinet and alto saxophone; and pianist Billy Mayerl. Recording for Columbia began almost immediately. Newton was required to sing with the band from the start: the day of the 'vocal refrain' had arrived.

In May, *Stop Flirting* opened at the Shaftesbury Theatre, with Adèle and Fred Astaire making their London debut. In America the show had been called *For Goodness Sake*. A high-spot was *The Oom-Pah Trot*, and when the Astaires danced that the audience went wild. An energetic one-step by Paul Lannin and William Daly, it was among the earliest recordings by the new Savoy Havana Band.

The stage was facing increasing competition from the 'silver screen', for which animated cartoons had been invented. Pat Sullivan's *Felix*, a black and white cat with a pointed face, was first seen in Paramount's *Felix Follies*, released in 1919.

In 1923, *Felix* became the subject of a song by Hubert W. David and Ed. E. Bryant, *Felix Kept on Walking*, which Newton recorded with the Havana Band. He also sang *Last Night on the Back Porch*, by Lew Brown and Carl Schraubstader; while Roy Turk and Lou Handman's *My Sweetie Went Away* was yet another recording by this attractive little band.

Pleased with the reception of the Havana Band, de Mornys soon installed a second band at the hotel, the now legendary Savoy Orpheans. Direction was handed to Dublin-born ex-military bandmaster William Debroy Somers, handsome, well-groomed and firmly in command.

The appointment might have proved disastrous. Bill Somers lacked the instinctive understanding of good band music possessed by such truly great leaders as Bert Ambrose, Lew Stone, Jack Hylton and Roy Fox. He revealed his limitations four years later, his own Debroy Somers Band hovering uneasily between dance and concert band, satisfying neither requirement and often stiffly precise.

What saved the Orpheans from mediocrity or an early demise was the quality of personnel. Before the British labour laws were tightened up, many superb American instrumentalists found employment in London. They worked harmoniously alongside their British colleagues, passing on something of their skill and faultless sense of rhythm. At least half of the Orpheans were American; all were first-class musicians.

The Savoy Orpheans made their maiden broadcast over 2LO in October, and began to record in November. Both Savoy bands were under exclusive contract to Columbia at a time when intense rivalry existed between that company and HMV. Yet the Orpheans made their first sides at Hayes, in flagrant violation of their contract.

In fact, the Orpheans visited Hayes twice in 1923; and no less than 27 times in 1924, almost double their visits to Columbia. Possibly Columbia finally gave up, because of nine recording sessions occurring between late September and the end of November that year, not one was for them.

How did the Orpheans get away with it? For their clandestine recordings of 1923 they called themselves the Albany Dance Orchestra; and throughout 1924 the Romaine Orchestra. But the Orpheans had a most distinctive sound and, as though to thumb their noses at Columbia, sometimes recorded the same tunes for both labels.

Columbia must have been aware of the deception. Musicians gossip like everyone else. One can only speculate why no action was taken. After November, 1924, it no longer mattered, because both bands signed up with HMV. Curiously enough, certain Orpheans recordings, issued on Zonophone, were still credited to the Romaine Orchestra.

It was not just the Savoy Orpheans who indulged in such unrepentant studio hopping. The Savoy Havana Band made records for Vocalion as the Savoy Harmonists, and for Vocalion's Aco label as the Whitehall Dance Orchestra.

The first 'Albany Dance Orchestra' recording was, perhaps appropriately, *Who Cares?* by Jack Yellen and Milton Ager, a song also interpolated during the run of Al Jolson's *Bombo*. Ager, born in Chicago on October 6, 1893, was turning out hits in 1918, such as *Everything is Peaches Down in Georgia*, for which he collaborated with lyricist Grant Clarke and fellow composer George W. Meyer.

Ager met Yellen in 1920, forming a profitable but remarkably stormy partnership which ended in 1930. He died in Los Angeles on May 6, 1979. Jack Yellen, born in Poland on July 6, 1892, but brought up in Buffalo, was another veteran. Back in 1910 he wrote a lyric for George L. Cobb's *I Used to be Lonesome*.

Another song recorded by the Orpheans for HMV was

Romany Rose, a pretty waltz by Worton David and Horatio Nicholls. Like *Who Cares?* it had no vocal.

The nine sides made for Columbia in 1923 were unexceptional. They included *Love Me Now*, Leo Fall's waltz from *Madame Pompadour*, which opened at Daly's in December, teaming Evelyn Laye and Derek Oldham.

Meanwhile, another bandleader, later to become very famous indeed, had begun to establish himself here. His name was Bert Ambrose. A Londoner, born in 1897, he had studied in his home city before moving to New York, a place he found to his liking, and where he remained for many years.

Ambrose played violin for New York symphony orchestras, but soon realised much more money could be made by playing dance music. In 1917 he became Musical Director of the very swank Club de Vingt; later he directed the resident band at the Palais Royal.

It was Luigi, proprietor of the Embassy Club, who lured Ambrose back to London in 1920. Located in Bond Street, the Embassy was a Society venue, frequently visited by the Prince of Wales. The head waiter, a Dane named Poulsen, later opened his own Cafe de Paris which, after a shaky start, was also patronised by 'David' and his coterie.

Early in 1922 Ambrose returned to New York, to play at the Clover Gardens; but Luigi was persistent, and by Christmas he had Ambrose back again. This time Ambrose remained for well over four years, his band being greatly admired by the Astaires. The association might have lasted longer, but Luigi misjudged his man. He strictly forbade Ambrose to broadcast and lost him to the May Fair Hotel.

Ambrose and his Embassy Club Orchestra only made a few records; all appeared on Columbia in the Spring of 1923. Perhaps Luigi disapproved of recording too. They included *Rose of the Rio Grande*, a fox-trot by Harry Warren, with a lyric by Edgar Leslie and Ross Gorman, the latter one of Paul Whiteman's players. Two of these songwriters are of greater interest than the song itself.

Edgar Leslie, born in Stamford, Connecticut, on December 31, 1885, had a distinguished career. However, his first lyrics had little merit, if his contribution to Halsey K. Mohr's *The Police Won't Let Mariucha Dance Unless She Move Da Feet*, an oddity of 1907, is any indication.

Leslie did better in 1909, helping to create Irving Berlin's early hit, *Sadie Salome, Go Home*. He was associated with a string of song successes in the Twenties, many with music by

Horatio Nicholls. As late as 1937 he was still abreast of popular musical tastes, writing the lyric for Joe Burke's much-recorded *It Looks Like Rain in Cherry Blossom Lane*. He died on January 22, 1976.

Warren is one of the all-time greats of popular music. Born in Brooklyn on December 24, 1893, his family name originally Guaragna, he worked at a film studio in his youth and later as a song-plugger. *Rose of the Rio Grande*, published in 1922, started him on his stardust road, and he produced a little charmer in 1924 with *Pasadena*.

He will long be remembered for the highly individual songs he composed for screen musicals with Al Dubin; but he was still in tune with his times in the mid-Forties, using lyricists of the calibre of Mack Gordon, Johnny Mercer, Leo Robin and Arthur Freed. He died on September 22, 1981, in Los Angeles.

A group appearing fleetingly on Columbia was the Broadway Five, with trumpeter Bert Heath (brother of the more famous Ted), and Percival Mackey at the piano. Mackey later joined Jack Hylton, but also conducted for some notable theatre productions, as well as forming his own band. It is unwise to judge from a few acoustical records, but on the evidence of Hubert W. David's *O Star of Eve* and Harry Akst's *Do I?* The Broadway Five seemed somewhat lacking in zest.

Some dance units still present unsolved mysteries. Who were Mr and Miss Brighten, co-directors of the Trocadero Orchestra? We know neither their first names nor how they were related. A small orchestra, mainly strings, it made just four sides for HMV and probably soon disappeared.

Two sides featured established German composers. *My Wayside Rose* was a really pretty fox-trot by Ralph Erwin, best remembered for *I Kiss Your Hand, Madame*, The Trocadero Orchestra gave quite a spirited performance, considering its instrumental limitations. *Love Bells* was a waltz by Ralph Benatzky.

Born on June 5, 1887, Benatzky composed a wealth of lilting melodies, many recorded by Marek Weber and his Orchestra in Berlin and issued here on HMV. He became better known in Britain when *White Horse Inn* reached the Coliseum in 1931.

In July, 1923, C. B. Cochran put on George M. Cohan's song and dance show *Little Nellie Kelly* at his New Oxford Theatre, with June (full name June Howard Tripp) as leading lady. Two of Cohan's songs, *You Remind Me of My Mother*

June, at one time Lady Inverclyde, made her stage debut as a 'sea nymph' when she was nine.

and *Until My Luck Comes Rolling Along*, were recorded for Regal by Harry Wood and his Dance Band.

Wood, a violinist, should not be confused with the American songwriter Harry McGregor Woods, who spent some of his time here. Born in Slaithwaite in 1868, he was Musical Director at Blackpool's Winter Gardens from 1917 to 1927. His band's non-vocal versions of both songs were rather pedestrian.

By this time, Jack Hylton was frequently at Hayes, recording for HMV or Zonophone every month of 1923 except November. His Zonophone records were credited to the Grosvenor Dance Orchestra. *The Co-optimists* had moved to the Prince of Wales' Theatre, and Hylton recorded one of their new songs, *Tampa Bay, You're Calling to Me*, by Laddie Cliff and Melville Gideon.

Hylton made over 60 recordings that year. They included Jessie L. Deppen's *Eleanor*, a remarkably pretty tune; *Saw Mill River Road*, another by Joseph McCarthy and Harry Tierney; and *Shores of Minnetonka*, an engaging fox-trot by Gus Kahn and Percy Wenrich. Lake Minnetonka, which inspired several songs, lies just south of Minneapolis, in the State of Minnesota.

Wenrich, born in Joplin, Missouri, on January 23, 1880, was once a highly regarded night club pianist, known as the Joplin Kid, composing some popular rags between 1903 and 1916. *When You Wore a Tulip*, a cheerful ditty of 1914, with a lyric by Jack Mahoney, later fitted comfortably into a Dixieland jazz setting. Wenrich died in 1952.

But the musical indignity of 1923 (which Hylton recorded) was *Yes! We Have No Bananas*, perpetrated by Frank Silver and Irving Cohn. With a ragbag melody filched from Handel, Balfe and heaven knows who else, together with a gloriously ungrammatical lyric, it tickled the public fancy after a rather slow start. Even Tin Pan Alley liked its fun; and if there was some money to be made too, so much the better.

Chapter Three

1924–25

'You Can Dance With Any Girl At All'

As the Twenties moved towards the half-way point, dance music began to reveal some quite definite characteristics. Fox-trots seem to have been played a little faster than they were at the start of the decade, and the tunes were inclined to be somewhat staccato, whereas waltzes were usually very sweet and dreamy. Few popular songs presented difficulties to anyone with half a voice, and most could be played by an amateur pianist with a modicum of training.

The Savoy Orpheans wasted no time in claiming their share of the record market, waxing more than 130 sides in 1924. They quickly become firm favourites over 2LO, undoubtedly helping to increase the sale of wireless sets. That year the number of licences issued passed the million mark.

The versatile Orpheans included genuinely hot numbers like *Eccentric,* by J. Russel Robinson, pianist of the Original Dixieland Jazz Band, among their many fox-trots, along with Grant Clarke, Edgar Leslie and Harry Warren's *Oh, Eva, Ain't You Coming Out Tonight?* which had some tasteful trumpet breaks by Vernon Ferry, one of the American contingent; *Burning Kisses,* a raggy composition by Percy Wenrich; and *Hum a Little Tune,* from our own Vivian Ellis, then only 20, with an exceptionally bright future before him.

Waltzes were never neglected by the bands of the Twenties and Thirties, despite the undue emphasis placed on fox-trots nowadays by those compiling albums of 'golden age' music. The Orpheans' rendition of *Dreamy Melody,* by Ted Koehler, Frank Magine and C. Naset, must have been ideal for romancing one's girl with lights down low. Koehler, long an active lyricist, died on June 17, 1973, aged 83.

Current shows added their measure of danceable songs. André Charlot's revue *London Calling* opened at the Duke of York's Theatre in September, and in it Gertrude Lawrence sang Noel Coward's *Parisian Pierrot.* Coward was then 25 and not yet 'the Master'. The Savoy Orpheans' recording competed with a light orchestral version by de Groot and the Piccadilly Orchestra. One is inclined to wonder which style Coward preferred, recalling his gibe about the potency of 'cheap' music.

London shows supplied the Savoy Havana Band with material for its records too. Ben Travers' musical play *The Three Graces* came to the Empire Theatre in January, with a score by Franz Lehár. Although never again achieving the magic of *The Merry Widow,* Lehár's music was always charming, and his pretty little *Gigolette* was easily transformed into a fox-trot.

In May, the Shaftesbury Theatre presented *Toni,* with Jack Buchanan, Elsie Randolph and June in the lead. Both Savoy bands recorded *Take a Step,* a fox-trot by Stephen Jones; the Orpheans did so as the Romaine Orchestra, their version being for HMV.

George Gershwin's *Primrose*, opening at the Winter Garden Theatre in September, offered two tunes tailor-made for dancing. The Havana Band recorded *Naughty Baby* and *Wait a Bit, Susie*, fox-trots typical of Gershwin's simpler style, although he had already composed *Rhapsody in Blue* a few months before *Primrose* opened. The London cast was headed by Heather Thatcher and Leslie Henson.

The Havana Band's recordings were actually made in August, by which time the line-up included a young American from Yale named Rudy Vallee. His voice was considered unsuitable for vocals, and his alto saxophone style somewhat soporific; but when he became a singing bandleader a few years later, the bobby-soxers, or whatever American teenagers were called in those days, went crazy over him.

The hit of 1924 was surely *Pasadena*, with Grant Clarke and Edgar Leslie's breezy lyric and a wonderful melody by Harry Warren. Both Savoy bands recorded it; the Orpheans doing so as the Romaine Orchestra. The Havana Band's version featured Ramon Newton, whose rather perfunctory style was quite typical of pioneer band singers.

The Havana Band cut its first sides for HMV in December. One was a fox-trot, *Driftwood*, by Gus Kahn and Lou Gold, a New York bandleader, little-known in this country.

As for waltzes that year, the Havana Band had plenty of choice. It recorded pleasantly relaxed versions of Victor Schertzinger's *Marcheta,* (first heard in 1913); Irving Berlin's *All Alone by the Telephone;* composer-publisher A. J. Stasny's *Waltz Me to Sleep in Your Arms* and Buddy de Sylva, Larry Spier and Con Conrad's *Memory Lane*, all suitable for cheek-to-cheek dancing or fireside listening with slippers and pipe.

A new band, with strong Canadian ties, was heard in the autumn, when Hal Swain was engaged by the New Princes Restaurant. His New Princes' Toronto Band recorded rather sparsely for Columbia from October, 1924, to February, 1926, Swain playing alto and tenor saxophones.

His trumpet player was Alfie Noakes, later to join Lew

Elsie Randolph frequently shared the lead with Jack Buchanan, whom she adored.

Yorkshire-born Hal Swain came back from Canada to direct the New Princes' Toronto Band, which included Alfie Noakes and Les Allen.

Stone, and Les Allan was on alto saxophone. He played with many bands, but eventually became a popular singer. Both men were Canadian, but Harold 'Hal' Swain was born in Halifax on May 9, 1894, and went to Canada as a young man, later serving in the Canadian army.

In 1927, Swain formed a new band for the New Princes Restaurant, retaining only his previous banjoist. He remained there until the Spring of 1928, then moved to the Cafe Royal. Few of Swain's 1924 recordings are of great interest. Perhaps the best-known tune was *Follow the Swallow*, a fox-trot by Billy Rose, Mort Dixon and Ray Henderson, waxed in October at the first session.

Jack Hylton soon became HMV's most-favoured bandleader. His recorded output was prodigious, and he had first pick of all the new tunes. Although required to record too much ephemeral trivia, his standards of arrangement and performance remained high. Midway through 1924 he made some changes, losing Alfred Gill but taking on Jerry Hoey (alto saxophone) and Percival Mackey (piano). In 1931, Hoey directed a band at the Piccadilly Hotel.

Hylton and Lawrence Wright formed close business and personal ties, many Horatio Nicholls songs being recorded by the Hylton band, including two newcomers, *Sahara*, a fox-trot, and *Riviera Rose*, a waltz, each with a Jean Frederick lyric. The latter song was featured in a broadcast to America made by the Savoy Orpheans on March 13, 1924, direct from the Savoy Hotel.

Isham Jones had several hits in 1924, among them *It had to be You*, with a Gus Kahn lyric. Hylton's recording had a vocal by Chappie d'Amato. Hylton also recorded a Yellen and Ager hit, the waltz *I Wonder What's Become of Sally?*

The majority of bands still used a vocalist sparingly or not at all. Things greatly improved for those desirous of hearing both verse and chorus when Layton and Johnstone arrived from American, making their London stage debut in *Elsie Janis at Home* at the Queen's Theatre, in June.

Turner Layton and Clarence Johnstone began their partnership in 1922, but London made them famous. Their voices blended well, accompaniment being provided by Layton, while handsome, white-haired Johnstone stood beside the piano. For ten years their records for Columbia were like a roll-call of Tin Pan Alley and theatre songs; they became the darlings of Society and among the highest paid Variety artists in Britain.

In Jack Hylton's absence, Noel 'Chappie' d'Amato directed the band for its first recording of Shepherd of the Hills, *but Hylton made another one three weeks later.*

Turner Layton was careful with his money, but Johnstone was a big spender, and things went disastrously wrong for him in 1935. Albert Sandler cited Johnstone as co-respondent in a divorce suit brought against his wife Raymonde, and that spelled the virtual end of the black singer's career in the racially intolerant climate of the Thirties. Adding the coup de grace, the Inland Revenue sued for unpaid tax, and Johnstone was declared bankrupt.

An incredibly successful partnership came to a close in November. Johnstone's wife divorced him and he married Raymonde Sandler. They went to America, living in obscurity and poverty in Harlem. Raymonde left him after eight years, and his last job was as janitor for an off-Broadway flophouse. He died, aged 68, in 1953.

Turner Layton carried on alone after Clarence Johnstone's disgrace.

Turner Layton, the more stable of the pair, carried on alone, his popularity undiminished. He was born at Washington, D.C., probably in 1892, and worked as a young man in W. C. Handy's publishing house. He is known to have recorded for Black Swan. An accomplished pianist and a gifted composer, he wrote a number of songs with lyricist Henry Creamer, *After You've Gone* (1918), *Dear Old Southland* (1921) and *'Way Down Yonder in New Orleans* (1922), being the best known.

A rather reserved man, quiet-spoken and good-mannered, Turner Layton continued to record for Columbia well into the Forties. He died on February 6, 1979.

One of the earliest recordings made by Layton and Johnstone was Irving Berlin's new waltz, *What'll I Do?* Another was *It Ain't Gonna Rain No Mo'*, a cheery novelty by ukulele-playing singer Wendell Hall. It was as inescapable in 1924 as *Horsey! Keep Your Tail Up,* by Walter Hirsch and Bert Kaplan, which Layton and Johnstone did not record, but the Savoy Orpheans did.

Overseas, Paul Whiteman enhanced an already enviable reputation. Although still recording popular songs like *Why Did I Kiss That Girl?* by Lew Brown, Ray Henderson and Bob King, he was determined to put his belief in 'symphonic jazz' to a practical test. In February, 1924, he directed an augmented orchestra at New York's Aeolian Hall, giving the premiere performance of Gershwin's *Rhapsody in Blue,* which had been orchestrated by Ferde Grofé and featured the composer as solo pianist. It was very well received.

While Whiteman embarked upon wider concepts of musical entertainment, other bandleaders pursued a less ambitious course. Paul Specht was still at the Hotel Alamac, where anything other than well-played dance music would soon have been discouraged. He recorded two conventional fox-trots for Columbia; Miller and Burtnett's *Oriental Love Dreams* and Yellen and Ager's *Bagdad.*

Throughout the decade, exotic titles flourished, offering eastern promises the music rarely fulfilled. In 1920, Paul Cunningham, Al Dubin and Irving Weill produced *Tripoli;* the following year Bartley Costello and Ted Fiorito lured us *By the Pyramids;* and in 1924, Earl Burtnett, Abe Lyman and Gus Arnheim (all bandleaders) trotted out *Mandalay.*

Horatio Nicholls never side-stepped a good thing, and in 1925 proffered *Araby,* waltzing back in 1927 with *Shalimar;* while among contenders for the popularity stakes of 1928 was *Constantinople,* for which Harry Carlton joined de Sylva, Brown and Henderson.

The words might be trite, but the tunes were catchy, which was all that mattered to most people, and the titles stimulated the imagination of sheet music cover artists. Albert W. Ketèlbey had similar ideas, composing *In a Persian Market* and *In a Chinese Temple Garden,* although, to be fair, his music usually did convey something of the atmosphere suggested.

Having aroused public interest in them so dramatically with *Sleep,* Waring's Pennsylvanians became a regular feature of Victor supplements. In 1924 they recorded *Give Me a June Night,* a happy fox-trot by Abel Baer and Cliff Friend.

Both men adapted successfully to changing styles in popular music and were still in the running during the early years of World War Two. Baer, a former conductor in Boston, was born in 1893. The song *There are Such Things,* a hit of 1943, teamed him with lyricist Stanley Adams and veteran composer George W. Meyer.

Cliff Friend was born in Cincinnati, Ohio, on October 1, 1893. At one time following the vaudeville circuit in an act that included Buddy de Sylva, he left the stage to try his luck as a songwriter. In 1940 he composed *Trade Winds,* which with its highly romantic lyric by Charles Tobias made a splendid vehicle for Bing's lazy baritone. Three years later, Tobias and Friend wrote *Don't Sweetheart Me.*

So This is Venice, marvelled Irving Kaufman, singing with Ben Selvin and his Moulin Rouge Orchestra at the start of 1924. Kaufman, a good all-rounder, adopted a rather grotesque English accent for that novelty by Grant Clarke, Edgar Leslie and Harry Warren, issued on Vocalion. In less frivolous mood, Kaufman was a very pleasant singer.

In contrast, the California Ramblers waxed a straight-forward fox-trot for Columbia in August; Irving Caesar and Vincent Youmans' *I Want to be Happy*, one of the best-known tunes from *No, No, Nanette*. The show had a pre-Broadway try-out before opening at the Globe Theatre in September.

The Ramblers' recording contained some fiery breaks by Bill Moore, a trumpet player who 'passed' for white, enabling him to appear at venues where blacks would have been barred or faced a hostile reception. He was an outstanding musician who played regularly with the Ramblers. Later his strong attack helped to enliven the band of 'Old Maestro' Ben Bernie.

Hawaiian-style dance music received a boost in 1924 with the launching of Victor's 'house' Hilo Hawaiian Orchestra. Among its earliest recordings were Eugene Platzman's *Waikiki is Calling Me* and Otto Motzan's *Moana Chimes*, both waltzes with Hawaiian guitar duets by Frank Ferera and Anthony Franchini.

Another 'studio' ensemble recording for the first time was Nathaniel Shilkret's Victor Salon Orchestra, modelled on de Groot's Piccadilly Orchestra, which Shilkret greatly admired. Dorothy Lee's *Out of the Dusk to You* was waxed at its initial session. An exquisite light orchestra, very much Shilkret's personal baby, it had a way with melodies that was almost caressingly sweet but never cloying.

HMV issued many of its sides as the Salon Orchestra, without reference to Shilkret. It recorded throughout the rest of the Twenties, less frequently (and less interestingly) in the Thirties, and was finally discontinued in 1940.

A tasteful arranger, Shilkret could play cornet, clarinet, piano, organ and celeste. He composed the music for *Lonesome Road,* with a lyric by Gene Austin (1927), and *Jeannine, I Dream of Lilac Time*, with L. Wolfe Gilbert (1928), as well as other songs.

Born Naftul Schildkraut on Christmas Day, 1889, he joined Victor in 1915 and became Light Music Director, providing suitable accompaniment for every kind of singer from Gene Austin to Gloria Swanson. His sound judgement, inventiveness and good taste were always in evidence. Records by the Hilo Hawaiian Orchestra and the Victor Salon Orchestra sold well in America and Britain.

1924 was not the brightest year for new songs, although it

Nathaniel Shilkret, Russian-born song composer and multi-instrumentalist who became Victor's Director of Light Music. He greatly admired de Groot.

had its moments. It may be regarded as a quiet interlude before 1925 arrived, rich in musical fare and introducing the dance sensation of the decade.

* * *

Was there ever a year like 1925 for lavish musical entertainment in London? To mention only the cream of the stage productions: *Betty in Mayfair* (Adelphi); *No, No, Nanette* (Palace); *Mercenary Mary* (Hippodrome); *Rose-Marie* (Drury Lane); *Katja the Dancer* (Gaiety), and *Dear Little Billie* (Shaftesbury). Theatregoers were spoiled for choice. Moreover, *The Co-optimists* were always offering something new.

In 1925, 1,642,000 wireless licenses were issued, and the two million mark was exceeded in 1926. Dance music had become a permanent source of entertainment: the Savoy bands shared the same programme on 2LO from 10.30pm to midnight.

Among the earliest records made by the Orpheans in 1925 was *Haunting Melody,* a dainty waltz by Ben Russell, Larry Spier and Larry Schloss. The sheet-music cover showed Debroy Somers directing the band.

No, No, Nanette opened in March, with Binnie Hale in the title role, familiarising the British public with the name of Vincent Youmans. Born in New York on September 27, 1898, he combined a thoroughly modern approach to popular music with excellent taste. This sparkling show remains a great favourite with amateur operatic societies.

Youmans scored again in 1927 with *Hit the Deck;* and six years later wrote the music for RKO's *Flying Down to Rio,* in which Ginger Rogers and Fred Astaire apparently danced on an aeroplane wing – a delightful example of cinematic illusion. But in the early Thirties, Youmans contracted tuberculosis and, after a constant struggle with ill-health, died at Denver, Colorado, on April 5, 1946.

The dance bands liked *No, No, Nanette. You Can Dance with Any Girl at All* and *Where has My Hubby Gone Blues?* made splendid fox-trots which the Orpheans recorded. They had lyrics by Irving Caesar, a busy New York librettist. Born on July 4, 1895, his association with the stage began about 1920, and in 1935 he started writing Hollywood scenarios.

Nine days after the curtain first rose on *No, No, Nanette*, a very different musical opened at Drury Lane. The enchanting

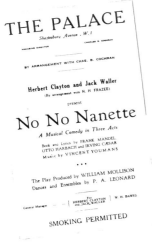

THE PALACE
Shaftesbury Avenue . W. 1

BY ARRANGEMENT WITH CHAS. B. COCHRAN

Herbert Clayton and Jack Waller
(By arrangement with H. H. FRAZEE)

present

No No Nanette
A Musical Comedy in Three Acts

Book and Lyrics by FRANK MANDEL
OTTO HARBACH and IRVING CÆSAR
Music by VINCENT YOUMANS

• • •

The Play Produced by WILLIAM MOLLISON
Dances and Ensembles by P. A. LEONARD

SMOKING PERMITTED

No, No, Nanette opened at the Palace Theatre on March 11, 1925, and soon had everyone whistling Tea for Two.

Rose-Marie had music by Rudolf Friml, lyrics by Otto Harbach and Oscar Hammerstein II, and highly romanticised Canadian settings. *The Indian Love Call* and *Rose-Marie*, both duets by Edith Day and Derek Oldham, were recorded by the Orpheans less than two weeks after audiences first heard them.

Facing fierce competition was Noel Coward's new revue *On with the Dance* at the London Pavilion, with Alice Delysia and Hermione Baddeley sharing the lead, and a song that simply could not fail, *Poor Little Rich Girl*. The Orpheans recorded it at Hayes; Paul Whiteman in New York.

From the current crop of popular songs, the Orpheans also recorded *Listening*, a pretty but long-forgotten waltz by Irving Berlin; *The Only, Only One for Me*, from Bud Green, James V. Monaco and Harry Warren; and *Panama*.

Panama underwent various transformations and name changes in the Twenties. Originally called *Madonna* and published in 1924, it was the work of Robert Katscher, a German composer. In 1925 it became the fox-trot *Panama;* and in 1926, Buddy de Sylva added a lyric and renamed it

Left – Three best-sellers on HMV's plum label in April, 1925.

Above – Hermione Baddeley: One of 'The Two Hermiones', the other being Hermione Gingold. Relations between these redoubtable stars of revue were sometimes less than cordial.

When Day is Done. As such, it became Bert Ambrose's signature tune.

When Day is Done was Paul Whiteman's favourite song, and he recorded it for Victor in September, 1926. A later recording, by his 21-man concert orchestra, was deplorably stiff in places. Whiteman died at Doylestown, Pennsylvania, on December 29, 1967. At the graveside, four days later, former sidemen played the tune as a farewell tribute to 'Pops'.

The dance sensation of 1925 was the Charleston, and the Savoy Orpheans made the first British recording in July, two months after Whiteman recorded it at Camden. Originally just called *Charleston*, with a skimpy lyric by Cecil Mack and a jerky, jazz-influenced tune by James P. Johnson, it was a high-spot of the all-black show *Runnin' Wild* at New York's Colonial Theatre back in 1923, but took nearly two years to become a Society craze.

James Price Johnson, a giant among jazz pianists, was born in New Brunswick, New Jersey, on February 1, 1894, and composed for many revues, as well as writing a host of piano pieces. Said to have taught Fats Waller how to play, Johnson died in New York on November 17, 1955.

The Charleston was demonstrated to Londoners in July by the husband and wife partnership of Robert Sielle and Annette Mills. Reports differ whether this was at the Kit-Cat Club or the Carnival Club in Dean Street. They danced it in evening dress, but it was obviously more suitable for the flappers' short skirts, by then just below the knee.

'By dancing much faster you're chancing disaster', warned Noel Coward. Although he may not have had the Charleston in mind, it was hardly a languid dance. A storm of controversy soon blew up. Barbara Cartland considered it somewhat vulgar; the Vicar of St. Aiden's, Bristol, condemned it hysterically. But the Prince of Wales became an expert; and the famous instructor Santos Casani and his partner performed it on the roof of a taxi in Regent Street.

Although the Charleston became synonymous with the Twenties at their most uninhibited, it was quite short-lived; almost out of fashion by 1927, and certainly not as vulgar as the Black Bottom which replaced it. The Savoy Orpheans' rendition was superb and, to my mind, the most interesting record they made.

Why the Savoy Havana Band recorded less frequently than the Orpheans is anybody's guess. It was always a lively outfit; perhaps too lively for Rudy Vallee, who did not stay long. In June, 1925, he returned to Yale, being replaced by Howard Jacobs, another New Englander.

One of the last recordings with Vallee was *Show Me the Way to Go Home*, a cheerful ditty by Irving King, with a vocal by Ramon Newton. Hot music lovers preferred *Everybody Stomp*, played as a fox-trot but a genuine jazz composition by Elmer Schoebel, pianist of the New Orleans Rhythm Kings. It was recorded after Vallee had left.

For Columbia, the Gilt-Edged Four, led by Canadian trumpet player Max Goldberg, recorded *Don't Bring Lulu*, by Billy Rose, Lew Brown and Ray Henderson. It had the racy humour and peppy rhythm associated with many good songs of the period. In the Fifties it was successfully revived by the ebullient Dorothy Provine.

Howard Jacobs: No real challenge to Rudy Wiedoeft.

But for the record industry, the most significant event of 1925 was the introduction of electrical recording. Victor and Columbia, working to different systems but closely in touch, kept this innovation secret until the time came to announce its success.

In November, the Victor Talking Machine Company held a 'Victor Day,' informing dismayed competitors that acoustical records were out-of-date. Aware that they had made their own catalogues obsolete, Victor and Columbia had been quietly recalling artists to remake more permanent recordings by the new method, a practice continuing throughout 1926.

Victor took the opportunity to launch their Victrola Orthophonic phonograph, with a concealed 're-entrant' horn. A little later, Columbia's brand new Grafonola also went on show. It was good news for record buyers but an unpleasant shock for other manufacturers. Not all were as affluent as the big two, and had to choose between going electrical or going bust.

There was no corresponding ballyhoo in Britain. HMV cut their first successful electrical record on June 24, 1925. It was made by Jack Hylton and his Orchestra, playing a quite insignificant song, *Feelin' Kinda Blue*, by Al Wohlman, Herman Ruby and Joe Cooper. Hylton was the vocalist. It had only a modest sale and is now extremely rare.

Incidentally, Hylton's last acoustic record was a song by Gus Kahn and Walter Donaldson, *Isn't She the Sweetest Thing?* In December he recorded two other Kahn and Donaldson hits, *That Certain Party* and *I Wonder Where My Baby is Tonight!*

Top – *Peggy O'Neil, who made her English debut at the Queen's Theatre, Manchester, in February, 1920. She had the name role in* Paddy the Next Best Thing.

Bottom – *Percival Mackey: At one time Hylton's pianist, he made Columbia's first electrical recording.*

When HMV made their first Orthophonic recording, Columbia were about to move from Clerkenwell Road to Petty France. Thus, they did not start recording electrically until October 1. Almost certainly, Percival Mackey's Band pioneered their 'new process'.

On that date, Mackey, who had been with Columbia since May, waxed Zelda Sears and Vincent Youmans' *Tie a String Around Your Finger*, one of the hits from *Mercenary Mary*, which opened six days later, with Peggy O'Neil, originally from County Kerry, in the lead. Miss Sears, born in Michigan on January 21, 1873, was a well-known actress. She died on February 19, 1935.

Mercenary Mary was a bright, modern show, full of good songs. Mackey recorded Louis Achille Hirsch's *I am Thinking of You* and Joseph Meyer's *Dipping in the Moonlight*, each with an Irving Caesar lyric; Con Conrad's *Honey, I'm in Love with You;* and *Mercenary Mary*, for which Conrad and William B. Friedlander collaborated.

Percival Mackey, born in London on June 1, 1894, was a concert-trained pianist with a fine sense of rhythm. He formed his own band early in 1925, but directed the Palace Theatre Orchestra at the start of *No, No, Nanette,* although later succeeded by Kennedy Russell, the famous ballad composer.

Mackey was also musical director for the Gershwins' *Lady, Be Good,* which began at the Empire Theatre in 1926. His band appeared on various labels, including the relatively minor Electron, Metropole and Octacros. After Ray Noble left for America in 1934, Mackey directed a few sessions for HMV's 'house' New Mayfair Dance Orchestra, then dropped out of the record supplements, becoming active in other spheres than as a bandleader. He died on November 23, 1950.

Mackey's 40-odd sides for Columbia in 1925 included three songs by Horatio Nicholls. The incredibly popular *Toy Drum-Major* (a masterpiece of trivia), and *Araby* were fox-trots with lyrics by Jean Frederick; *Babette*, a waltz, had a Ray Morelle lyric.

Babette was not, as is sometimes assumed, a tribute to Betty Warren, whose real name is Babette Hilda Hogan. She was 20 when this song appeared and in the cast of *The London Revue* at the Lyceum. In 1933 she married Lawrence Wright, 17 years her senior, but they were divorced a few years later. In fact it was casually named after a waitress in the Isle of Man hotel where it was composed.

For Byron Gay's almost unbearably dreary *Just a Little*

Betty Warren: In December, 1936, she became leading lady in 'Balalaika', a smash hit.

Drink, Mackey provided doo-wacka-doo interpolations from the brass and musical quotes from *In Cellar Cool* and *Drink to Me Only with Thine Eyes*. He supplied a smoother arrangement of Gus Kahn and Charles Rosoff's *When You and I were Seventeen,* a pretty waltz by a suprisingly obscure composer.

The return of Bert Ralton late in 1925 meant that two Havana Bands were playing in London. Ralton's band soon began to record again for Columbia; it included Jack Jackson, one of the best trumpeters this country ever produced. He became a popular bandleader and much later a highly original disc jockey. Many people will recall his *Record Roundup*.

Ralton's first recording date produced *Brown Eyes, Why are You Blue?* by Al Bryan and George W. Meyer. A second session included Al Bryan and Ted Snyder's *Lillian*, a fox-trot, and Hero de Rance's *Memory's Melody,* a waltz.

Meyer was born in Boston on January 1, 1884, but moved to New York. He composed his first songs in 1909, had a big hit in 1914 with *When You're a Long, Long Way from Home* (understandably popular in wartime Britain), and was still busy over 30 years later. He died in New York on August 28, 1959.

Mail Order store advertisement of November, 1925. Less of a bargain than suggested, the horn gramophone was actually on its way out.

Snyder, a music publisher, had been Irving Berlin's business partner back in the roaring days of ragtime, while the distinctively named Hero Freda Sybil de Rance, a Londoner born in 1907, was a pianist, singer and song composer. She had a major success in 1929 with *Journey's End*, with a lyric by Rex London, which was recorded by Raymond Newell and Peter Dawson.

Hal Swain's New Princes' Toronto Band recorded two attractive waltzes in 1925. *Sometime* had a lilting tune by Ted Fiorito and a lyric by Gus Kahn. It was sung by José Collins, who in 1917 had been *The Maid of the Mountains*. The song enjoyed a new lease of life in 1949, when Jo Stafford made a beautiful recording for Capitol, accompanied at the piano by George Greely.

Fiorito, who had many other hits, was born at Newark, New Jersey, in 1900. A pianist, he jointly directed the Oriole Orchestra with Dan Russo. Resident at the Oriole Terrace in Detroit, it began about 1922 and was greatly liked. Eventually, Fiorito went solo, leaving the Oriole Terrace to direct a band at the prestigious Edgewater Beach Hotel in Chicago. He died in July, 1971.

The second waltz recorded by Hal Swain's band came from a serious orchestral work, *At Twilight*, by the distinguished Czech composer Zdenek Fibich. Jan Kubelik transformed it into a languorous piece for solo violin and christened it *Poème*.

Poème became a great favourite with salon orchestras and was undeniably charming. In 1933 it underwent another change, when William Scotti made an adaptation (with due acknowledgement to Fibich), and Paul Francis Webster added a lyric. The result was *My Moonlight Madonna*.

During 1925, many records appeared on Columbia credited to the Hannan Dance Band. Quite a few of these had originated in New York, but others were made by a 'house' band in London, directed by Stan Greening, an arranger who could play banjo, piano and guitar.

Two enjoyable Hannan sides, under Greening's direction, featured tunes from *Katja the Dancer*, which opened in February with Lilian Davies in the name role. *Just for a Night*, a waltz, and *Leander*, a fox-trot, had delightful Jean Gilbert melodies. *Leander* had a lengthy and stylish trombone solo by Ted Heath, for years in demand as a session player. Why Hannan? Probably that will always remain an unsolved mystery.

At the start of 1924, John Birmingham and his Band, then

Jack Payne: In later years he married the concert pianist Peggy Cochrane and became a BBC disc jockey.

resident at the prestigious (if rather shabby) Hotel Cecil in the Strand, decided to move on. Their place was taken by a man unknown to the general public, who had to assemble a suitable band in some haste. His name was Jack Payne, and after several years of obscurity he was on the threshold of dazzling success.

John Wesley Vivian Payne was born in Leamington Spa on August 22, 1899, but grew up in Birmingham. With his mother's encouragement he developed into a talented pianist, but at 18 joined the Royal Flying Corps, in which he became a pilot. Demobilised in 1919, he formed a small band, and after some success with Midland gigs moved to London, still in demand for one-nighters.

His Hotel Cecil breakthrough led to regular broadcasts over 2LO and a few records. In August, 1925, he made four sides for Zonophone, one being *Yes, Sir! That's My Baby*, by Gus Kahn and Walter Donaldson. Payne made no more records until the summer of 1926, then appeared regularly on Regal from February, 1927, to January, 1928, by which time an even bigger slice of luck was coming his way.

In 1925, Tin Pan Alley took us to the *Bam, Bam, Bamy Shore*, although Alabama only has a small area of coastline around Mobile Bay. Mort Dixon and Ray Henderson's song was recorded for Victor by Roger Wolfe Kahn and his Orchestra, then resident at the Hotel Biltmore, in New York.

The son of millionaire banker Otto Kahn, young Roger followed Sir Thomas Beecham's excellent example and bought himself a band. Usually more sweet than swingy, it nevertheless provided temporary anchorage for jazz stalwarts like Manny Klein (trumpet), Miff Mole (trombone), Joe Venuti (violin) and Arthur Schutt (piano). Personnel changed frequently in the Kahn band during its short existence. More a dilettante than a true professional, he broke it up in 1928.

Serious musicians have often laughed at the number of people it could take to write a simple song. *I'm Knee-Deep in Daisies* needed five: Joe Goodwin, Jack Little, Jack Stanley, Paul Ash and Larry Shay, but nothing spectacular resulted. It was recorded for Victor by George Olsen and his Music, with a vocal duet by alto saxophonist Fran Frey and trumpeter Bob Rice.

Born in Portland, Oregon, on March 18, 1893, Olsen went early into the band business. His entire band appeared on stage in several Broadway musicals, notably Eddie Cantor's *Kid Boots* at the Earl Carroll Theatre in 1923 (music by

Harry Tierney), and *Sunny* at the New Amsterdam in 1925. Olsen probably retained affectionate memories of *Sunny* in particular, as his recording of *Who?* sold a million copies, the vocal (by Fran Frey, Bob Rice and Jack Fulton), setting the fashion for vocal trios.

Olsen's basically simple, zestful style, ideal for the Twenties, sounded increasingly dated when the Thirties brought in smoother, more sophisticated arrangements. Instead of moving with the times, he became a restaurateur, and died in 1971 on his 78th birthday.

Sunny, combining the considerable talents of Otto Harbach, Oscar Hammerstein II and Jerome Kern, began to charm London audiences in 1926. Meanwhile, one could hear its two biggest numbers, the title song and *Who?* on New York recordings by Eddie Elkins.

Elkins was playing on the Pacific Coast at the close of World War One, but moved east to New York, directing the resident band at the Knickerbocker Hotel from 1921 to 1926. Most of his Columbia records were correctly labelled over here, but for some reason *Sunny* and *Who?* were relegated to Regal and he was disguised as the Raymond Dance Band, a pseudonym masking the identities of various bands in the second half of the Twenties.

Columbia of London seem to have been addicted to this practice. 'The Denza Dance Band' could be one of many bands, among them those of Leo Reisman and Harry Reser, as well as Ben Selvin's Cavaliers and the California Ramblers. Under this guise, the Ramblers made a spirited recording of *Sweet Georgia Brown* (later a great jazz favourite), by Ben Bernie, Kenneth Casey and Maceo Pinkard.

So determined was Columbia to hide the American origin of such recordings that phoney British matrix numbers were printed on the labels. It all seemed rather pointless, because the sales potential of major bandleaders was obviously greater than that of the non-existent 'Denza'.

Quite undisguised, Fred Waring continued to woo the college set. His recording of *Collegiate*, a fox-trot by Nat Bonx, Moe Jaffe and Lew Brown, appeared in the Spring and sold well. When Harold Lloyd's new screen comedy *The Freshman* had its August premiere, Waring's Pennsylvanians presented a fast-paced show as a prologue, which was as well-received as the Pathé movie it preceded.

Despite his concert jazz pretensions, Paul Whiteman was still recording finger-snapping, appealing dance music. *I*

Miss My Swiss, My Swiss Miss Misses Me, a tongue-tangling novelty by L. Wolfe Gilbert and Abel Baer, caught the public fancy in 1925. Apart from John Sperzel's vocal, some yodelling by Frank Zimmerman supplied an appropriate Alpine touch.

I Miss My Swiss was trivial but cheerful, unlike the lachrymose *Pal of My Cradle Days*, a maudlin testimony to maternal love by Marshall Montgomery and Al Piantadosi. Whiteman's version had a vocal by Lewis James.

New Yorker Piantadosi had a penchant for schmaltz. In 1913 he created the tear-drenched *Curse of an Aching Heart,* abetted by lyricist Henry Finck. It was as bad as that absurdity of 1877 by the Reverend Robert Lowry, *Where is My Wandering Boy Tonight?*

But Whiteman redeemed himself with *Ukulele Lady*, a winner for Gus Kahn and Richard A. Whiting, played without 'concert' frills and sung by the Southern Fall Coloured Quartet.

Unfortunately, it triggered off a host of copyists, the Alley always being reluctant to abandon a lucrative theme. In 1926 we had to endure *Tune Up the Uke*, *Ukulele Lullaby*, *Ukulele Dream Man, Ukulele Baby* and even, heaven help us, *Under the Ukulele Tree.*

You didn't have to buy the records if you didn't like the songs, but I wonder how many people began to loathe that harmless Hawaiian native guitar?

Chapter Four

1926

"Charleston, Charleston, Show Me The Way"

'I am told that America's first "School of Syncopation" has been opened in New York,' began a *Daily Mirror* item in July, 1926. 'Instruction is to be given in jazz instruments of every kind, and the lessons at the school have been modelled on the lines of those given in academies of conventional music. Will the next step be a Jazz Chair at a university?'

It will be noted that the newspaper regarded jazz, for which read dance music, as unconventional. Popular music was rarely taken seriously by Fleet Street, the dissension engendered by the Charleston often inspiring facetious comment. But the Charleston, then at the peak of its popularity, was already being challenged by a newcomer from America, the short-lived and inelegant Black Bottom.

Dance musicians discovered a new magazine in 1926. *The Melody Maker* started in January as Lawrence Wright's house publication, produced in the basement of his Denmark Street office. Its first editor was Edgar Jackson, who later relinquished the post to become a record reviewer. The writer recalls his trenchant criticism of the latest emanations from Stan Kenton, Woody Herman and others, back in the early Fifties.

In March, the *Melody Maker* became an independent journal, always ready to expose exploitation and injustice in a notoriously insecure profession. Coverage of the home scene was comprehensive, although hilarious errors sometimes occurred when writing about Americans. Memory treasures such howlers as 'Glen Millar,' 'Bix Bidlebeck' and 'Mugsy Spaniard.' But overall the *Melody Maker* was just what the British musician needed: an intelligent, often combative paper highlighting his own particular problems and interests.

London was still Mecca for American bandleaders. Vincent Lopez had played at the Kit-Cat Club in 1925; and Paul Specht's Canadian Club Orchestra had a short stay there in 1926, under the direction of Orville Johnson.

While here, the Canadian Club Orchestra recorded *The Prisoner's Song* for Columbia, demonstrating how an imaginative arrangement and very relaxed playing could improve a simple waltz. Guy Massey, its composer, had actually done time. His song first appeared in 1924, providing a Victor best-seller for Vernon Dalhart (real name Marion Try Slaughter), a popular hillbilly singer of the Twenties.

The Savoy Orpheans changed leaders several times in 1926, but Debroy Somers was still in charge at the beginning of the year, when a non-vocal recording of *Five Foot Two,*

Eyes of Blue, a fox-trot by Sam M. Lewis, Joe Young and Ray Henderson, showed the band was still maintaining a high standard. Equally peppy was *Then I'll be Happy,* by Sidney Clare, Lew Brown and Cliff Friend, which had a vocal by Ramon Newton.

Sometimes a Spanish influence was heard, in particular the music of José Padilla and Tolchard Evans. Little is known about Padilla, who probably lived in Paris, but he had

Advertisement in October, 1926, for a new magazine, featuring songs which had earlier been hits.

four big hits in the Twenties: *El Relicario, La Violetera, Valencia* and *Ça, c'est Paris.*

It was Mistinguett who made the one-step *Valencia* famous at the Moulin Rouge in 1925, using the lyric by Lucien Boyer and Jacques Charles. In February, 1926, it was duetted by Lorna and Toots Pounds in Charles Gulliver's revue *Palladium Pleasures*, having received an English lyric from Eric Valentine. In Britain, the song became immensely popular, the Savoy Orpheans' recording having a Ramon Newton vocal. Spanish-style music had long been popular here, the tango first attracting Londoners in 1912, although it had closer links with Argentina.

But *Valencia* was challenged by *Barcelona,* which caught the flavour of Spanish music to perfection, as might be expected for its composer was no run-of-the-mill tune pedlar. Tolchard Evans was born at Haringay in 1901. His first name was actually Sydney, and Tolchard was his mother's maiden name.

His career as a songwriter lasted for at least 40 years, beginning shortly after the Great War, but from the mid-Twenties onward, he was also a resident bandleader, first at Westcliff and then at Southend. In 1931, his song *Lady of Spain* was one of the hits of the year, and altogether he is said to have composed around a thousand songs. Their lilting melodies made some as suitable for light orchestras as for dance bands. He died at Willesden on March 12, 1978.

Barcelona, his jaunty one-step, had a lyric written for Americans by Gus Kahn. The non-vocal Orpheans version, made in April, 1926, was waxed at Somers' last session before he left to form his own band, being then 36. Reginald Batten replaced him temporarily, while Ramon Newton began to direct the Havana Band. Batten resumed direction of the Havana two months later and Newton took over the Orpheans until succeeded by Carroll Gibbons early in 1927.

By the mid-Twenties every attractive girl was somebody's 'baby', or so Tin Pan Alley led us to believe. As usual overworking a popular theme, songwriters gave us *Bye-Bye, Baby, Naughty Baby, Everybody Loves My Baby, Tonight's My Night with Baby* and *There Ain't No Maybe in My Baby's Eyes.* There were many others, good, passable or excruciating; even an intriguing *Alibi Baby,* by Irving Caesar and Stephen Jones, from a Gaiety Theatre production called *Poppy.*

Harry Akst had his 'Baby' too. For *Baby Face* he used lyricist Benny Davis, and soon had a hit on his hands. It was

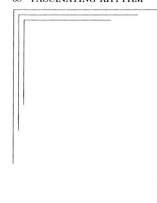

Tolchard Evans is believed to have composed a thousand tunes, but Lady of Spain *is the one we remember.*

just a routine fox-trot, but the Orpheans put a gloss on it. They recorded it in October, during Ramon Newton's tenure as director, with a vocal duet by Newton and Jim Cassidy, for the 'vocal refrain' was becoming more common.

Harry Akst was born in New York on August 15, 1894. His father, a serious musician, taught him to play the piano well enough to become a concert artist, but he turned instead to song composition, being employed for a time in Irving Berlin's publishing firm.

He began to write songs soon after his war service, producing nothing of consequence until 1923, when he composed *A Smile will Go a Long, Long Way,* with a Benny Davis lyric. He did much better in 1925 with *Dinah,* enlisting the veteran partnership of Sam Lewis and Joe Young.

Evergreen *Dinah* was recorded sentimentally by the immensely popular Revelers male voice quintet in 1925; swingily by the Benny Goodman Quartet in 1936; and flippantly by Danny Kaye (who called her 'Deenah'), in the post-war years. *Baby Face* outlived its time too, having an enthusiastic American revival in 1947.

At the close of 1926, the Orpheans recorded *Neapolitan Nights*, a waltz by J. S. Zamecnik from the Fox film *Fazil,* starring the silent screen stars Charles Farrell and Greta Nissen. The lyric was by Harry D. Kerr, who died, aged 77, on May 20, 1957. For once, the Orpheans were directed by Ben Evers, and not Newton.

In 1929, two years after the demise of the Orpheans, Evers, an arranger, assembled a band also called the Savoy Orpheans, although it had different players and no connection with the Savoy Hotel. It soon broke up, leaving behind a few sides by Dominion, of infamous memory. Evers died of a heart attack on September 27, 1931.

In the autumn of 1926, Carroll Gibbons, a founder member of the Savoy Orpheans, began to direct a section of the band from the piano. Called the Sylvians, and minus the brass, it played for dancers at the Berkeley Hotel, which was under the same management as the Savoy. For recording purposes brass was restored, the Sylvians then becoming a slightly smaller edition of the parent band.

Among a handful of HMV sides made that year, the Sylvians included *Everything will Happen for the Best*, a fox-trot by Buddy de Sylva and Lewis E. Gensler. Non-vocal, but with some stylish piano by Gibbons, it came from *Queen High*, a musical play by de Sylva and Laurence Schwab, which did moderately well at the Queen's Theatre in London, and much better at the Ambassador, in New York.

The Sylvians also recorded a number from *Lido Lady*, a musical play by the famous British revue writer Ronald Jeans, embellished by the songs of Rodgers and Hart. *Here in My Arms* made less impact than most numbers by that supremely gifted pair.

The career of Richard Rodgers is already well-known. Born in Long Island on June 28, 1902, his father was a doctor and his mother a fine amateur pianist. He is said to have been initially influenced by Jerome Kern, his association with Lorenz Milton Hart beginning in 1919 while both were at Columbia University. Rodgers died in New York on December 30, 1979.

Despite superb contributions to the musical theatre, after a daunting early struggle, the Rodgers and Hart partnership had its stormy interludes. Hart was the elder, born in New York on May 2, 1895. His lyrics had polish and sophistication; often with a cutting edge that only Cole Porter later matched; but he was moody and unreliable. Hart's creative work was virtually at an end, so erratic had he become, before he contracted pneumonia and died on November 22, 1943.

Mid-Twenties fashions and mannerisms prompted a sardonic comment from Edgar Leslie and James Monaco. *Masculine Women and Feminine Men* was recorded early in 1926 by the Savoy Havana Band, then still being directed by Reginald Batten. The vocalist (inevitably) was Ramon Newton.

No band should be judged solely by its records, many of which may not have been the leader's choice, but those made by Bert Ralton and his Havana Band were undeniably more routine than remarkable. *Picador*, by Horatio Nicholls, another song in the Spanish manner, had a rather odd lyric by Ray Morelle. The 'incidental singing' was by Fred Douglas as Harry Glen. *By the Light of the Stars*, dreamy sentimentality by George A. Little, Arthur Sizemore and Larry Shay, seemed more suitable for a salon orchestra.

Lawrence Wright called himself Everett Lynton for *I Never See Maggie Alone*, a comedy number suitable for the Halls, which became a smash-hit for Ralton, who sang it with his band. To confuse matters, the Savoy Havana Band recorded it a few weeks later.

Ralton's Havana Band also recorded *I'm a Little Blackbird Looking for a Bluebird*, by Grant Clarke, Roy Turk and George W. Meyer. This catchy novelty came from *Dixie to Broadway*, a New York show of 1924.

Engagement rates were falling, and although Ralton received many offers he became dissatisfied. In addition, the Ministry of Labour was making difficulties for foreigners seeking long-term work permits. In September, Ralton went to South Africa, taking Jack Jackson and Billy Mayerl with him.

It was an ill-starred venture. A few months after their arrival, Ralton was accidentally shot while on safari and died on January 16, 1927, being remembered for his likeable if restless personality and expertise with the soprano saxophone.

Most Horatio Nicholls songs had a happy ring, but *Speak* combined a lugubrious Ray Morelle lyric with a mournful tune. A waltz, it was recorded in February by Hal Swain's New Princes' Toronto Band at its penultimate session. This dirge sounded better as an orchestral piece, as played by the J. H. Squire Celeste Octet, then commanding huge fees wherever it appeared.

Devonshire-born J. H. Squire's Celeste Octet was a bill-topper in the days when light orchestral music was enormously popular.

The New Princes Restaurant had two good bands residing concurrently. Alfredo's only made a scattering of records, at infrequent intervals, for Winner. In the Spring of 1926 they included two outstanding numbers by the Gershwins, the title song and *Fascinating Rhythm*, from *Lady, Be Good*, which opened at the Empire Theatre in April, bringing back the Astaires.

Alfredo, whose real name was Alfred Gill, came from Newark, New Jersey. At the end of 1930 he disbanded, forming instead his Gypsy Orchestra, which drew much of its repertoire from Central European tzigane music. It recorded for HMV and Decca, toured and broadcast frequently. Alfredo died in 1966.

Jack Hylton's treatment of popular songs was full-blooded rather than fiery. He liked jazz, but wisely left its performance to others. In 1926 he recorded such transitory ditties as *When the Red, Red Robin Comes Bob, Bob, Bobbin' Along*, with words and music by Harry Woods, (who was born in North Chelmsford, Massachusetts, on November 4, 1896; went to Harvard; had a rather off-hand attitude to songwriting, despite many successes; and died at Phoenix, Arizona, on January 7, 1970); *Behind the Clouds*, a happy song by Buddy de Sylva and James F. Hanley; the delicious *Sleepy-Time Gal*, uniting Jospeh R. Alden, Raymond B. Egan, Ange Lorenzo and Richard A. Whiting; and Ted Waite's amusing novelty, *I've Never Seen a Straight Banana*.

Amid the gems and dross waxed by Hylton was *Oh! Miss*

Alfred Gill: Later he donned broad-brimmed hat and earrings for his 'Gypsy' image, but he had been 'Alfredo' when he first began to make records in the summer of 1925.

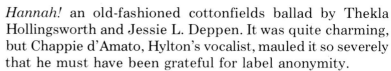

Binnie Hale, otherwise Beatrice Mary Hale-Monro. She made her debut in 1916 at the Empire Theatre in Follow the Crowd.

Hannah! an old-fashioned cottonfields ballad by Thekla Hollingsworth and Jessie L. Deppen. It was quite charming, but Chappie d'Amato, Hylton's vocalist, mauled it so severely that he must have been grateful for label anonymity.

Sunny opened at the London Hippodrome in October, with Binnie Hale (as 'Sunny'), Jack Buchanan and Elsie Randolph. Inevitably, Hylton recorded *Sunny* and *Who?* the biggest Kern and Hammerstein hits from this very successful show.

Hylton installed bands at several fashionable venues. When the Kit-Cat Club opened in 1925, he put in one under the direction of Al Starita, who was later to take charge of the Piccadilly Players at the Piccadilly Hotel, where Ray Starita was given the Piccadilly Revels Band to direct.

The Starita brothers were Bostonians of Italian extraction, except for Rudy, who was born in Naples. He doubled on drums and xylophone; Al played clarinet and alto saxophone; Ray clarinet and tenor saxophone. They figured prominently in the London band scene and were well-liked.

The Kit-Cat Band first recorded for HMV in June, 1925, continuing to do so until May, 1927, when it went over to

Above – *Al Starita, director of the Kit-Cat Band and the Piccadilly Players.*

Right – *Clem Lawton joined Jack Hylton in the summer of 1927. His ponderous brass bass gave way to the string variety early in the Thirties.*

Far right – *Jay Whidden, violinist from the State of Montana who became a Society bandleader. On many of his records he was the vocalist.*

Columbia, ceasing to record in March, 1928. It was sometimes labelled as Jack Hylton's Hyltonians. Basically a ten-man unit, it was augmented at times for recording purposes.

During its comparatively short existence, this band made a large number of records. One, in August, 1926, was *Breezin' Along with the Breeze*, the work of Haven Gillespie, Seymour Simons and Richard Whiting, a song which remained popular long after its first appearance.

The Piccadilly Revels Band made its recording debut late in December, four rather nondescript tunes being issued by Regal under the Raymond Dance Band collective pseudonym. At the start of 1927 it was upgraded to Columbia, recording under its true name until February, 1928. The line-up included Philip Cardew, doubling clarinet and alto saxophone; Clem Lawton, brass bass (a ponderous instrument replaced in most bands by the string variety in the early Thirties); and Rudy Starita, playing drums and xylophone.

Cardew was also the arranger. Born at Wimbledon in 1903, he had been to the Royal Academy of Music, and was a member of the Automobile Racing and Flying Clubs at Brooklands. In 1932 he became one of Henry Hall's staff arrangers, remaining with the BBC Dance Orchestra in that capacity until the end of 1936.

The Piccadilly Revels, it should be explained, were two floor shows, one at dinner and the other at supper time, consisting of first-class variety acts, with Ray Starita's band taking a prominent part in the festivities.

The Hotel Metropole had a cabaret too, called the Midnight Follies. From early in 1926 to the autumn of 1927, the resident band was that of Jay Whidden, a violinist and song composer from Montana, who formed his first British band shortly after World War One. After leaving the Metropole, he found an equally comfortable berth at the Carlton.

From March, 1926, to September, 1927, Whidden recorded for Columbia, afterwards appearing on various labels, notably Imperial and Decca. Early in the Thirties he returned to the States. In 1926 he recorded Roy Turk and Lou Handman's *You've Got Those Wanna-Go-Back-Again Blues*. Perhaps he ended up with them too.

Among better tunes waxed were R. H. Hardman's *My Carmenita,* an authentic Spanish one-step, and *Twilight on the Missouri,* a typically dreamy waltz (by Ralph Jack, Ray Vincent and Leo Herbert) extolling an American river. Whidden also recorded a fleeting novelty on the last day of

Cabaret at the Hotel Metropole in April, 1927. Producer Carl Hyson was probably still married to Dorothy Dickson at this time. Elsa Macfarlane was a prominent 'Co-optimist'.

Top – *Vivian Ellis: His inspired collaboration with A. P. Herbert gave us* Bless the Bride *in 1947.*

Centre – *Sidney Firman, whose London Radio Dance Band preceded those of Jack Payne and Henry Hall.*

Bottom – *Pasquale Troise played banjo for the London Radio Dance Band. Later he formed his Mandoliers and recorded for Decca.*

December. *Too Many Tots Make You Totter* was a caution against insobriety, not an endorsement of family planning. It was by Haydn and Francis, whoever they may have been.

Sigmund Romberg's light opera *The Student Prince* began to charm His Majesty's Theatre audiences in February, with baritone Harry Welchman in the lead. Romberg's entrancing music was mostly considered unsuitable for dance arrangements, but Percival Mackey recorded *Deep in My Heart, Dear*, and the *Serenade*.

On the other hand, talented and ambitious Vivian Ellis wrote music as attractive to dancers as to theatregoers. *Shake a Little Shoulder* and *Charleston, Charleston, Show Me the Way*, with lyrics by Desmond Carter, came from *Just a Little Kiss*, a musical comedy which opened at the Shaftesbury in September. They were lively tunes, giving the Mackey band an opportunity to step up the tempo.

In 1925, *Gentlemen Prefer Blondes*, a first and cynical novel by Anita Loos, became a best-seller. Buddy de Sylva and Lew Gensler wrote a song with the same title in 1926, which Mackey recorded in the autumn. Gentlemen actually marry brunettes averred Miss Loos, writing her sequel to that effect a couple of years later. It did not sell so well.

Of particular interest was the formation in 1926 of the London Radio Dance Band, a BBC 'house' aggregation foreshadowing the more ambitious bands of Jack Payne and Henry Hall. Directed by Sidney Firman (who died on December 14, 1932, at the early age of 32), it made its broadcasting debut on February 16. Firman was the sole violinist; Jack Padbury doubled alto saxophone and clarinet; the banjoist was Pasquale Troise.

Born at Naples in 1895, Troise remained with the band until it broke up. In March, 1928, Padbury took over from Firman, but shortly afterwards the band was succeeded by Jack Payne's which, although not 'house,' was tied to a BBC contract.

Troise joined Padbury's sextet at the Cosmo Club early in 1929 and was still a member at the end of 1930. Not long after that he formed his Mandoliers, featuring Birrell O'Malley, a concert-trained tenor, disguised as Don Carlos. Troise became very popular and recorded for Decca. He died in London on March 21, 1957.

1926 was a happy year for Irving Berlin, who liked to commemorate personal events with his song titles. In February, 1912, he had married Dorothy Goetz, but she died five months later of typhoid fever, contracted while they were honeymooning in Cuba. Berlin wrote *When I Lost You* in her memory.

It was 14 years before he married again, this time to the young heiress Ellin Mackay, against her father's wishes. The marriage worked out well, but it was eight years before Clarence H. Mackay lost his antipathy to his son-in-law.

No wonder, therefore, that Berlin was *At Peace with the World,* as duly recorded for Victor by Roger Wolfe Kahn and his Orchestra, with vocalist Henry Burr. Conceivably, *Don't Wait Too Long* had been some gentle advice to Berlin's eventual bride. It made a pleasant recording for Layton and Johnstone.

Irving Berlin was 38 and a wealthy man. Born Israel Baline, in Siberia, on May 11, 1888, he was four when his family emigrated to America. They lived in acute poverty on New York's tough East Side, but Berlin (as he called himself from 1907), was determined to break free of the mean streets.

He became a newsboy, then a singing waiter, and eventually worked for Ted Snyder's publishing firm, later to be made a partner. The Wall Street Crash almost ruined him, but by pouring out songs of superb quality, many for stage and screen musicals, he regained his prosperity. Whatever the future trends in popular music, and at present the standard is abysmal, it will be long before the name of Irving Berlin fades from memory. He died on September 22, 1989, Ellin having passed away in 1988.

Ben Selvin and the Cavaliers had *Someone to Love* in 1926, in the form of a song by Gus Kahn and Ted Fiorito. It was one of Selvin's records which Columbia credited to the Denza Dance Band.

Few American bands could match the Savoy Orpheans or Jack Hylton's show band for versatility. At the Waldorf Astoria, for example, Harold Leonard and his Orchestra played routine music in an unimaginative manner. Their plushy locale would have frowned upon fireworks, but it was possible to let oneself go on records, as Ambrose's May Fair Orchestra was to demonstrate so effectively.

Leonard's records appeared here on Brunswick, a typical example being *Hugs and Kisses*, a fox-trot by Raymond Klages and Louis Alter, which would have lent itself readily to an up-tempo arrangement. Instead it was given a perfunctory performance, with Harry Maxfield's high-pitched vocal.

Top – 'Don Carlos', who sang with Troise and his Mandoliers, was actually Christopher Thomas Birrell O'Malley. A concert-trained tenor from Edinburgh, he was as much at home in opera and oratorio.

Bottom – A pre-World War One photograph of Irving Berlin, who died in his 102nd year.

Alter, born at Haverhill, Massachusetts, in 1902, started out as a cinema pianist, became staff arranger to a music publisher, and later accompanied stage celebrities. His subsequent career as a songwriter led him to Hollywood.

His songs were perfectly acceptable, but he revealed his limitations when seeking to emulate Gershwin with his *Manhattan Serenade*, which appeared in 1928. It may have caught the moods of Manhattan, but sounded harsh, jerky and sometimes strident. Nat Shilkret recorded it with an augmented Salon Orchestra, but not even he could provide a smooth performance.

Harold Leonard may have made tedious listening, but much good music was issued by Brunswick during its long existence. Launched in October, 1923, by Chappells, it was taken over in 1927 by British Brunswick. In December, 1930, Warner Brothers acquired the label, and in June, 1933, it was purchased by Decca, who finally phased it out in the mid-Sixties.

Broad humour was always part of the Pennsylvanians' stock-in-trade. Much of it was of the cheap and cheerful variety, geared to the high spirits of co-eds, of whom Waring had once been one. Pat Ballard's *Any Ice Today, Lady?* was typical, sung by members of the band, in particular Poley McClintock, an old friend of Fred Waring's from their gig days at Penn State.

Hawaiian-style music had a few more years to go before the singing cowhands took over. For Arthur Coleman's *Sweet Hawaiian Dreams* and F. W. Vandersloot's *Hawaiian Sunset*, both waltzes, the Hilo Hawaiian Orchestra added the xylophones of Joe and George Hamilton Green, two very active 'session' brothers.

The music originated in New York, and the 'sound' was hardly authentic, but record buyers were not over-critical in the Twenties. It was a balm for tired city dwellers, and with a little imagination one could almost hear the surge of the incoming tide.

Chapter Five

1927

'Do The Black Bottom With Me'

The 3,000 miles a second New York-London Hit!

SHEPHERD
OF THE HILLS

FOX-TROT ∴ BALLAD
With Ukulele Accompaniment.

Music by . . .

HORATIO NICHOLLS

Composed on board S.S. "MAJESTIC" at sea.

Words by EDGAR LESLIE

Written on Broadway, New York City,

And transmitted to London *via* Transatlantic Telephony Service.

Played by JACK HYLTON AND HIS BAND

Copyright.

Lawrence Wright.

Printed in England.

Price 2/- net

Code SHEP

'Do you dance?' asked an HMV advertisement in 1927. 'There is a fascination about well-played dance music. The melody is there and an unfailing rhythm, but around them is woven a texture of quaint effects, so numerous and unexpected as to give one great respect for the clever people who think them all out.'

Dance music might be 'quaint,' but at least this naive description did not call it jazz. Records sold well, despite the relatively high prices of leading makes. In January alone, Columbia sold over two million discs.

On January 1, The British Broadcasting Company became a Corporation and John Reith, its first Director-General, was knighted. The BBC celebrated the New Year with two hours of dance music from the Albert Hall, played by Jack Hylton and his Orchestra.

Musical classicists and many churchmen disliked such music, the latter regarding it as a symbol of moral decline. But the public flocked to the London Palladium, where at least four bands presented shows in 1927: Bert Firman and his Devonshire House Band; Jack Hylton and his Orchestra; the Savoy Havana Band and Bert Ambrose's May Fair Hotel Orchestra.

The Charleston was on the way out, so Leyton Council lifted a ban on dancing it in halls under their control, having previously considered it too dangerous. The *Melody Maker* commented unfavourably on dancing trends. In a July editorial, Edgar Jackson wrote: 'Modern ballroom dancing has narrowed itself down to within the confines of the fox-trot, now a standard dance; the Charleston, anything but standard; and the Black Bottom, which has become a terpsichorean hotch-potch.'

Introduced by de Sylva, Brown and Henderson into George White's *Scandals* at New York's Apollo Theatre in 1926, the Black Bottom soon became 'old hat', but it is curious that Jackson ignored the waltz, which was always very popular.

On August 23, Hal Swain and Alfredo, still resident at the New Princes Restaurant, were the first bandleaders to broadcast over 5GB, an Experimental Station at Daventry, which only went on the air two days previously.

Swain began to record for Regal in June, continuing to do so until 1930, when he switched to Broadcast and in 1931 to Imperial. His first Regal record was *Muddy Water*, by Jo Trent, Harry Richman and Peter de Rose. Swain took the

vocal spot himself. Joe Daniels was in this eight-man unit, still remembered for his fiery Hotshots, who recorded for Parlophone in the post-war era.

About three weeks before his historic broadcast, Swain recorded de Sylva, Brown and Henderson's *Lucky Day*, also from the current edition of George White's *Scandals* – a revue which was hardly scandalous – but for some reason by-passed *The Birth of the Blues,* a better song.

Alfredo recorded for Winner from the summer of 1925 to October, 1927, but his 54 sides were meagre compared with the output of many bands. Some were of little worth, unless one enjoyed such ephemera as Charles Tobias, Al Sherman and Harry Woods' *Me Too – Ho! Ho! Ha! Ha!* or Irving King's *The More We are Together,* the anthem of the Frothblowers, a fraternity with its own insignia and rules, flourishing after the war among those with money to spare for hard drinking.

Of greater interest was Alfredo's recording of *Do the Black Bottom with Me,* by George W. Meyer, which saluted the latest dance craze in lively fashion.

Lawrence Wright was at his most enterprising in 1927. One could then advertise on the front page of Saturday's *Daily Mail,* so Wright bought the entire page on October 8, to launch his latest Horatio Nicholls song, *Souvenirs.* The lyric was by Edgar Leslie, who became his American agent that year.

Norman MacPhail Blair, better known as Maurice Elwin. He recorded under all kinds of names, but often anonymously.

The advertisement cost Wright £1400, but obviously paid off. The ballad was a best-seller here and did well in America too, its melody equally suitable for light orchestral treatment or as a dance band arrangement. One minor, but interesting recording was made for Guardsman by the Cabaret Dance Orchestra, a 'house' band directed by Harry Bidgood, with a vocal now known to be by Tom Barratt, although believed earlier to be by Maurice Elwin.

Bidgood and Barratt also recorded *Mountain Greenery*, one of the most joyous songs created by Rodgers and Hart. It came from *The Girl Friend,* which opened in September at the Palace Theatre, with Emma Haig in the lead.

Guardsman first appeared in 1914 and made its final bow in May, 1928. During the Twenties it was showy in white and gold. Bidgood, who not only assembled their 'house' band but almost certainly provided the arrangements, became Light Music Director for Vocalion.

Maurice Elwin was born at Uddingston, near Glasgow, in 1898. A thoroughly dependable vocalist, he could handle dreamy ballads or up-tempo swingers with equal aplomb. I am indebted to Cavan O'Connor (who knew him well) for the information that Elwin's real name was Norman MacPhail Blair. He recorded under that name for Zonophone, but appeared on many labels under various pseudonyms, or simply anonymously.

In 1927, the Vocalion Gramophone Co. Ltd. abandoned the upper end of the record market to concentrate exclusively on popular music. The ten and twelve-inch Vocalion and Aco records were discontinued and a new, eight-inch disc called Broadcast was introduced. The red, white and gold label was only two inches in diameter and, by means of closer grooving, a playing time equivalent to that of a ten-inch disc was achieved. Electrical recording by the Marconi process was excellent and, at only 1s 3d (just under 7p) it was good value for money.

Apart from Bidgood's many session bands, genuine ones appeared on Broadcast. Among the earliest was that of Victor Vorzanger, a Hungarian violinist, who had recorded early in the Twenties for Aco and Scala. In the summer of 1927 he was at the East Ham Palais de Danse.

Vorzanger made only four sides for Broadcast (in October) before ceasing to record altogether. Judged by these it was a lively band with good soloists, and it is curious that no more recordings were made. *Oh, Baby, Don't We Get Along?* and *It All Depends on You* were by de Sylva, Brown and Henderson;

a third was Horatio Nicholls' *Souvenirs;* and the last a typically bouncy Yellen and Ager number called *Crazy Words, Crazy Tune.* Although styled as Victor Vorzanger's Famous Dance Band, it was hardly one of the élite.

On the first two sides the vocalist was John Thorne, a rather tragic figure who failed to achieve his full potential. Born at Manchester in 1893, his real name Thomas Greenhalgh, he went to Merchant Taylors School. Enlisting in 1914 and wounded five times, he was awarded the Military Cross and the Distinguished Conduct Medal.

Thorne, a concert-trained baritone whose 'serious' records won critical approval, was dogged by ill-health. As a session singer he was frequently employed by Bidgood, coming over well on sweeter ballads, although a rollicking fox-trot was never his forte. He died on September 17, 1939.

The saxophone became the symbol of between-wars dance music. 'We've boyish busts and Eton crops/We quiver to the saxophone,' wrote one minor poet in 1926. People who disliked dance music complained of the saxophone's 'moan,' an epithet hardly applicable to such a powerful instrument. In 1927 the dancing licence of the Liberal Club in Wallasey was only renewed on the strict understanding that visiting

Victor Vorzanger's Famous Dance Band, which made four sides for Broadcast in 1927, after which Vorzanger ceased to make records.

*Ray Starita, in the days of the
'moaning' saxophone.*

bands must not play saxophones. Their sound was considered too penetrating and likely to disturb the neighbours.

Al Starita, whose alto saxophone was never heard to moan, directed the Kit-Cat Band throughout 1927, treating *C'est Vous,* a lingering waltz by Abner Greenberg, Abner Silver and Harry Richman, with the same respect afforded Yellen and Ager's cheery little fox-trot *Ain't She Sweet?* which became the theme music of *Foxy Lady*, a TV comedy series of the early Eighties, starring Diane Keen as a provincial newspaper editor.

The Kit-Cat Club got into trouble, but not because of 'penetrating' saxophones. Night clubs were often raided by the police, illicit gambling or violation of the drinking laws being the usual charges. The Kit-Cat was raided in 1927 and decided to become a Society restaurant, still employing the best of the bands.

No such problems beset the Piccadilly Hotel; and its Revels Band, under Ray Starita's direction, recorded frequently for Columbia. In the autumn it was reduced from 11 men to seven, but the redundant players were brought back for records.

After an excellent Broadway run, Sigmund Romberg's *The Desert Song* opened at Drury Lane in April, with Edith Day and Harry Welchman sharing the lead. *Blue Heaven*, just as frequently called *The Desert Song Waltz,* and an irresistible tune, was heard everywhere. Created by Otto Harbach, Oscar Hammerstein II, Frank Mandel and Romberg himself, it quite justified the collective effort. The Piccadilly Revels Band recorded it in March, exactly seven day before the curtain first rose.

During the Thirties, brisk, happy-go-lucky songs would gradually be supplanted by smoother, often rather mournful ballads, as the Depression began to influence Tin Pan Alley. But that was still to come. Meanwhile, Ray Starita could record *Does She Love Me? Positively, Absolutely!* by Sam Coslow and Jean Herbert; and *Is She My Girl Friend? How-de-ow-Dow!* by the ubiquitous Yellen and Ager, in the punchy style that was still in favour.

Many songs survived the Twenties to become standards, or were revived many years after their original appearance. For example, *In a Shady Nook, By a Babbling Brook* became as closely identified with Donald Peers as *I'm Only a Strolling Vagabond* did with Cavan O'Connor, both ballads thus receiving an extended lease of life.

An advertisement of 1927. Brunswick underwent several changes of ownership, but survived (ultimately in L.P. form) until about 1967.

In a Shady Nook, by Harry Pease and Ed Nelson, was recorded in 1927 by Jay Whidden and his New Midnight Follies Band, with Whidden's own vocal. Whidden also recorded Billy Rose, Al Jolson and Dave Dreyer's *Me and My Shadow,* which was revived shortly after World War Two.

Layton and Johnstone must have recorded nearly every hit from both sides of the Atlantic while they were together. *Bye, Bye, Blackbird,* a triumph for Mort Dixon and Ray Henderson, was the kind of song they performed extremely well. They also helped to popularise *Anytime, Anywhere,* a new British waltz by Clifford Seyler and Reginald Morgan.

Reginald Dudley Morgan, born at West Norwood in 1900, had studied at the Royal Academy of Music, winning medals and awards as a pianist. He wrote music for several films, as well as other songs, but never had another success like *Anytime, Anywhere.*

Top – *Carroll Gibbons: His friendly drawl endeared him to radio listeners.*

Bottom – *Dolores del Rio: The waltz* Ramona *was dedicated to her.*

Irving Berlin created some outstanding songs at this period in his career. One of the most enduring was *Blue Skies,* typifying his deceptively simple, melodic approach to song-writing. Not all Berlin songs were unforgettable after one hearing, but *Blue Skies* made an immediate impact.

The Debroy Somers Band recorded it in March, its leader beginning a fresh association with Columbia that lasted until late in the Thirties. Somers actually tried HMV first, but the sides he made were rejected. It was ironic that he went to Columbia, considering how often he had flouted their contract while directing the Savoy Orpheans.

Carroll Gibbons began to direct the Orpheans in January and several changes occurred. Frank Guarente joined as sole trumpeter (there had previously been two), and the violins of Teddy Sinclair, Reg Pursglove and Sidney Kyte were added. Ramon Newton, who had been violinist, vocalist and briefly director, still sang for the band.

Guarente was a real asset. Earlier in the Twenties he had been with the Georgians, a hot quintet within Paul Specht's band. Such units were by no means unusual. Whiteman employed his star players in this manner to give some credibility to his King of Jazz cognomen; and the Bob Cats played Dixieland jazz as part of the Bob Crosby orchestra.

Guarente had left Specht to form his own New Georgians, and play on the Continent. He joined the Orpheans in January, and stayed until Wilfred de Mornys finally called it a day.

Reginald William Pursglove, a Londoner, born on November 21, 1902, won a Carnegie Scholarship at the Guildhall School of Music. He played in a theatre orchestra before becoming an Orphean. In 1930 he formed his own orchestra, securing engagements at the Malmaison Restaurant, Embassy Club and Quaglino's.

Kyte was equally accomplished. Born in Stamford Hill on June 1, 1896, he studied viola, violin, and piano at the Royal Academy of Music, and formed his first band after a nine-year stint with the Life Guards ended in 1923. In October, 1931, he took a band to the Piccadilly Hotel, leaving in June, 1936, to begin a stage tour. He died on July 29, 1981.

In 1926, Fox Films made *What Price Glory?* with Mexico's own Dolores del Rio playing *Charmaine,* inspiring a beautiful waltz by Ernö Rapee, with a lyric by Lew Pollack. Film and song were alike popular; the Savoy Orpheans' recording appearing in the summer of 1927, with a Ramon Newton vocal.

Ernö Rapee was born in Budapest on June 4, 1891, and

graduated from the Conservatory in 1909. In 1913 he was appointed Musical Director of the Hungarian Opera Company in New York. He guest conducted the Berlin, Budapest and Vienna Philharmonic Orchestras, and in 1932 became Musical Director of the Radio City Music Hall. Renowned for his graceful songs, he died on June 26, 1945.

Two real charmers recorded by the Orpheans in 1927 were Rodgers and Hart's *The Blue Room,* from *The Girl Friend,* and the Gershwins' haunting *Someone to Watch Over Me,* from *Oh, Kay!* which opened at His Majesty's Theatre in September and brought home Gertrude Lawrence from her Broadway triumph.

Both *The Blue Room* and *Someone to Watch Over Me* had vocals by the Hamilton Sisters and Fordyce, but the Orpheans ignored *Do-Do-Do,* which Miss Lawrence had recorded herself, with a touch of naughtiness that was quite irresistible, for Victor at Camden, in October, 1926.

Throughout the decade, new dances came and went with a mayfly brevity. If you weren't doing the Raccoon or wishing you could shimmy like your sister Kate, you could have a go at the Varsity Drag, or check to see if the Breakaway really was 'as easy as pie'. In 1927 it was time to try the Yale Blues, although that did not last long either.

Gertrude Lawrence, for whom Noel Coward had a high regard. Her 1908 debut was as a child dancer in Dick Whittington *at the Brixton Theatre.*

Vivian Ellis, ever alert to changes in musical fashion, composed his own *Yale Blues*, and Collie Knox, a young Irish journalist, wrote the lyric. It wasn't really a blues, of course; just another bright little song, recorded (non-vocal) by the Orpheans at Hayes in September, and in New York in January, 1928, by Waring's Pennsylvanians.

Few white men really understood the blues, although jazz clarinettist Mezz Mezzrow probably got nearer than most. Its origins lay deep in the sadness and isolation of American negroes; in an 8- or 12-bar form it became the basis of jazz music at its most moving.

It was hard to escape from de Sylva, Brown and Henderson, who rarely wrote a dull song. *Here am I, Broken-Hearted* was not nearly as sad as the title implied, and the Sylvians played it with gusto. They also recorded Frank Swain's waltz *Just a Rose in Old Killarney*, which sounded distinctly passé in 1927.

The Sylvians made their last record on December 13; but the Savoy Havana Band ceased to record three months earlier, and the Orpheans never went to Hayes after November 30.

The Savoy Havana Band made some splendid records just before the axe fell. *There Ain't No Maybe in My Baby's Eyes*, a typically happy Walter Donaldson song, with a lyric by Gus Kahn and Raymond B. Egan, was played Charleston-style; *At Sundown*, entirely by Donaldson, received equally vigorous treatment; and there was a pleasantly relaxed performance of Harry Woods' *Side by Side*.

For waltz lovers, the Havana Band recorded two by Edgar Leslie and Horatio Nicholls: *My Tumbledown Cottage of Dreams* and *The Whispering Pines of Nevada*. In 1927, this pair seemed to turn out one successful song after another.

When Reginald Batten took the Savoy Havana Band to the London Palladium in June, it may well have triggered off an inevitable clash between Wilfred de Mornys and the management of the Savoy and Berkeley Hotels. The latter objected to the bands providing public entertainment and decided to forbid it. Their intransigent attitude was matched by determination on the part of de Mornys not to yield.

It was a clash of wills and nobody won. There would be no more stage shows, but no bands either. In November, de Mornys refused to renew his contract. The Sylvians disappeared immediately; the Savoy Havana Band, renamed the Original Havana Band, despite different players, carried on until early in 1929. Under Newton's direction it made some quite acceptable records for Broadcast.

The Savoy Orpheans also lingered on, but not for long. Carroll Gibbons renamed them the Original Savoy Orpheans and played some German engagements, but afterwards broke the band up. Ben Evers' abortive attempt to launch a bogus Savoy Orpheans band resulted in a lawsuit. The Twenties still had a little way to go, but an era ended at the close of 1927.

In September, Peter Yorke played some syncopated piano music over 2LO, favourably impressing the Melody Maker, which considered he had 'a good attack and distinct rhythm'. He joined Jack Hylton in January, 1929, as pianist and arranger, staying until the end of 1931.

Peter Yorke, F.R.C.O., was born in London on December 4, 1902. At Trinity College of Music he studied organ and composition, afterwards leading his own semi-pro band for a time. He freelanced after leaving Hylton until he formed a broadcasting orchestra in 1936, and three years later a concert orchestra. Following his war service he assembled a new concert orchestra, often graced by the exquisite alto saxophone solos of Freddy Gardner. It made many records for Columbia. Yorke died on February 2, 1966.

The Hylton band appeared at the Hippodrome in *Shake Your Feet,* a revue which opened in July, 1927. The cast included Laddie Cliff, Gwen Farrar and Billy Mayerl. That month, Jack Jackson joined Hylton, replacing Charlie Pemell who, having been with the band since its inception, went to Percival Mackey.

Jackson, born at Barnsley in 1907, had studied trumpet at the Royal Academy of Music. He played for obscure bands until engaged by Bert Ralton in 1925. In 1931 he left Hylton for a spell with Jack Payne before forming his own band in 1933.

As a bandleader he was regarded by his men as likeable but lazy, unlike Payne, who was loathed as a disciplinarian. After a lengthy stay at the Dorchester, Jackson began to tour, but in 1940 took up residence at the May Fair. He disbanded in 1947, and died in Jersey on January 15, 1978.

Jack Hylton's records in 1927 concentrated on good songs, avoiding the witless trash so frequently masquerading as humour. Unlike the Orpheans, he recorded *Do-Do-Do*, using a vocal trio of himself, Hugo Rignold and Chappie d'Amato. They harmonised very well and a trio was thus employed on many occasions.

Above – *Joe Gilbert, lyricist and composer. On sheet music always shown as Jos. Geo. Gilbert.*

Right – *Flying over Blackpool Tower in September, 1927, to publicise* Me and Jane in a 'Plane.

The tuneful trio sang *Ain't That a Grand and Glorious Feeling?* an explosion of happiness by Yellen and Ager; and *Me and Jane in a 'Plane*, a really inspired Edgar Leslie lyric matching an exuberant tune by a young English composer named Joe Gilbert (always shown on sheet music as Jos. Geo. Gilbert).

Gilbert's song came at a time of increasing public interest in air travel, and an aeroplane was appropriately used to push sales. Lawrence Wright, who published the song, hired a big, slow biplane on Sunday, September 4, which circled Blackpool Tower, the Hylton band playing lustily, while copies of the sheet music were dropped to holiday makers below.

That was resourceful enough, but for sheer ingenuity the manner employed to launch *Shepherd of the Hills* took some beating. Inspired by the name of a racehorse, Wright composed the melody while crossing the Atlantic on the *Majestic*. In New York he got an 'instant' lyric from Edgar Leslie and, by prior arrangement, contacted Hylton on February 10.

The Transatlantic Telephony Service had only linked America and Britain on January 7. Invited members of the press watched in the *Melody Maker* office as Hylton took down details of the song, partly dictated by Wright and partly sung by Ennis Parkes who, with Joe Gilbert, had accompanied Wright to New York.

A distinctive arrangement – the *Melody Maker* considered it 'symphonic' – was done at very short notice by Leighton Lucas, and the new Horatio Nicholls ballad was heard at the Alhambra Theatre the same evening. *Shepherd of the Hills*, described as 'the best and the worst popular number ever composed', was really neither; just a catchy tune and a Tin Pan Alley lyric of no great merit. But with such publicity, how could it fail?

The sheet music cover, printed in red and bearing a portrait of Hylton, described *Shepherd of the Hills* as 'the 3000 miles a second New York – London hit.' The telephone call cost Wright £140, no mean sum in 1927 but peanuts compared to the reward he reaped.

Next day Hylton was injured in a car crash while driving to Hayes through dense fog to record the song. The band was directed instead by Chappie d'Amato, who sang the chorus. On March 2, Hylton made a fresh recording with his own vocal. Both versions went on sale.

Seventh Heaven, a Fox Film co-starring Charles Farrell and Janet Gaynor, was released here in 1928, but its theme song preceded it. Hylton's lush version of *Diane, I'm in Heaven When I See You Smile* did full justice to Rapee's wistful melody.

Hylton used no vocalist for *Diane* and neither did he for *I'm Looking Over a Four-Leaf Clover*, a carefree ditty by Mort Dixon and Harry Woods, recorded at the Kensington Cinema, with Claude Ivy's Wurlitzer organ added to the band. Ivy later became Decca's staff pianist. For *Meadow Lark* by Hal Keidel and Ted Fiorito, Hylton took the vocal spot himself.

Although Hylton had once been 'the Singing Mill Boy', he always sounded harsh on records. In 1927 he was 35, with 13 years to go as a bandleader and many more as an impresario. His gifts as a showman were already in evidence as the Twenties approached their final phase.

While Hylton kept both press and public entertained with his antics, Ambrose took the most important step of his entire career. On March 27, 1927, the luxurious May Fair Hotel opened in Berkeley Square, and Ambrose left the

Fox's Seventh Heaven *rocketed Janet Gaynor to stardom in 1927, beginning a screen partnership with Charles Farrell which went on into the early years of the talkies.*

Embassy Club to become Musical Director. For this he was paid a staggering £10,000 a year, making him the highest paid bandleader in Britain.

By instinct and training, Bert Ambrose was ideal for the May Fair, where music had to be soft enough for dancers to hear their own heavy breathing, and the tempo subtly adapted for their terpsichorean limitations. Ambrose enjoyed catering for Society; and Society liked Ambrose.

It was different when he went to the recording studio. He was then aiming at a public which wanted less inhibited performances, stopping short of outright jazz. Ambrose actually liked jazz, admiring the expertise of its exponents. His front-line players could blow up quite a storm, aided by a superb rhythm section; but it was always dance music.

With such a princely salary, Ambrose could have become wealthy, but he was a compulsive gambler, playing for high stakes and lacking a winning streak. Sometimes, after a particularly bad night at the tables, even the band payroll was at risk. In his final years, Ambrose was extremely hard up, dependant on the goodwill of others, and became a tragic figure before he died on June 12, 1971.

After making no records since 1923, Ambrose recorded half a dozen sides for Brunswick in June, 1927. His 11-man May Fair Orchestra included hot trumpeter Henry Levine, born in London on November 26, 1906, but taken to New York as a baby. Levine went back to New York later in 1927, becoming a distinguished jazz and dance musician. In the late Thirties he helped to form the Chamber Music Society of Lower Basin Street, a distinctively named and innovative jazz band which broadcast regularly over NBC and made many records.

Others in the new Ambrose band were Jack Miranda, doubling alto saxophone and clarinet; Joe Crossman, an outstanding tenor sax player who later joined Lew Stone; and Sydney Lipton, a violinist who became a Society bandleader too, finding a comfortable niche at Grosvenor House.

Of the six sides recorded, possibly the most interesting was *The Birth of the Blues*, a light-hearted explanation of jazz origins by de Sylva, Brown and Henderson, with a vocal by the Hamilton Sisters and Fordyce.

In July, Jack Payne and his Hotel Cecil Band appeared for a week at the Holborn Empire. The *Melody Maker* was impressed: 'The band is good, the programme is good, the arrangements are exceptionally good.' Payne first began to

broadcast from the Cecil in 1927, but no-one knew then that the hotel's days were numbered. On February 28, 1930, it closed, the new owners, Shell-Mex, having decided to erect offices on the site.

Broad comedy, so much a part of Payne's band shows, went on records too. Campbell and Connelly's *Since Tommy Atkins Taught the Chinese How to Charleston* – the mind boggles! – had a vocal by Payne himself; but better songs were also waxed. *In a Little Spanish Town,* a sunny waltz by Mabel Wayne, aided by Sam Lewis and Joe Young, had another, typically high-pitched Payne vocal; and *I'm Coming, Virginia* gave the band a chance to show its mettle.

Published in 1926, *I'm Coming, Virginia* became a jazz standard. Donald Heywood wrote the lyric; Will Marion Cook the music. Born in Washington, D.C., on January 27, 1869, Cook was a talented black bandleader and composer. His all-negro musical comedy *In Dahomey,* starring Bert Williams, was a sensation at the Shaftesbury Theatre in 1903. In 1919, Cook himself was in London, directing his Southern Syncopators, with the distinguished jazzman Sidney Bechet as featured soloist. Will Marion Cook died in New York on July 18, 1944.

Left – Bert Ambrose: £10,000 a year at the May Fair Hotel, but how much lost at the gambling tables?

Centre – Hot trumpeter Henry Levine, a founder member of the Chamber Music Society of Lower Basin Street.

Right – Jack Miranda doubled alto saxophone and clarinet for Ambrose 1927-28.

From 1925 to 1928, Zonophone's Light Music Director was Bert Firman, a violinist, who was born in 1906. His 'house' bands included the Rhythmic Eight, continued by his brother John, who succeeded him. Bert Firman also found time to direct resident bands at the Carlton Hotel (1924-1926) and Devonshire Restaurant (1926-1927), both recording profusely for Zonophone.

Music at the Devonshire Restaurant was played from 9pm to 2am and the band had no brass. For recording purposes, trumpeters Charles Rocco or Frank Guarente (both Orpheans), and sometimes trombonist Ted Heath were brought in. John Firman was the regular pianist until the band broke up. He then formed his own, including alto saxophonist Jerry Hoey, and played at Verrey's Restaurant.

Away from the restrictions of the Devonshire, Bert Firman's band could better demonstrate its capabilities. Among its 1927 recordings were *Persian Rosebud,* a new Edgar Leslie and Horatio Nicholls fox-trot, and *There's Everything Nice About You*, teaming lyricists Alfred Bryan and Arthur Terker with composer Pete Wendling, a New Yorker, born in 1888.

After leaving Zonophone, Bert Firman became a full-time bandleader, playing in London, Monte Carlo and America. He was certainly active until the end of the Thirties, but apart from four sides each for HMV and Parlophone in 1937, made no more records in England.

Hit the Deck opened at New York's Belasco Theatre in April, and ran for a year. In November it also began in London, at the Hippodrome, starring Stanley Holloway and Ivy Tresmand. Among Vincent Youmans' hits were *Hallelujah!* with a lyric by Leo Robin and Clifford Grey, and *Sometimes I'm Happy,* with an equally good lyric by Irving Caesar. Both were recorded by Percival Mackey's Band in September for Edison Bell's new Electron label, which only lasted until 1930.

Back in February, while still under contract to Columbia, Mackey saluted Willard Robison, a bandleader whose songs were highly regarded in America, although they seem to have aroused less interest over here. *The Music of a Mountain Stream,* a fox-trot, was just an agreeable pastoral ditty, with a vocal by Fred Douglas.

Drifting and Dreaming, with Douglas again the vocalist, was recorded at the same session. Haven Gillespie wrote the lyric; but it required the combined efforts of Egbert van Alstyne, Erwin R. Schmidt and Loyal Curtis to compose a simple, if languorous waltz tune.

Ivy Tresmand began as a chorus girl at the Comedy Theatre in 1915.

Van Alstyne was a veteran songwriter. Born on March 5, 1882, in Marengo, Illinois, he played the church organ as a child of seven. Later, he studied at Chicago Musical College. He eventually teamed up with Harry Williams, but they had a hard struggle until they came up with *Navajo* in 1903.

They wrote a real winner two years later with *In the Shade of the Old Apple Tree,* and in 1907 the charming ballad *Your Eyes Have Told Me So.* During the Great War, van Alstyne collaborated with Gus Kahn. His songwriting career seems to have ended with the Twenties.

Electrical recording brought cinema organists into the catalogues, and Jack Courtnay appeared on both Columbia and Regal in the late Twenties, playing a Christie Unit organ at the Elite Cinema, Wimbledon. For Columbia he recorded *Shalimar,* an oriental winner in waltz-time by Edgar Leslie and Horatio Nicholls. This song also appeared on Victor, played by Waring's Pennsylvanians, with a vocal by Tom Waring.

British songwriters often complained that the American market was closed to them, but Lawrence Wright proved otherwise. Astute enough to use good American lyricists, he made his songs as welcome in New York as in London. American publishers were neither parochial nor prejudiced. If a British ballad was a money-spinner, they wanted it.

With a sound 'Co-optimist' reputation already, Melville Gideon branched out as a crooner. In the autumn he went home to New York, where he made some records at the Victor studios for HMV. They included two lovely songs: *The Hours I Spent with You,* by Sam M. Lewis, Joe Young and 'Little' Jack Little, and *My Heart Stood Still,* a Rodgers and Hart gem from *A Connecticut Yankee,* then at the Vanderbilt Theatre.

Back in January, Gideon had recorded a song by Irving Berlin, written in 1926, obviously as a tribute to Ellin Mackay. How many young ladies have received as tasteful a compliment as *Because I Love You?*

Crooners seem to have arrived about mid-decade. Gideon was an appealing example of the genre; so was his fellow countryman Gene Austin, who was born in 1900 and died on January 24, 1972. Austin, a Victor recording star, had at least two big hits in 1927, *Lonesome Road,* with his own lyric and Nat Shilkret's music, and *My Blue Heaven,* in which George Whiting and Walter Donaldson purred with cozy domesticity.

Lonesome Road, a rather mournful spiritual, suited Austin's

Top – *Laura la Plante shared top billing with Joseph Schildkraut in Universal's silent version of* Show Boat, *but was overshadowed by the Paul Whiteman Band in Universal's* The King of Jazz. *She had originally intended to be a violinist.*

Bottom – *Jack Smith's soft-voiced singing earned him the soubriquet of 'The Whispering Baritone'. He came to London in 1927.*

soft-voiced, very relaxed style, and in 1929 was interpolated into the first screen version of *Show Boat*, made by Universal, with Joseph Schildkraut and Laura La Plante sharing top billing.

Whispering Jack Smith entertained London audiences with his hushed baritone in 1927. A New Yorker, born in 1899, his vaudeville appearances won him a tremendous following, and he could be remarkably effective in songs like *Me and My Shadow*. In 1927, his Victor recordings included *The Best Things in Life are Free,* a memorable song by de Sylva, Brown and Henderson, from *Good News*, a college musical better understood by young America than by the average Briton. It came to the Carlton Theatre in August, 1928, but had only a short run. Jack Smith, many of whose records sold well here, died in May, 1951.

Charles Lindbergh's cross-Atlantic flight in 'The Spirit of St. Louis' inspired several tunesmiths. To be really effective, a topical song had to be launched quickly. Lindbergh took off from New York on May 20, landing at Le Bourget 33 hours later. On May 26, *Lucky Lindy*, by L. Wolfe Gilbert and Abel Baer, was recorded in New York's Liederkranz Hall and soon on sale. It was performed by the 'house' Victor Orchestra, Nat Shilkret conducting, with a vocal quintet including 27-year-old Richard Crooks, soon to become a famous concert and operatic tenor.

The Troubadours was a Victor 'house' band from the early Twenties to 1931, directed by Hugo Frey or Nat Shilkret. For *Baby Feet Go Pitter Patter*, Shilkret directed, and the Revelers (here a quartet), sang the vocal refrain. Franklyn Baur, Charles Harrison, Elliott Shaw and Wilfred Glenn also recorded individually at times. *Baby Feet* was the Alley at its sentimental worst, with Gus Kahn for once composer as well as lyricist.

Shilkret's assistant, Leonard Joy, frequently directed studio orchestras or provided accompaniment for singers. Joy directed the Hilo Hawaiian Orchestra for recordings of *Hawaiian Nights* and *Aloma*, neither the work of a Hawaiian. *Hawaiian Nights* was a waltz by Lee S. Roberts, formerly an executive of the QRS company, which made piano rolls. His first hit song – and it was a very big hit – was *Smiles*, published in 1917, which established the reputation of lyricist J. Will Callahan.

On the other hand, *Aloma* was one of a number of light pieces by the serious composer Robert Hood Bowers. For both recordings the Hilo Hawaiians were reduced to a quintet, including Frank Ferera's steel guitar, but when a fuller sound was required the orchestra was considerably enlarged.

The regular dance bands sometimes came in for adverse criticism, particularly when visiting this country. Johnny Hamp came under fire from the *Melody Maker* in October, 1930, after playing at the Kit-Cat. 'The Kentucky Serenaders' records on HMV have been known for a long time and, if seldom sensational, have usually been good average American commercial style', began the writer, before delivering a blast of unfavourable comment. Anything Hamp could do, we could do better, summarised his attitude.

It must be admitted that Hamp usually did sound tame, but once in a while he let himself go. His Victor recordings of *Black Bottom* (1926) and *I'm Afraid You Sing that Song to Somebody Else* (1927), both non-vocal, not only swung well but featured hot solos. As a rule, though, he stuck to an agreeable, undemanding style, realising that the majority of people preferred their dance music to be sweet and simple.

Nobody understood that better than Guy Lombardo, who began to produce 'the sweetest music this side of heaven' in the mid-Twenties, and lived to see all the highfliers blow their last, while his Royal Canadians played on: clipped brass, exaggerated vibrato saxes and languid rhythm. What is more, many jazzmen liked the band: Louis Armstrong, in particular, holding it in high regard; but then Satchmo made many uncompromisingly commercial records of his own.

A typical Kentucky Serenaders recording of 1927 was *The Sunrise will Bring Another Day for Me*, a fox-trot by Lester Santley and Cliff Friend. Too much in this unambitious style could be monotonous; too many high-pitched Joe Cassidy vocals wearisome; but a little Hamp did no-one any harm. He fitted in somewhere between the showband lushness of Jack Hylton giving his all to a waltz, and Bert Ambrose in overdrive with Sylvester Ahola tearing into a trumpet break.

Somewhat similar to the Kentucky Serenaders were Waring's Pennsylvanians, both appealing to college youngsters; Fred Waring did however move with the times, and his novelties had more impact. But curiously enough, the Pennsylvanians actually reached back 15 years in June, 1927, to record *The Sweetheart of Sigma Chi.*

This tribute to a college fraternity – each had its Greek letters, secret grip and identifying pin – was created by Byron D. Stokes and F. Dudleigh Verner. In the restless Twenties

Jan Garber, 'the Idol of the Air Lanes', led a sweet band which sometimes blew hot.

the song seemed as faded and fragrant as linen folded in lavender, but something of its charm lingered on. The record sold well; and six years later the shoestring Monogram company made a film of that name, starring Buster Crabbe and Mary Carlisle.

Earlier mention of Guy Lombardo also brings to mind Jan Garber, who led a band playing in similar style during the Thirties. Because it so often toured, it was dubbed a roadshow version of the Royal Canadians. But it is unfair to dismiss Garber as a 'Mickey Mouse' bandleader, although at least one British musicologist (not Brian Rust) has done so.

Garber was born in November, 1894, and not long after the Great War joined one of Meyer Davis' many bands. Later he linked up with Milton Davis (the surname is coincidental) to direct jointly the successful Garber-Davis Orchestra, which recorded for Victor. When this broke up he went it alone, but in the early Thirties formed a partnership with Freddie Large, a Canadian who became a close friend. After Large's death Garber retired, dying at Shreveport, Louisiana, on October 5, 1977.

Although Garber's touring band may have resembled Lombardo's, he directed a wartime unit which swung well and was greatly respected. Garber was more versatile than is usually acknowledged. A disciplinarian, he demanded personal smartness and punctuality; his well-rehearsed bands always had a polish. Wherever he went, Garber was always sure of a good reception.

The records he made for Victor in the late Twenties, shortly before switching to Columbia, are often of great interest, revealing a thorough understanding of hot music. *You Don't Like It – Not Much!* a fox-trot by Ned Miller, Art Kahn and Chester Cohn, is an excellent example. It had a vocal duet by Harry Goldberg and Webb Hahne. The song flaunted itself briefly in 1927 and then was forgotten.

Nobody ever called Ben Selvin a 'Mickey Mouse' bandleader, although much of his output was decidedly sweet. In 1927 he made a 12-inch Columbia record of Egan and Whiting's nine-year-old waltz *Till We Meet Again*. On this occasion Ben Selvin was disguised as Eddie Thomas's Collegians, and there was a vocal duet by Irving Kaufman and Vaughn de Leath.

Born on September 26, 1896, Vaughn de Leath was a Canadian, but little is known about her. She was the first woman singer to broadcast, but her performance over New York's 2XG in 1919 got the station in trouble, wireless entertainment then being forbidden.

She was a rich-voiced contralto, capable of handling a sugary ballad or hard-hitting torch song with equal assurance, and she recorded for Victor in her own name from 1927 to 1929. Records by such contemporaries as Ruth Etting and Annette Hanshaw have appeared on long-playing albums, and it would be pleasant to have some by Vaughn de Leath similarly reprised, before she is completely forgotten. She died on May 28, 1943.

Although Ira Gershwin wrote many lyrics for his brother George, other song composers used him too. He provided the lyric for Philip Charig's *Sunny Disposish* in 1926, and it was recorded the following February by Jean Goldkette and his Orchestra. Charig, a New Yorker, was born on August 31, 1902. For many years his music appeared in Broadway and London shows.

Goldkette directed good bands that could have been better. A French concert-trained pianist, born in Valenciennes on March 18, 1899, he emigrated to America as a youth. In the early Twenties he became a bandleader, secured a Victor recording contract, and remained with Victor until he ceased to record in the summer of 1929.

Much that Goldkette waxed was commercial, but he made some hot sides of considerable interest, *Clementine (from New Orleans)*, recorded in September, 1927, being a notable example. At one time or another, Bix Beiderbecke, Tommy and Jimmy Dorsey, Eddie Lang, Frankie Trumbauer and Joe Venuti all played for Goldkette, but frequently had little opportunity to shine.

Goldkette's career peaked in 1926-7, when he began to realise the possibilities of his superb band, but it became too costly to keep together and he broke it up before the end of 1927. He soon re-formed, but ceased to be a full-time leader in 1929, making spasmodic reappearances but concentrating mainly on his other business enterprises. He died at Santa Barbara, California, on March 24, 1962.

Also predominantly commercial was Fred Rich, who temporarily left New York's Hotel Astor to play for a few weeks in London at the start of 1928. Born in 1898, Rich drew on the best talent available for his bands, and as well as the Dorseys, Lang and Venuti, who seem to have played for almost everybody, used trombonist Jack Teagarden, the brilliant but erratic trumpeter Bunny Berigan, and British-born trumpeter Bob Effros.

Rich recorded officially for Columbia, but made clandestine sides elsewhere. *Dream Kisses*, a fox-trot by Jack Yellen and M. K. Jerome, recorded non-vocal in December, was issued here by Imperial, Rich being effectively disguised as the Golden Gate Dance Orchestra. There was nothing exceptional about the performance. Fred Rich died in 1956.

Although the reverse side was also credited to the Golden Gate Dance Orchestra, the treatment of *Zulu Wail* was remarkably different. A song by Frank Skinner and Irving Bibo, it was played in Yale Blues style by the California Ramblers, whose hot performance showed how an element of jazz injected into a dance tune made for exciting listening.

Many Society bandleaders dispensed schmaltz for the undiscerning, thus earning the unenviable 'Mickey Mouse' soubriquet, but Vincent Lopez hardly fell into that category. Admittedly a rather flashy pianist, whose signature tune, *Nola*, had been composed by Felix Arndt in 1915, Lopez formed his first band in 1918. He introduced his broadcasts, and some of his records, with 'Lopez speaking'.

A Lane in Spain, by Al Lewis and Carmen Lombardo, and *I'll Just Go Along*, by Gus Kahn and Ted Fiorito, were recorded by Vincent Lopez and his Casa Lopez Orchestra, and issued here on Brunswick. Vocals were by a trio, the Keller Sisters and (Al) Lynch. Both were simple, pretty fox-trots, embellished by good solo breaks and well-planned arrangements, the band sounding warm and relaxed.

Paul Whiteman was far from marking time in 1927. He was still directing a band full interest, with the added attraction of his Rhythm Boys Trio. He had signed up Bing Crosby and Al Rinker in Chicago, in December, 1926; Harry Barris completed the trio in April, 1927.

The Rhythm Boys' impact on the public was quite remarkable, but their affected vocal mannerisms often sound ludicrous today. Listening to them now, one gets an occasional hint of the 'Old Groaner' who began to charm us in 1931; meanwhile, Whiteman had again demonstrated that he was still king of entertainment, if not of jazz.

Chapter Six

1928

'Blue Bird, Sing Me A Song'

Just as the microphone abolished the acoustic recording horn, so the soundtrack quickly ended the reign of the silent film. In 1927, De Forest Phono Films made a series of short 'talkies', centred around stars of stage and variety; and in Warner's *The Jazz Singer*, Al Jolson sang and spoke a few words.

Then came *The Singing Fool*, a smash-hit for Warner in 1928. People rushed to hear Jolson wringing every drop of bathos from *Sonny Boy*, which de Sylva, Brown and Henderson swore they had written as a joke.

Most, if not all records were now made electrically, and several minor labels disappeared, while fresh ones were introduced. Aeolian's Little Marvel and Crystalate's Mimosa were discontinued, but Crystalate launched the seven-inch Victory, for which Jay Whidden's Carlton Hotel Band made some sides, including Nacio Herb Brown's instrumental *Rag Doll*.

Born at Deming, in Luna County, New Mexico, on February 22, 1896, Brown's earliest songs included his fox-trot *When Buddha Smiles,* recorded by Paul Whiteman in 1921. Throughout the Twenties and Thirties his lyricist was Arthur Freed. In 1927 his *Doll Dance* proved too intricate for many amateur pianists; in 1929 he wrote the entire score for *Broadway Melody,* an early MGM musical with interludes of crude Technicolor; and in the Thirties hits by Freed and Brown were a regular occurrence.

As late as 1948, Brown was still composing an occasional ballad, joining Edward Heyman to write the title song for *On an Island with You*, a minor musical by MGM, after which he probably retired. He died in San Francisco, on September 28, 1964.

Arthur Freed, who became an MGM producer, was born in Charleston, South Carolina, on September 9, 1894. As a young man he contributed to New York revues, and at one time in Hollywood managed the Orange Grove Theatre. He died on April 12, 1973.

Dominion Gramophone Records Ltd. began with high hopes in 1928 and a singularly mendacious advertisement: 'Clear as a mirrored reflection, the tones of vocalist and instrumentalist are revealed on Dominion records. There is no scratch and no blare; but reproduction so true that it equals the actual performance.'

In fact, poor quality shellac made the surface noise appalling, and reproduction was atrocious. With a cream label depicting a gramophone disc encircling the globe, and costing 1s 3d (around 7p) each, the ten-inch Dominions first

New Electrical Recordings

APRIL, 1928

New Dance Records Issued Mid-March.

10-inch Double-sided Plum Label Records 3/- each

SAVOY ORPHEANS
At the Savoy Hotel, London.

B. 5409 { Lonely Nights in Hawaii (*Seaman-Smoled*) Waltz
I'll think of you (*Sper-Coslow*) Waltz

NAT SHILKRET AND HIS ORCHESTRA
B. 5437 { Wherever you are ("Will-o'-the-Whispers") (*Dowling-Hanley*) Fox-Trot
Headin' for Harlem ("Will-o'-the-Whispers") (*Dowling-Hanley*) Fox-Trot

RED NICHOL'S STOMPERS
B. 5433 { Make my cot where the cot-cot-cotton grows (*Le Soir-Doll-Klein*) Fox-Trot
Sugar (*Yellen-Ager*) Fox-Trot

GEORGE OLSEN AND HIS MUSIC
B. 5428 { Worryin' (*G. Fairman*) Waltz
JOHNNY HAMP'S KENTUCKY SERENADERS
I'm afraid you sing that song to somebody else (*Mahr-Verges*) Fox-Trot

TED WEEMS AND HIS ORCHESTRA
B. 5412 { From Saturday Night till Monday Morning (*Dublin-Marr*) Fox-Trot
She'll never find a fellow like me (*O'Keefe-Archer*) Fox-Trot

DON BESTOR AND HIS ORCHESTRA
B. 5429 { Baby your Mother (*Donnelly-Morse-Burke*) Fox-Trot
NAT SHILKRET AND HIS ORCHESTRA
Nothin' (*Turk-Handman*) Fox-Trot

WARING'S PENNSYLVANIANS
B. 5436 { I scream, you scream, we all scream for ice cream (*Johnson Moll-King*) Fox-Trot
Wob-a-ly Walk (*Warren-Green*) Fox-Trot

BOBBIE LEECAN'S NEED-MORE BAND
B. 5430 { Apaloosa Blues (*Leecan*) Fox-Trot
BENNIE MOTEN'S KANSAS CITY ORCH.
Sugar (*Pinbard*) Fox-Trot

*With Vocal Refrain

As late as April, 1928, HMV were still emphasising their records were made electrically, although the acoustic method had ceased in 1925.

appeared in October. Jay Wilbur (born Wilbur Blinco at Leamington Spa), a pianist and arranger, as Musical Director, assembled some humdrum 'house' bands, but few 'name' artists were attracted, although Elsie Carlisle ill-advisedly recorded *My Man o' War*, which was considered so objectionable it had to be withdrawn. Gross mismanagement and public apathy forced Dominion into receivership. The end came in July, 1930.

On the other hand, Radio records were well-made and consistently interesting. In an eight-inch format, they were introduced by Edison Bell in February, to compete with Broadcast. 'A diminutive but very assertive little newcomer,' commented the *Melody Maker*. Edison Bell claimed they were 'in a class by themselves', cheerfully ignoring their rival. Initially, the tiny label was navy blue, but it became bright gold in the summer of 1931, as did Winner. In April, 1932, production ceased.

From 1927-1933, Edison Bell's Musical Director was Harry Hudson, who quickly roped in Alfredo to record for Radio. He also began to assemble session bands every bit as lively as those directed by Harry Bidgood, his opposite number at Broadcast.

Harry Hudson's Melody Men brought together some of London's most accomplished musicians. To record *Blue Bird, Sing Me a Song*, with a Benny Davis lyric and a pretty

Left – Jay Wilbur left Dominion before the end came to become Light Music Director for Crystalate.

Above – Although Elsie Carlisle's naughty record for Dominion was frowned upon, she earned golden opinions for her duets with Sam Browne.

tune by James F. Hanley, the line-up included Sylvester Ahola, a powerful trumpet player from America, of Finnish extraction, and Sid Phillips, playing alto saxophone (but equally renowned as clarinettist and arranger), together with a young Italian violinist named Annunzio Mantovani.

Harry Hudson, who died on July 27, 1969, had been an entertainer on the variety halls, teamed with the baritone Stanley Kirkby as Kirkby and Hudson. His former partner began to record for Radio, though not always under his own name. As Walter Miller he sang *Just a Little Fond Affection* and *In Old Vienna,* for which Lawrence Wright became respectively Everett Lynton and Horatio Nicholls. Both were hits, the lyricist being Edgar Leslie.

Kirkby claimed kinship with Louise Kirkby Lunn, a famous operatic contralto. He made records for many labels over a long period and at one time had his own concert party. Like Peter Dawson, he could tackle most kinds of song and give a good account of himself.

Radio's big brother, Winner, used session bands too. Murray's Melody Makers were a lively little combo, assembled by Hudson and led by Murray Dempsey, who had played trumpet in Jack Payne's Hotel Cecil Band. *Are You Happy?* by Yellen and Ager, had a vocal by Harry Hudson; but *The Trail of the Tamarind Tree*, a fox-trot by Horatio Nicholls – how Denmark Street loved the Orient! – went at a fast clip without the interruption of Edgar Leslie's lyric.

Hudson had to keep on his toes if he were to avoid unfavourable comparison with Broadcast's enterprising session bandleader. Harry Bidgood's Broadcasters was one of the earliest 'house' bands to appear on Radio's competitor. Early in 1928 it played Al Piantadosi's latest tale of woe, *Tired Hands.* Bidgood's arrangement did wonders for a hack tune, but John Thorne must have longed for something better to sing.

A Londoner, born in 1898, Harry Bidgood was one of the sons of Thomas Bidgood, composer of the famous march *Sons of the Brave.* He studied at the London College of Music and when war came did a three year stint with the East Surrey Regiment. In the early Twenties he was de Groot's pianist, but in 1926 was appointed Vocalion's Light Music Director.

When Crystalate bought out Vocalion he worked under Jay Wilbur and created Primo Scala's Accordion Band, which escaped from the recording studio to start broadcasting

AHOLA NOW PLAYING CONN

THE NEW ERA TRUMPET

Now available in two Models :—

56ᴮ with ro-

AHOLA
(Principal Trumpet, Bert Ambrose's Orchestra) says :

" After trying the various well-known makes of Trumpet throughout the world, I have finally chosen the Conn as the ideal instrument."

In harmony with the modern vogue for smarter lines, greater beauty, lighter weight, and higher efficiency, Conn has manufactured the "NEW ERA" TRUMPET. Apart from the features of general appearance, these two models posses

Left – Sylvester Ahola, equally at home with Bert Ambrose or in a symphony orchestra.

Below – Stanley Kirkby (bottom left) with his Concert Party. His real name was James Baker.

Anona Winn was still entertaining radio audiences after World War Two.

Eddie Gross-Bart: Drummer and vocalist, he was directing his own band at the Ambassadors' Club in 1930. He died in 1988.

in 1940. Bidgood became Music Director at the Columbia British studios, conducting music for George Formby films, and in 1945 turned to Variety, becoming well-known to radio listeners. Small, versatile and energetic, he died in 1955.

Sylvester Ahola, in regular demand as a session player, joined Ambrose at the May Fair on October 18, 1928. 'Hooley' helped to provide discreet accompaniment, under Carroll Gibbons' direction, for Anona Winn's HMV recording of *I've Got a Feeling for Somebody,* a new ballad by Phil Charig. In the same backing group was Van Phillips, whose clarinet and alto saxophone had been heard with the Savoy Havana Band.

Anona Edna Winn (Mrs. Frederick Lamport), a frequent broadcaster, was born at Sydney in 1907 and studied at the Sydney Conservatorium of Music and the Albert Street Conservatorium, Melbourne. She was equally accomplished as singer, lyricist and short story writer.

Ahola and fellow American Perley Breed, a multi-reedist who also joined Ambrose, were added to Al Starita's Piccadilly Players for recordings only. Both were with Starita when *I'm Afraid of You* was waxed. A fox-trot by Eddie Davis, Lew Daly and Archie Gottler, it had an Eddie Gross-Bart vocal. In New York it was recorded by Paul Whiteman, who let Bing Crosby have the vocal spot all to himself.

The Piccadilly Revels Band ended early in 1928 and Ray Starita went to the Ambassadors' Club, taking brother Rudy with him. His new unit also added brass for Columbia records, and it is this practice which makes it difficult to imagine how such bands sounded away from the studios.

Ray Starita provided relaxed performances of Sunny Clapp's *Girl of My Dreams* and de Sylva, Brown and Henderson's *Together*, both waltzes, the latter featuring Ahola's trumpet and a vocal by Eddie Collis. This band was also under Hylton's overall control.

Hylton's own band visited Germany twice in 1928 and was well-received. It went first in January, playing at the Scala Theatre, Berlin. Towards the end of the year it returned, entertaining Scala audiences for a whole month. Hylton took with him Sam Browne, who had joined him in August; and Browne was heard on *I Kiss Your Hand, Madame,* a suavely romantic effusion by Fritz Rotter and Ralph Erwin, recorded for HMV in Berlin.

Sam Browne has been overshadowed by the Al Bowlly cult, but he was a good, versatile singer who made hundreds of records (mostly anonymously) with real and session bands, cinema organists, and even large theatre orchestras. He also recorded under his own name for Radio and other labels.

Born in Stepney on July 25, 1899, he sang for obscure British and European bands until Hylton gave him the step-up he needed. Browne stayed with Hylton for 18 months, found constant touring irksome and went to Ambrose, with whom he recorded until October, 1937. His amusing duets with Elsie Carlisle became very popular and some were recorded.

During World War Two he joined Bebe Daniels and Ben Lyon in *Hi, Gang!* but when the Fifties blew out his kind of music in a storm of rock 'n' roll he fell on hard times, dying in Whittington Hospital, Highgate, on March 2, 1972.

Browne did not replace the vocal trio of Hylton, Rignold and d'Amato, which was still used frequently. *'s Wonderful,* the Gershwins' show-stopper from *Funny Face,* was recorded by them in August, while that musical comedy was still on Broadway. It opened at the Prince's Theatre in November, giving London audiences another good reason to adore the Astaires.

Sam Browne's recorded output (mostly anonymous) was prodigious. He was a thoroughly dependable band singer, but collectors seem obsessed with Al Bowlly.

Left – *Records for Christmas, 1928, but as in earlier years, descriptions of them were often painfully fulsome.*

Below – Funny Face: *Another good reason to adore the Astaires.*

Above – *Paul England: A talented revue singer, he sounded out of place with the Hylton band.*

Centre – *Reginald Foort, the BBC's staff organist, who was succeeded by Sandy Macpherson.*

Right – *Fred Elizalde: He liked it hot, but the Savoy Hotel didn't, and neither did the BBC.*

A few months earlier, Hylton went to the Palladium, there recording several songs with revue artist Paul England and Reginald Foort's Wurlitzer. Neither *Firefly* nor *Sing Me to Sleep with a Twilight Song*, both by Leslie and Nicholls, quite suited England's style, and the clarity of the recording left much to be desired.

Not every new band enjoyed its engagement at a big London hotel, and that directed by Manila-born Fred Elizalde had a most unhappy time. Opening at the Savoy in December, 1927, it played such outright hot music that the hotel's waltz-loving patrons were outraged. When Elizalde began to broadcast, the BBC received an avalanche of hostile mail.

Nothing went right for Elizalde. The BBC took him off the air; the Savoy ejected a band thar blew hot but never sweet; and a tour of the north and Scotland proved disastrous. Finally, Fred and his elder brother Manuel called quits, and eventually left the country.

The Elizaldes suffered from being too much ahead of their time, and for refusing to compromise, but before they gave up they did us a great service by bringing over Al Bowlly from Germany. He ended up as a street singer when the band broke up, but his future was brighter (despite a tragic ending) than he could possibly have envisaged while he was busking on the London pavements.

Meanwhile, Jack Payne took a giant step forward. In March, 1928, he succeeded Sidney Firman as the BBC's tame bandleader, although the band was his, unlike that of Henry Hall, who replaced him. Payne's last records with his Hotel Cecil Band were made for Regal in January, Irving Berlin's haunting *The Song is Ended* being an appropriate inclusion. His first broadcast with his BBC Dance Orchestra occurred on March 2; and in June he began to record for Columbia.

His varied radio programme suited many kinds of listener, leaving a daunting reputation for Hall to follow. Routine dance melodies were played somewhat unadventurously, but the band could belt out hot choruses too, aided by a brilliant young arranger who joined Payne in 1928. His name was Ray Noble. Perhaps there was a surfeit of broad comedy, on and off records, but Payne sometimes turned to unusual items, as in November, when he recorded Grofé's entire *Mississippi Suite.*

Some of Ambrose's records made in 1928 equalled or bettered anything many American bands could do. De Sylva, Brown and Henderson's *Without You, Sweetheart;* Jack LeSoir and Ray Doll's *Singapore Sorrows;* Will J. Harris and Victor Young's *Sweet Sue, Just You;* and Mort Dixon and Harry Woods' *I'm Riding to Glory* all revealed gutsy, incisive front-line work and a springy, driving rhythm.

But Ambrose's first experience of HMV was discouraging. During his 12-month contract he had to accept what Jack Hylton rejected, and as Hylton recorded prodigiously that left very little. Only 17 sides had been cut when his contract ended in January, 1929, and unwilling to accept another's leavings any longer, Ambrose switched to Decca.

Decca's bright-blue and gold label first began to spin in 1929; recording at the Chenil Galleries studios was in need of improvement, and there were few 'names'. Before long it began to challenge the leading record makers; meanwhile, Ambrose was able to choose his own material and to record frequently.

A short-lived but appealing little band was installed at Ciro's by Debroy Somers, recording for Broadcast from April to September, 1928. Ciro's Club Dance Band, 'conducted by its Famous Director', was how the labels coyly announced it, but it was not Debroy Somers (under contract to Columbia), but either Harry Bidgood or Ramon Newton who actually directed.

It made some interesting records. Noel Coward's *A Room*

Paul Robeson: His political beliefs offended Americans and eventually ended his career.

Cyril Ramon Newton, seen here in the mid-Thirties when he was being heard over European commercial radio stations.

with a View began as a duet by Jessie Matthews and Sonnie Hale in *This Year of Grace,* which opened in March at the London Pavilion; *Ol' Man River* was Paul Robeson's song in the sumptuous *Show Boat,* which began to thrill Drury Lane audiences two months later; a triumph for Hammerstein and Kern.

Less prestigious ditties included Kahn and Donaldson's *My Ohio Home* and Leslie and Nicholls' *My Inspiration is You,* the last recording the band made. All had vocals by Ramon Newton.

In the early Thirties, Newton directed provincial bands, gradually dropping out of sight, but he was much in the news until then. From the autumn of 1928 to the Spring of 1929, he directed the Original Havana Band, which also recorded for Broadcast. As usual, he was the only singer. The first recording was *Get Out and Get Under the Moon,* a rather old-fashioned song by Charles Tobias, Billy Jerome and Larry Shay.

Jerome, in his time actor, singer, lyricist and song composer, was born at Cornwall-on-the-Hudson, New York, on September 30, 1865. In 1906 he joined Jean Schwartz to create *Chinatown, My Chinatown;* six years later he had a big hit with the less enduring *Row, Row, Row,* with music by James V. Monaco. He died on June 25, 1932.

Newton's rather perfunctory vocals appeared on the Debroy Somers Band recordings too, one being *Today, Tomorrow, Forever,* an uninspired opus by Leslie and Nicholls which quickly faded away. Somers' was a most perplexing band to hear, as its recording of W. R. Collins' novelty *Laughing Marionette* illustrated, playing as neither a concert nor a dance band, but somewhere between the two.

Another brief dance craze began in the late summer, when the curtain first rose at the Carlton Theatre on *Good News,* which featured de Sylva, Brown and Henderson's *Varsity Drag.* The tune was recorded by Alfredo's Band for Electron.

Most bandleaders are now recalled only by their recorded music, but the personality of big, bluff Bill Cotton (only professionally called Billy), remains vivid in many memories. His radio (and later television) band-shows were prefaced by a raucous 'Wakey-Wakeee!' Cotton had a natural gift for comedy, and although he could be tough, his men liked him.

When the new Astoria Ballroom opened in Charing Cross Road on January 15, 1927, with its sky-blue and gold decor, it was Billy Cotton's London Savannah Band which took up residence, having previously been at the Southport Palais de Danse.

Billy Cotton was born in London on May 6, 1899, and served in the Royal Flying Corps. In the Thirties he raced at Brooklands; and he died on March 26, 1969, just after completing his autobiography, which was as forthright as the man himself. In 1921 he led a band at the Ealing Palais de Danse, and he was a dance bandleader until the early Thirties, when he turned to Variety. Despite the accent on comedy, the Cotton bands recorded some splendid dance music, occasionally surprisingly hot.

The Savannah Band had some first-rate players in 1928. The lead trumpeter was Sid Buckman, born in Stratford, East London, on April 26, 1904, who later joined Roy Fox; sole trombonist was Joe Ferrie, later to play and sing with Lew Stone; and Sydney Lipton was on violin.

Cotton's first records appeared on Metropole and Piccadilly. Metropole began in April, 1928, and lasted about two years. The simple label, depicting Big Ben, bore the punning motto: 'A striking record'. Piccadilly was Metropole's cheaper label,

Still spinning in August, 1928, but two years later Metropole were out of business.

Albert Sandler lived in acute poverty as a child. His 'Palm Court' style made him famous, but Raymonde went off with Clarence Johnstone.

Dorothy Fields, who wrote lyrics for Jimmy McHugh and Jerome Kern. She is seen here with brothers Herbert (left) and Joseph.

launched at the same time. Popular items were featured on a black, white and gold label, portraying Eros. Recording quality was adequate only, and Piccadilly spun its last in April, 1932.

One of Cotton's earliest sides for Piccadilly was *That's My Weakness Now,* by Bud Green and Sam H. Stept, made popular by Helen Kane, the 'boop-oop-a-doop' girl. It was Stept's first hit. Born at Odessa in 1897, he was taken as a child to Pitsburg, Ohio. In his twenties he had his own small band, but moved to New York, becoming both songwriter and music publisher. Sammy Stept was still composing songs in 1950, one of his last being *Seems Like Yesterday.* The title was unconsciously prophetic. When *Rock Around the Clock* exploded over the airwaves in 1954, his kind of music soon became part of yesterday.

Jimmy McHugh's pretty song *I Can't Give You Anything But Love* was recorded by various bands, among them those of Sam Lanin and Johnny Hamp in America, and the 'house' ones of Harry Hudson and Harry Bidgood in England. It was also waxed by Albert Sandler's Park Lane Hotel Orchestra, but as this was in the 'Palm Court' style which made Sandler famous, Dorothy Fields' lyric was unheard on this Columbia recording.

The song was featured in the revue *Blackbirds of 1928* at New York's Liberty Theatre, and was Miss Fields' first major song success. Born on July 15, 1905 at Allenhurst, New Jersey, she was the daughter of famous comedian Lew Fields. She collaborated frequently with McHugh, and later with Jerome Kern, and died on April 28, 1974.

Jimmy McHugh was a Bostonian, born on July 10, 1894, who worked briefly in his home city as a song-plugger in Irving Berlin's branch office. Success came quickly when he moved to New York and began to compose popular songs. Many of his later ones were heard in Hollywood productions. In the Forties his principal lyricists were Harold Adamson and Frank Loesser. He died in Beverly Hills on May 23, 1969.

Another popular song recorded by Sandler in 1928 was *Mistakes*, a big hit in waltz-time for Lawrence Wright in his Everett Lynton guise. Sandler's recorded output is mostly outside a work on dance music, but he did occasionally turn to Tin Pan Alley. Of Lithuanian Jewish extraction, he was born in London in 1906 and studied at the Guildhall School of Music.

He became famous for his broadcasts from Eastbourne's Grand Hotel and London's Park Lane Hotel, and later for his concerts from the BBC's imaginary 'Palm Court of Grand Hotel' on Sunday evenings. He still enjoyed a great following at the time of his death on August 30, 1948.

Although becoming forgotten, David de Groot was an

This photograph of de Groot was autographed in March, 1929, after he had left the Piccadilly Hotel. His rendition of The Londonderry Air *had made Miss Beatrice Gardiner cry!*

DE GROOT

equally popular violinist and leader. In 1928 he left the Piccadilly Hotel, having directed the resident orchestra for 20 years, taking his Trio for a week at New York's Palace Vaudeville Theatre, embarking on a tour of the Gaumont British theatre circuit, and even broadcasting from Radio Hilversum, a newly formed Dutch commercial station.

Born in Rotterdam on October 25, 1880, de Groot eventually took British citizenship. He studied at the Amsterdam Conservatory, became solo violinist and leader at the Amsterdam Opera House, and in 1903 played at the Paris Exhibition. He came to London in October, 1907, to play at the Royal Opera House, Covent Garden, going to the Piccadilly Hotel the following year.

De Groot made an enormous number of records, all for HMV, and some were of dance music, although played in salon style. A disciplinarian and perfectionist, he could transform a commonplace tune into a minor gem. In 1929 his Trio (violin, cello and piano) toured South Africa; and in 1931 he became Musical Director of the New Victoria Theatre. But his health began to fail, and he died in his Baker Street home on May 22, 1933.

Among the last records made by the Piccadilly Orchestra was the waltz *Worryin'*, which did well in 1928 for its lyricist and composer George Fairman. De Groot's portrait appeared on the sheet music cover.

Roses of Yesterday sounds like a faded old waltz, but was actually a nostalgic fox-trot by Irving Berlin. It was given a touch of distinction by the soprano Lilian Davies (late of *Katja the Dancer*), who recorded it for HMV. Born in Cardiff on January 18, 1895, her brilliant stage career was prematurely terminated by her death at the age of 37 on March 3, 1932.

A rather wistful mood crept into *A Garden in the Rain*, with its lovely melody by Carroll Gibbons and lyric by James Dyrenforth. It was recorded for HMV by George Metaxa, a former Rumanian civil servant of Greek extraction, who became a musical comedy star. The orchestral accompaniment was directed from the piano by the composer.

Carroll Richard Gibbons was born in Clinton, Massachusetts, on January 4, 1903, and studied at the Boston Conservatory of Music. He came to London in 1924. After the dissolution of the Savoy Orpheans he became Director of Light Music for HMV, leaving in 1929 to compose for MGM in Hollywood.

John Kirby and Emma Haig in Virginia. *An American, Miss Haig made her London debut in 1927 in* The Girl Friend.

In 1931 he returned to London and became co-director of the Savoy Hotel Orpheans with Howard Jacobs, but soon became sole director, remaining in this capacity until his death in London on May 10, 1954. With his pleasant drawl, friendly personality and exquisite piano style, Gibby was one of the most likeable of all the Americans who directed British bands.

Chicago-born James Dyrenforth acted in New York and London, but also wrote for revues, musical comedies and films. He wrote lyrics for Johnny Green, Philip Charig and Kenneth Leslie-Smith. A member of the Savage Club, he spent much of his time in London.

The musical comedy *Virginia* opened at the Palace Theatre in October, 1928, starring Emma Haig. The principal songs, *Dreams of Yesterday,* a waltz, and *Roll Away, Clouds,* both created by Douglas Furber, R. P. Weston, Bert Lee, Jack Waller and Joseph Tunbridge, were recorded by Layton and Johnstone, in their usual lively manner.

An uninspired ballad, unenthusiastically sung, *The Angelus was Ringing* appeared on Imperial, with Cavan O'Connor disguised as Pat O'Dell. Far better songs were created by lyricist Stanley John Damerell and composer Robert Hargreaves. The former, a Londoner, also contributed to newspapers and magazines.

Cavan O'Connor: After service in World War One he won a scholarship to the Royal College of Music. He is recorded there as Clarence O'Connor.

Born in Nottingham on July 1, 1899, of Irish parentage, Cavan O'Connor saw active service with the Royal Horse Artillery and was wounded in 1915. After demobilisation he won a scholarship to the Royal College of Music.

A powerful tenor when permitted to demonstrate his range, he was the vocalist on countless session band recordings, although rarely acknowledged. He also made scores of records for every conceivable label under pseudonyms as diverse as Con Conway, Earl Parry, Francesco Odoli, Harry Carlton and Allan O'Sullivan.

He became a household name in 1935 when he began to appear in the BBC's weekly show *The Vagaband Lover*, although at first he was disguised for that too. In 1929 he had married Rita Tate, niece of the distinguished song composer James W. Tate, and she was the pianist in an instrumental trio which accompanied O'Connor on a Rediffusion L.P. he made in 1978.

This grand old trouper was still much in demand for private functions when in his eighties. For me, as for many others, he will always be remembered for his theme song, *I'm Only a Strolling Vagabond*.

Despite much disparagement by collectors of pre-war dance records, the waltz was always very popular. Two distinguished examples were recorded for Victor by Gene Austin: Irving Berlin's *I Can't Do Without You* and Nathaniel Shilkret's *Jeannine, I Dream of Lilac Time,* with a lyric by L. Wolfe Gilbert (1886-1970).

Sensational in 1928 was the rocketing success of *Ramona,* actually published in 1927. For this, L. Wolfe Gilbert wrote a triumph of romantic yearning, matched by Mabel Wayne's caressing waltz melody. *Ramona* was dedicated to lovely Dolores del Rio, whose United Artists film of that name was released in 1928. She recorded the song herself for Victor.

Blonde Mabel Wayne, born in Brooklyn on July 16, 1904, was an ex-vaudeville entertainer who became a talented composer. She first made her mark in 1925 with *Don't Wake Me Up,* aided by L. Wolfe Gilbert and Abel Baer. In 1926 came *In a Little Spanish Town,* with a lyric by Sam M. Lewis and Joe Young; *Chiquita* (lyric by Gilbert) helped to brighten up 1928. It was recorded (for Victor) by Victor Arden and Phil Ohman's dance orchestra (both were pianists), with a vocal by Lewis James.

In 1930, Mabel Wayne joined Billy Rose to write *It Happened in Monterey,* another hit; and in 1934 she teamed up with Al Hoffman and Maurice Sigler for *Little Man, You've Had a Busy Day,* a surefire winner among child songs. She was still busy at the close of the Forties.

Among the many recordings of *Ramona* was one on the Perfect label, allegedly by the Lennox Dance Orchestra, a collective pseudonym for various bands. On this occasion it was Willard Robison and his Deep River Orchestra providing a warm-toned, easy-paced performance, with a vocal by Frank Bessinger.

Perfect, another label owned by Pathé Frères Pathéphone Ltd., only lasted from December, 1927, to December, 1928. Showy in red and gold, it depicted two nude figures kneeling against the rays of the rising sun, with the Pathé cockerel above them; a striking, if abstruse piece of symbolism.

Irving Berlin's *Marie* appeared in 1928, recorded by Nat Shilkret and the Troubadours, with a Lewis James vocal. The song became a runaway success for Tommy Dorsey in 1937 (also on Victor), members of the band chanting a sort of obbligato to Jack Leonard's vocal.

But *Chloe* was the surprise of the year. Indeed, this must be reckoned one of the most unusual songs of all time. Subtitled *The Song of the Swamp*, it had an almost surrealistic lyric by Gus Kahn, far removed from his often banal sentimentality. The finger-snapping tune was by Neil Moret.

Moret, real name Charles N. Daniels, first came to public notice in 1901 with a piano piece called *Hiawatha.* He was a prolific and talented composer, and it is surprising that in 1925 he claimed credit for *Moonlight and Roses*. Originally *Andantino*, it was the work of Edwin H. Lemare, a distinguished English organist, with a lyric added by Ben Black.

A very hot version of *Chloe* appeared on Duophone, credited to the Wabash Dance Orchestra, but actually featuring Red Nichols. It had a vocal by Phil Baker and is now a collectors' item. Daniels died in San Francisco on January 23, 1943.

Ernest Loring Nichols was born on May 8, 1905, in Ogden, Utah, not a place normally associated with jazz. He became a highly esteemed cornet and trumpet player, leading his Five Pennies, who often greatly exceeded that number. He died in Las Vegas on June 28, 1965.

Like many minor record labels, Duophone had only a short existence. Launched by the Duophone Syndicate in December, 1925, with a simple, deep purple label, it offered performances by some notable American bands, concealed under pseudonyms. But in May, 1930, it ceased to spin.

Red Nichols: His band appeared on Duophone records as the Wabash Dance Orchestra.

Guy Lombardo: His Sweetest Music This Side of Heaven *lasted at least forty years.*

As for *Chloe*, she remained popular for years until, unkindly parodied by Spike Jones and his City Slickers, she vanished, perhaps forever, into the swamps of oblivion.

Having left Victor for Columbia, Jan Garber and his Orchestra belted out a fox-trot in a manner that owed nothing to Guy Lombardo and was a joy to hear. *Tin Ear* was composed by Bob Effros, a Briton of Greek extraction, who was born at Dulwich in 1903, took his fiery trumpet to America, and eventually became President of the American Federation of Musicians. However, on Garber's recording the trumpet soloist was Harry Goldfield.

Garber might be dispensing brimstone but the Royal Canadians provided treacle for Columbia. *Where the Shy Little Violets Grow,* a fox-trot, was unadulterated sweet corn by Gus Kahn and Harry Warren, tailor-made for the Lombardo band, with Lebert Lombardo leading the brass and brother Carmen the reeds.

Gaetano 'Guy' Lombardo, born in London, Ontario, on June 19, 1902, directed his Royal Canadians for around 40 years with an almost unvarying style. Carmen, who sang with the band and also composed songs, died in 1971; Guy in Houston, Texas, on November 3, 1977. Although Garber, 'the idol of the air lanes', may have had a similar approach to sweet music, it was our own Maurice Winnick who became the Lombardos' most faithful copyist. Whatever its detractors may have said, 'the sweetest music this side of heaven' meant money in the bank.

A song like Dorothy Fields and Jimmy McHugh's *Collegiana* was bound to appeal to Waring's Pennsylvanians, who recorded it with a vocal duet by Fred Waring and brother Tom. *Laugh, Clown, Laugh,* a waltz in melancholy mood by Sam Lewis and Ted Fiorito, gave Fred Waring a chance to vocalise solo with the band.

His rather unsatisfactory attempts to compose concert music notwithstanding, Louis Alter was a capable songwriter, and *Blue Shadows*, with a lyric by Ray Klages, a pleasant song. It was recorded by Johnny Hamp's Kentucky Serenaders, with a Frank Munn vocal. Although a peppy fox-trot, Hamp's version offered no surprises. This was equally true of George Olsen's recording of *Ten Little Miles from Town*, a fox-trot by Gus Kahn and Elmer Schoebel, with Fran Frey, Bob Borger and Bob Rice forming the vocal trio.

Let's Do It and *Let's Misbehave* were song titles which seemed to sum up the attitude of the Bright Young People, whose capers helped to sell newspapers in the Twenties. Both songs were wholly the work of Cole Porter and intended for *Paris*, at New York's Music Box Theatre; however, only *Let's Do It* was actually used.

They were recorded for Victor by Irving Aaronson's Commanders, *Let's Do It* with a vocal duet by Phil Saxe and Jack Armstrong; *Let's Misbehave* with Saxe on his own. Aaronson recorded for Victor from 1926 to 1929, one of his vocalists being Tony Pestritta, later famous as singer and bandleader Tony Pastor. At about the same time, Artie Shaw was among the reeds.

Cole Porter, who was born in Peru, Indiana, on June 9, 1891 (or 1892 or 1893: there seems to be much disagreement about the year), came from a wealthy family, and his personal and professional life has been thoroughly documented. Whatever his human frailties, he had great courage, and as lyricist and composer ranks among the leaders. Porter had been writing songs of a sort since 1916, but it was *Paris* which made people start to notice him. He died on October 15, 1964, but, like Irving Berlin, is unlikely to be forgotten for many years yet.

One of the most distinctive of all the Twenties dance bands was still riding high in 1928, with four years to go before tragedy brought about its dissolution. The Coon-Sanders Nighthawks had been formed in 1918 by Joe L. Sanders and Carleton A. Coon, then just out of the army.

The Nighthawks was one of the earliest American bands to go on the air. Before long its late-night broadcasts were on a multi-State hook-up, so clamorous was audience demand. This was as much a testimony to the infectious humour of its friendly co-directors as to the jazz-influenced, exquisitely arranged music the band played so stylishly. It was a very happy band, recording often for Victor, but it never came to London.

Typical of its 1928 recordings were *Little Orphan Annie*, by Gus Kahn and Joe Sanders, a whimsical but never mawkish novelty; *What a Girl! What a Night!* typical of Nighthawk exuberance and solely by Sanders; *Here Comes My Ball and Chain*, a highly original number by Benny Davis and J. Fred Coots, zestfully played; and *Rhythm King,* by Jo Trent and Joe Hoover. The first three had Sanders vocals; the fourth side one by Coon. All were waxed in Chicago.

Joe Sanders was born in Thayer, Kansas, on October 15, 1896. His prowess as a baseball pitcher earned him his 'Old

Left-Hander' nickname. He was an accomplished pianist and a fine singer. His brilliant arrangements, very forward-looking for their time, helped to put the band among the élite.

Carleton Coon, the band's drummer, frequently duetted with his partner. Born in Rochester, Minnesota, on February 5, 1894, he learned about black music first-hand when his family moved to Missouri and he became friendly with riverside workers.

Always abreast of its times, or even slightly ahead of them, this was a band which could play sweetly but was never schmaltzy, and favoured a hot approach. Its players were neither virtuosi nor 'names'. It was a well-integrated band that swung superbly and sounded like no other. It still had a huge following when Coon was rushed into a Chicago hospital; his death on May 4, 1932, shocked his partner and stunned the fans.

Joe Sanders broke up the Nighthawks almost at once. He formed a new band later and carried on for years, dying on May 15, 1965; but there could never be another band like the one which had played so joyously in the wee small hours. On that sad day in Chicago a legend began.

Chapter Seven

1929

'Dance Away The Night'

Alarmed by the increasing incidence of song-plugging over the air, the BBC ordered in March, 1929, that the titles of dance tunes must not be announced. It was a ludicrous attempt to combat a serious problem, and hostile reaction from listeners was inevitable. In November the ban was abruptly lifted.

Back in the Spring of 1928, Hal Swain had finally left the New Princes Restaurant to direct an entirely new band at the Cafe Royal. Among the four dozen sides he made for Regal in 1929 was Grant Clarke and Harry Akst's pretty song *Am I Blue?* with Swain's own vocal.

Swain's Cafe Royal band was a nine-man outfit, sometimes augmented for recording purposes by the cinema organ of either Oliphant Chuckerbutty or Ernest Frederic Curzon. Such recordings were usually made at the Shepherd's Bush Pavilion, where Curzon, a talented composer, was the resident organist.

Alfredo made nearly as many sides as Swain in 1929, all for Edison Bell's Radio and Winner labels. For the former he recorded the waltz *Carolina Moon*, with its Benny Davis lyric and a mellow tune by Joe Burke. Although the record had the currently fashionable vocal trio, the band performance was unusual, inasmuch as it began as an out of tempo waltz and ended as a red-hot stomp.

Born in Philadelphia on March 18, 1884, and educated at the University of Pennsylvania, Joe Burke was determined to become a songwriter, unlike many popular composers whose early careers were often quite varied. In 1916 he teamed up with James E. Dempsey and Ernie Burnett to create *Down Honolulu Way*, and in 1924 joined Benny Davis and Mark Fisher for *Oh, How I Miss You Tonight*. His major breakthrough occurred in 1929 when he wrote the score for *Gold Diggers of Broadway*.

Burke's collaborations with Benny Davis, Al Dubin and Edgar Leslie resulted in some outstanding hits. He was well to the fore until the mid-Thirties, after which his output tailed off. *Rambling Rose*, his last song, appeared in 1948, and he died at Upper Darby, just outside Philadelphia, on June 9, 1950.

Alfredo's contributions to Winner included *Softly, as in a Morning Sunrise,* one of the smoothly romantic songs by Oscar Hammerstein II and Sigmund Romberg from *The New Moon.* Already enjoying a long run at New York's Imperial Theatre, this sparkling show opened at Drury Lane in April, with Evelyn Laye in the lead. Today, *The New Moon* is more readily recalled by MGM's screen version of 1940, co-starring Jeanette MacDonald and Nelson Eddy, which television revives from time to time.

Other memorable songs from *The New Moon* were *Lover, Come Back to Me* and *Marianne*, both played as fox-trots by Paul Whiteman, who had gone over to Columbia; and *One Kiss*, performed in his blandest Palm Court manner by Albert Sandler. Sigmund Romberg, a Hungarian, was born in the small town of Nagykaniszsa on July 29, 1887, and emigrated to America in 1909. His engagement by the Shuberts to write scores for their musical shows rescued him from obscurity and he became much in demand, although rarely given an opportunity to compose quality music.

The Student Prince, The Desert Song and *The New Moon* stand out amid a surfeit of mediocrity, but his career was a long one and he collaborated with such well-known composers as J. Fred Coots, Leo Fall, George Gershwin, Jean Schwartz and Oscar Straus. In 1954 *The Girl in the Pink Tights* opened in New York, but it was a posthumous production, Romberg having died in that city on November 9, 1951.

Some indication of the incredible popularity of de Sylva, Brown and Henderson at this time can be gauged by the recordings made in 1929 by Jack Hylton and his Orchestra. *Button Up Your Overcoat, My Sin, To Know You is to Love You, You're the Cream in My Coffee, Little Pal* and *Why Can't You?* all had Sam Browne vocals, while for *You Wouldn't Fool Me, Would You?* and *I Want to be Bad* (written from a girl's viewpoint), a vocal trio was employed, including Browne.

London audiences had a chance to see two de Sylva, Brown and Henderson shows that year, *Hold Everything* opening at the Palace Theatre in June and *Follow Through* at the Dominion in October. The songs were obviously better liked than the musicals, neither of which had a very long run.

From *Blackbirds of 1928* came *Diga Diga Doo*, a piece of mildly naughty nonsense by Dorothy Fields and Jimmy McHugh, played at high speed by the Hylton band, with almost barking brass bracketed by tom-tom drums in an imaginative arrangement by Leo Vauchant.

Fields and McHugh's *I Must Have That Man* would have sounded better without Browne's vocal. Bands were beginning to employ girl singers, but all too frequently males were still being saddled with material which for them was patently absurd.

Browne sounded more at ease in *The Breakaway*, originally danced by David Rollins and Sue Carol in Fox's *Movietone Follies of 1929*. Created by Archie Gottler (who had a part in the film), Sidney Mitchell and Con Conrad, dance and song soon faded away, but listeners to BBC Radio's Saturday morning *Breakaway*, hosted by Bernard Falk, will be familiar with Hylton's recording, which is the signature tune.

The advent of 'talkies' soon resulted in a torrent of musicals, too many of which were low-budget quickies featuring players of limited talent. But despite absurd plots and stilted acting, these long-forgotten 'squawkies' were often enlivened by good songs, the cream of popular composers and lyricists having been drawn into the Hollywood dragnet.

MGM's *The Broadway Melody*, starring Bessie Love, Charles King and Anita Page, was undeniably crude, judged by later standards, but it had a beautiful score by Nacio Herb Brown, who introduced some splendid songs, aided by Arthur Freed. A high-spot of the film was *The Wedding of the Painted Doll*, which Hylton recorded with Browne's vocal. Two other hits were the title song and *You were Meant for Me*, paired on a pleasing Brunswick record by Earl Burtnett and his Biltmore Orchestra.

The London stage could still offer strong competition, whatever the attractions of the silver screen. *Mr Cinders*, a particularly bright example, opened at the Adelphi in February, with Binnie Hale and Bobby Howes sharing the lead. Lyricist Clifford Grey was co-author, and the music was by Vivian Ellis and Richard Myers. Two of the biggest hits were *Spread a Little Happiness* and *Ev'ry Little Moment,* which Ray Starita and his Ambassadors' Club Band recorded, both with vocalist Eddie Gross-Bart, in October, 1928, four months before the West End opening, but presumably issued after the show began.

Another hit was recorded by Jack Payne and his BBC Dance Orchestra, and more than one sideman must have stifled a grin while their much disliked leader was singing *I'm a One-Man Girl* with his high-pitched tenor. Assuredly, girl vocalists were badly needed.

Inevitably, stage successes were later transformed into screen musicals, an early example being *Rio Rita*, first seen at the Ziegfeld Theatre in February, 1927. It became a Radio film, starring Bebe Daniels and John Boles. The score was by Harry Tierney, using his regular lyricist, Joe McCarthy. *You're Always in My Arms,* a waltz, had a vocal by Jack

A Columbia advertisement of March 1930, although Mr Cinders *had actually opened at the Adelphi in February, 1929.*

Bebe Daniels, who with husband Ben Lyon captivated British radio and later television audiences with their Life with the Lyons.

Payne, but *Sweetheart, We Need Each Other*, a fox-trot, was entirely instrumental.

Cole Porter was rapidly becoming a lyricist and composer whom no-one could disregard. Recorded by Jack Payne, with his own vocal, *What is This Thing Called Love?* was featured in *Wake Up and Dream*, which began at New York's Selwyn Theatre in December.

I May Be Wrong, But I Think You're Wonderful was a good song that never faded away until all good songs went out of fashion. I have personal recollections of Dinah Shore's lively Columbia version in the early post-war period. Written by Harry Ruskin and composed by Henry Sullivan, it was recorded in 1929 by the Debroy Somers Band, with a vocal trio.

Born in Worcester, Massachusetts, on December 7, 1893, Sullivan wrote music for two Dion Titheradge revues of 1932,

Top – *Tommy Kinsman: His band-leading activities extended into the era of the long-playing record.*

Above – *Fats Waller, one of the most likeable figures in the pre-war world of jazz and popular music.*

Bow Bells, starring Binnie Hale, at the London Hippodrome, and *Fanfare* at the Prince Edward Theatre.

Honey was just a pleasant song of its time, and soon forgotten. The work of Seymour Simons, Haven Gillespie and Richard A. Whiting, it was recorded by Tommy Kinsman and his London Frivolities Band for Piccadilly, disguised as the Florida Club Dance Band. Famous for its bottle parties, the Florida Club was just a step away from Berkeley Square. Kinsman, like Joe Loss, went on directing bands long after the golden age had ceased to be.

Ramon Newton's Original Havana Band broke up in the spring. Among its last sides for Broadcast was *My Blackbirds are Bluebirds Now*, a cheery ditty by Irving Caesar and Cliff Friend. After this, Newton ceased to be a recording artist and began to direct provincial bands, although he was later heard over continental commercial radio stations.

Ain't Misbehavin' always conjures up memories of Fats Waller, who created it with lyricist Andy Razaf. First heard in *Hot Chocolates*, an all-black revue at New York's Hudson Theatre, in June, 1929, it was recorded by Percival Mackey and his Dominion Theatre Orchestra, in a small batch of sides made for Broadcast. Mackey was, at that time, musical director for *Follow Through*.

Thomas 'Fats' Waller, born in Waverley, New York, on May 21, 1904, was the son of a Harlem baptist minister. A superb organist and pianist, and a genuinely happy man, his over-indulgence in the good life, combined with his tremendous bulk, resulted in his early death on December 15, 1943.

Waller created three more song classics in 1929, *My Fate is in Your Hands, Honeysuckle Rose* and *Blue, Turning Grey, Over You*, all with lyrics by Razaf. Over the years he sang other people's songs too, in a style peculiarly his own, and also recorded much genuine jazz. Hard-drinking, a great clown and a great artist, Fats Waller has become one of the almost legendary figures of popular music and jazz.

To His Majesty's Theatre, in July, came Noel Coward's *Bitter Sweet*, challenging the Broadway productions which had dominated the West End throughout the Twenties. Starring Peggy Wood, George Metaxa and Ivy St. Helier, it had a very long run, and soon everyone was humming *I'll See You Again*, composed in a taxi during a 20-minute traffic hold-up. This beautiful waltz song was recorded for Piccadilly by Percival Mackey's Band, prior to his appointment at the Dominion Theatre.

RKO's *Syncopation* was a minor musical, starring Barbara Bennett and Bobby Walton, and featuring Waring's Pennsylvanians. From it came *Jericho*, a jazz-influenced song by Leo Robin and Richard Myers, recorded by Al Starita's Piccadilly Players. His new vocalist, deep-voiced Betty Bolton, gave an outstanding performance, putting to shame other versions by male singers.

In contrast, *My Mother's Eyes*, recorded at the same Columbia session, was pure schmaltz by L. Wolfe Gilbert and Abel Baer, redeemed by a good arrangement and Harry Shalson's fine vocal.

A Londoner, born in 1898, Henry Edward Shalson became a popular variety artist and a successful song composer. In 1924 he was the singer and pianist at the Golden Square, a small London dance club; and in 1927 he began to record for Brunswick. Neither Shalson nor Betty Bolton made many sides with the Piccadilly Players, and those mentioned were their last. The band itself ceased to record in November.

Honky Tonk, an early Warner musical, was built around the considerable talents of Sophie Tucker, who sang Yellen and Ager's *He's a Good Man to Have Around* in her own inimitable style. One of the Piccadilly Players' last records, it would have been fine for Betty Bolton; instead the vocal spot went to Eddie Collis, for whom it was quite unsuitable.

In January, Ambrose and his May Fair Hotel Orchestra made their last four sides for HMV before abandoning Hayes unregretfully for Decca's Chelsea studios. A first-class arrangement, forceful playing and a vocal trio did wonders for *Me and the Man in the Moon*, an otherwise unremarkable song by Edgar Leslie and Jimmy Monaco.

James V. Monaco, born in Genoa on January 13, 1885, arrived in New York State as a child and became a professional pianist while still in his teens. Among his earliest songs was *Oh, You Circus Day!* (lyric by Edith Maida Lessing), featured in *Hankey-Pankey* at the Broadway Theatre in 1912. He had other hits with *Row, Row, Row* (lyric by Billy Jerome) and *You Made Me Love You* (lyric by Joe McCarthy) that year.

Busy throughout the Twenties, Monaco began to compose songs for films early in the Thirties, and was still capable of writing a good tune in 1945, when he joined Mack Gordon for *I Can't Begin to Tell You*. It was probably his last song, as he died in Beverly Hills on October 16, 1945.

No longer overshadowed by Jack Hylton, Ambrose sought out the best of current songs to wax for Decca, among the

PEGGY WOOD

Peggy Wood, an American, scored a personal triumph in Noel Coward's Bitter Sweet *after Evelyn Laye refused to appear in the show.*

Maurice Chevalier made his Hollywood debut in Paramount's Innocents of Paris. *Margaret Livingston had a part in this film. On August 16, 1931, she became Mrs Paul Whiteman.*

earliest being *A Precious Little Thing Called Love,* by Lou Davis and J. Fred Coots, another record using a vocal trio.

Fortune smiled early on Coots. Born in Brooklyn on May 2, 1897, he was only 25 and hardly known when he composed the score for *Sally, Irene and Mary,* which had a modest run at New York's Casino Theatre. He wrote much for the stage, little if anything for Hollywood, and many individual songs, remaining active at least until the end of the Forties.

Ambrose added his own individual touch to material from screen and stage productions. Paramount's *Innocents of Paris* was Maurice Chevalier's Hollywood debut; Leo Robin and Richard Whiting gave him *Louise* to sing with irresistible Gallic charm.

Thou Swell had been in *A Connecticut Yankee* at the Vanderbilt Theatre in 1927. An exuberant ditty, described by Dr. Sigmund Spaeth as 'a delightful combination of Arthurian English and American slang', it had a sensational revival in MGM's 1948 biopic extravaganza *Words and Music*, allegedly the story of Rodgers and Hart, in which it was sung with incredible verve by little June Allyson.

The 'talkies' inspired de Sylva, Brown and Henderson's *If I had a Talking Picture of You*, featured in Fox's *Sunny Side Up*, co-starring screen sweethearts Janet Gaynor and Charles Farrell.

With songs like these, played by one of the finest British bands ever assembled, Bert Ambrose earned himself an enviable reputation, probably making HMV regret they had practically driven him into the studio of a competitor, just as Luigi had caused him to forsake the Embassy Club for the May Fair Hotel.

'House' bands continued to flourish on major and minor labels alike. The Rhythmics appeared on Sterno, assembled by Nat Star, who was Light Music Director, giving a smooth performance of *I'll Always be in Love with You*, a waltz by Herman Ruby, Bud Green and Sammy Stept, with a vocal by Cavan O'Connor. In 1966 the song was included in an album of romantic melodies recorded for RCA by country singer Eddy Arnold.

Sterno was launched in 1926 by W. D. Sternberg, boss of the British Homophone Co. Ltd. The red and gold label depicted a spread Union Jack on which reclined the British lion, listening to a portable gramophone. Reproduction has been described as 'boxy', but Sterno issued some quite attractive records until its demise in May, 1935.

Cavan O'Connor made some solo sides for Broadcast as Harry Carlton, two being of particular interest. Freed and Brown's evocative waltz *The Pagan Love Song* came from MGM's *The Pagan*, starring Ramon Novarro. *Tondeleyo* was inspired by a character in a play called *White Cargo* (filmed in 1930), based on Vera Simonton's novel *Hell's Playground*. A highly melodramatic ballad, with a better than usual tune by Noel Gay, it was given a full-blooded rendition.

In dreary contrast, *The Heart of the Sunset*, a fox-trot with a Jean Frederick lyric, and *My Flame of Love*, a waltz, were uninspired pot-boilers by Horatio Nicholls. They were paired on Imperial, then rather drab in contrasting shades of bluish-purple, with O'Connor (as Pat O'Dell) striving to inject some life into them and failing dismally.

Creating an illusion that Broadcast had many bands under contract, Harry Bidgood assembled studio units with various exotic titles. The New York Night Birds was one of these, directed by Bidgood from the piano. It recorded *Miss You*, straightforward sentimentality by the brothers Harry, Charles and Henry Tobias, with a vocal by the very popular Lou Abelardo, and *Where the Sweet Forget-Me-Nots Remember*, a much more schmaltzy effusion by Mort Dixon and Harry Warren, wasting the talent of John Thorne.

Tom Barratt: He sang with the band of Sir Robert Peel, Bart., for some Sterno recordings.

These sides appeared in Broadcast Twelve's new ten-inch *Super-Dance Series*, which claimed a playing time equivalent to a 12-inch disc, hence the name. First seen in 1929, the tiny label was eye-catching in pale pink, orange, white and gold.

The Radio Rhythm Boys, directed by Harry Hudson, were featured on Radio, and a lively little band they formed too. *Painting the Clouds with Sunshine* and the brisk but rather old-fashioned *Tip-Toe Through the Tulips*, both fox-trots by Al Dubin and Joe Burke, helped to make Warner's *Gold Diggers of Broadway* a roaring success. Filmed in early Technicolor, the movie starred Conway Tearle, Nancy Welford, Nick Lucas, Winnie Lightner, Ann Pennington and Lilyan Tashman. Hudson's vocalist, once thought to be Billy Milton, was actually Eddie Gross-Bart, who had good diction and an excellent sense of rhythm.

Dubin and Burke also supplied this film with the waltz *Go to Bed*, issued here on the dark-blue Parlophone label. It was recorded by the Eugene Ormandy Orchestra, a studio dance band directed by a distinguished conductor more readily associated with the Minneapolis Symphony Orchestra and the Philadelphia Orchestra. Born in Hungary on November 18, 1899 he died in March, 1985. The vocalist was Harold 'Scrappy' Lambert, who became a bandleader early in the Thirties.

Parlophone was started (as Parlophon) in Germany in 1922 by Carl Lindström, but acquired by Columbia in 1927. Four years later it was included in the merger which created EMI, and lasted (ultimately in long-playing form) until 1980.

As HMV's Director of Light Music, Gibbons not only provided instrumental accompaniment for various artists, but assembled dance bands which he directed from the piano. Carroll Gibbons and his Playmates was one of these, a small unit with his own exquisite piano work much in evidence. *Mean to Me,* a fox-trot by Roy Turk and Fred Ahlert, was typical of such recordings, easy listening, but somewhat marred by Alma Vane's rather 'precious' vocal.

Fred E. Ahlert was born in New York on September 19, 1892, and abandoned a law career to compose songs. Among his best-known are *I'll Get By* (1928), with Turk; *Walking My Baby Back Home* (1930), with Turk and Harry Richman; *Where the Blue of the Night* (1931), with Turk and Bing Crosby; and *I'm Gonna Sit Right Down and Write Myself a Letter* (1935), with Joe Young. Appointed President of the American Society of Composers, Authors and Publishers (ASCAP) in 1948, Ahlert died in New York on October 20, 1953.

During the second half of the Thirties, Billy Milton compered sponsored shows for European radio stations.

The Mayfair Dance Orchestra had been a money-spinner for HMV, and it was decided to introduce a New Mayfair Dance Orchestra. Under Gibbons' direction it cut its first sides in November, 1928. Using many of London's finest players, Gibbons made about three dozen sides before relinquishing his post to direct music for British films. His assistant, Ray Noble, then took over, and under Noble the New Mayfair Dance Orchestra became internationally famous.

Among the last recordings made by this 'house' band under Gibbons' direction were his own compositions *Encore* and *I'll be Getting Along*, with vocals by Billy Milton.

Noble had already directed this promising new band occasionally before he became Light Music Director, but unlike Gibbons rarely featured himself as pianist. He used the same top-flight players whenever possible, and a galaxy of equally distinguished (but anonymous) singers, including George Baker, Eve Becke, Webster Booth, Sam Browne, Dorothy Carless, Cavan O'Connor, Jack Plant, Stuart Robertson and Val Rosing. From November, 1930, however, he began to employ Al Bowlly regularly, and when in 1934 he was invited to front his own band in New York, he took Bowlly and Irish drummer Bill Harty with him.

Ray Noble was born in Brighton on December 7, 1903, and studied at the Royal Academy of Music. In 1926 he won a *Melody Maker* arranging competition, which led him to becoming Jack Payne's staff arranger. His songs became world famous, and he made the New Mayfair Dance Orchestra a favourite with American record buyers too. So influential did he become, that the HMV 'house' band was renamed first Ray Noble and his New Mayfair Dance Orchestra and finally Ray Noble and his Orchestra.

A proficient pianist, a gifted arranger and an outstanding song composer, Noble never fronted a true band in this country. He met with mixed fortunes in America, and on his retirement came home, dying in London on April 2, 1978.

Among the handful of records made by Noble's 'house' band in 1929, two are of passing interest. *My Heart is Saying*, entirely instrumental, had the distinctive lilt of a Vivian Ellis composition, while *She's My Slip of a Girl*, with an early vocal by Pat O'Malley, was entirely the work of Henry Cyril Watters, who won a *Melody Maker* song competition with it and left a bank stool to become a professional composer for films.

Despite an occasional guest appearance on records with Ray Noble or Jack Hylton, one can hardly describe Webster

Ray Noble: Feuding with Glenn Miller helped to break up his Rainbow Room orchestra.

Top – *Webster Booth originally intended to become an accountant. It was Peter Dawson who suggested HMV should give him a test.*

Above – *Carl Brisson, Danish boxer turned film star and cabaret singer. He recorded for HMV and Decca.*

Booth as a dance band vocalist, but he did record many popular songs. His first recordings were made for HMV in December, 1929, and included *Let Me Dream in Your Arms Again,* a new ballad by Joe Gilbert and Horatio Nicholls, and the waltz *Dance Away the Night,* by Harlan Thompson and Dave Stamper. Orchestral accompaniment was directed by Ray Noble.

First heard in Fox's early screen musical *Married in Hollywood,* which was graced by an Oscar Straus score, *Dance Away the Night* began as a duet by the stars, Norma Terris and J. Harold Murray, supported by a 60-strong chorus. It was more suitable for Webster Booth's warm, powerful tenor than Nicholls' song.

Born in Birmingham on January 21, 1902, Leslie Webster Booth was once a boy soprano at Lincoln Cathedral. Later he jettisoned a career in accountancy to join the chorus of the d'Oyly Carte Opera Company. He will always be remembered for his duets with the soprano Anne Ziegler, whom he married in 1938. They appeared together in various stage and screen productions, spending some years in South Africa. Webster Booth died at Llandudno on June 21, 1984.

Marie Burke's rendition of *Bill* and *Can't Help Lovin' Dat Man* helped to make *Show Boat* memorable. Later, Columbia had her singing the more tuneful popular ballads. She soft-pedalled her strong soprano for *Little Log Cabin of Dreams,* which had an Eddie Dowling lyric and a characteristically graceful melody by James F. Hanley, whom Spaeth regarded as of 'the miniature school'.

Born Marie Rosa Holt in London on October 18, 1894, she married and later divorced the ex-coalminer turned operatic tenor Tom Burke. In 1919 she made her debut at the London Pavilion in C. B. Cochran's *Afgar,* and had a singularly distinguished stage career. Her daughter Patricia, born in 1917, became a successful actress.

More than one boxer has left the ring to enter show business. Carl Pedersen did so to become the matinee idol Carl Brisson. He could sing quite pleasantly and made records for HMV and Decca. For the former he sang *There's Something About You that's Different,* from his British film *A Song of Soho.* It was a tripping little number by Fred May and Jay Whidden.

Brisson was born in Copenhagen on December 24, 1895, becoming first Denmark's amateur lightweight champion and later middleweight champion of mid-Europe and Scandinavia. In 1916 he made his Danish stage debut as a dancer, with his sister Tilly, and his London debut occurred five years later at the Finsbury Park Empire in a sketch called *The Clown*. He became internationally famous as a stage, screen and cabaret star, known as *The Dimpled Dane* or *The White Gardenia Man*.

Happy Days and Lonely Nights, recorded by Layton and Johnstone, was a briefly popular ballad by Billy Rose and Fred Fisher, with a sad theme. It contrasted with the defiant *I'm Too Young to be Careful*, by Al Bryan and George W. Meyer, which Jennie Howard recorded for Piccadilly. The latter song came from First National's *Drag*, renamed *Parasites* for British distribution, starring Richard Barthelmess.

However, the nonsense song of the year was surely Harry Carlton's *Shinaniki Da*. Jack Hylton recorded it with a trio including himself and Sam Browne; the Debroy Somers Band featured Phil Arnold. Neither version could compare with the way Lily Long belted it out for Radio, aided by a loud and brassy studio band. Miss Long seems to have been a rather obscure figure, but her record was sheer delight.

If one preferred girl singers to dispense 'lavender and lace' sentimentality rather than broad humour, then Vaughn de Leath's *Old-Fashioned Lady* was an ideal choice. Created by Al Lewis and Abner Silver, it was recorded for Victor, with an instrumental septet directed by Leonard Joy.

Joy also directed the High Hatters, yet another Victor 'house' band, for the cheerfully ungrammatical *You've Got Me Picking Petals off o' Daisies*, a de Sylva, Brown and Henderson fox-trot from *Sunny Side Up*. The anonymous vocalist was Frank Luther, whose solo records for Victor, as Bud Billings, appeared here on Zonophone.

Not many people today will recall silent screen star Lupe Velez, known as *the Mexican Spitfire*. She could certainly sing, as her Victor recording of *Where is the Song of Songs for Me?* effectively demonstrated. Issued here on Zonophone, and a haunting ballad by Irving Berlin, it came from her United Artists part-talkie *Lady of the Pavements*. Sadly, she committed suicide on December 14, 1944, because she was pregnant but unmarried.

Although genuine British bands did appear on Piccadilly, some of the recordings had been made by American studio ensembles, taken from the Grey Gull catalogue. The fox-trots *Stepping Along*, by William Kernell, who wrote many songs for films, and *My Fate is in Your Hands*, an Andy Razaf – Fats Waller collaboration, are known to be of Grey Gull origin.

Bandleader and singer Smith Ballew: Buddy Blue and his Texans *on Imperial records.*

Heigh-ho, everybody, this is Rudy Vallee!

These sides were credited to the White Star Syncopators, a collective pseudonym used by Piccadilly for various British and American bands. On this occasion, Mike Mosiello (trumpet) and Andy Sanella (alto saxophone and clarinet) were in the band, both being much-used session players.

In so many instances, the songs of this period were infinitely more entertaining than the minor musicals in which they were first heard. Probably the best thing about Paramount's *Applause* was singer Helen Morgan, who starred. It featured a fox-trot, *I Love You, Sweetheart of All My Dreams*, by Art and Kay Fitch and Bert Lowe, later recorded in New York by Adrian Schubert and his Salon Orchestra, with a vocal by Scrappy Lambert, issued here by Imperial.

Born in the 1890s, Schubert was Musical Director for the Plaza-Mills record group, which included Domino, Jewel, Oriole and Regal, from 1922 to 1930, after which he moved to Crown. Imperial's so-called Hollywood Dance Orchestra concealed many sides by Schubert, including the best-selling *I'm Following You*, a rather touching little song by Dave Dreyer and Ballard MacDonald.

Apart from its melodic appeal, this record had the added interest of a trombone solo by Tommy Dorsey; the vocalist was Smith Ballew, who was born on January 21, 1902, went to Texas University, played banjo with various bands, later directed one of his own, and occasionally acted in films.

I'm Following You was featured in MGM's *It's a Great Life,* released in 1930, with Rosetta and Vivian Duncan, Jed Prouty and Lawrence Gray. The Imperial record, flaunting a new colour scheme of bright red, black and gold, still turns up quite frequently.

Radio's *The Vagabond Lover* was a vehicle for Rudy Vallee, who played his alto saxophone, sang, and directed his Connecticut Yankees. Although years later he developed into a likeable character actor, Vallee gave a stiff performance in this film, supported by Sally Blane and Marie Dressler.

The movie did at least have several pleasant songs: Ken Smith and Edward Heyman's *I'll be Reminded of You;* Leon Zimmerman and Vallee's *I'm Just a Vagabond Lover* and Harry Woods' *A Little Kiss Each Morning,* all of which Vallee also droned nasally for Victor to the plodding accompaniment of the Connecticut Yankees, a band almost never given anything worthwhile to do.

Vallee had already become a nationwide radio celebrity, always beginning his NBC shows with 'Heigh-ho, everybody, this is Rudy Vallee', in his twangy, New England accents. A pharmacist's son, he was born Hubert Prior Vallee on July 28, 1901, at Island Pond, Vermont, and studied at both Maine University and Yale. He was nicknamed Rudy after Rudy Wiedoeft, a virtuoso American alto saxophonist, something which Vallee himself never became.

Vallee was still active in the early Eighties, but by mid-decade he had become seriously ill, and he died suddenly at his North Hollywood home on July 3, 1986, while watching the Statue of Liberty re-dedication ceremony on television.

Leo Reisman and his Orchestra were featured in Jerome Kern's *Good Morning, Dearie* at New York's Globe Theatre in 1921. After a spell with Columbia, Reisman began to record for Victor in March, 1929, and he remained with Victor until October, 1933.

Born in Boston on October 11, 1897, Leo F. Reisman's early career was as a violinist playing symphonic or light orchestral music in Baltimore, but he came to public notice after he formed a dance orchestra in Boston. Later he had many others under his control. For over four decades he directed Society bands, his particular forte being a lush presentation of show tunes. Kern, no mean judge of such music, had a high regard for Reisman.

Among the band's earliest Victor recordings was *I Kiss Your Hand, Madame*, with Fritz Rotter's original lyric suitably adapted by Sam Lewis and Joe Young. Restrained, warm-toned brass and velvety strings enhanced the charm of Ralph Erwin's melody, and in Ran Weeks the band had a sympathetic vocalist.

Doing the Boom-Boom was recorded six months later. A routine song by Archie Gottler, Sidney Mitchell and Con Conrad, it was given a technically irreproachable treatment but had no memorable qualities. On that occasion the vocalist was Lou Levin.

Although catering for the most part to a wealthy clientele desirous of smooth, sweet dance music, Reisman earned himself an undeserved reputation as a lover of jazz in the Thirties, when his popularity was at its highest point, by making some records with the famous Ellingtonian growl trumpeter Bubber Miley. In fact, Miley was wished upon him by Victor, and Reisman loathed the records which resulted. Reisman died on December 18, 1961.

MGM's *Devil May Care* starred Ramon Novarro, Dorothy Jordan and Marion Harris, and this early musical gave Ben

Selvin and his Orchestra a brace of romantic ballads to record for Columbia. *Charming* and *The Shepherd's Serenade*, with lyrics by Clifford Grey and music by Herbert Stothart, were played in Selvin's sweet but never cloying style, the vocalist being Smith Ballew.

Paramount's long forgotten musical *The Rainbow Man* co-starred Eddie Dowling and Marion Nixon. From it came *Sleepy Valley*, a waltz which had a brief burst of popularity and was much recorded. The lyric was by Andrew B. Sterling; the lilting melody by James F. Hanley.

Ben Selvin and the Cavaliers recorded it for Columbia. A version by the Hurtado Brothers' Marimba Band appeared here on Imperial; light orchestral performances were waxed by de Groot and Albert Sandler for HMV and Columbia respectively. Perhaps it was only what Raymond Chandler would have called a tinsel waltz, but heard today on an old record, *Sleepy Valley* still retains a rather faded charm.

The gaiety of a decade which had disported itself to the Charleston, Black Bottom, Yale Blues, Varsity Drag and Breakaway ended abruptly in October, 1929, with the Wall Street Crash. Before then the music had already begun moving towards the smoother, more sophisticated arrangements of the Thirties, the banjo and brass bass going out of favour.

But much else would change too. Back in 1920, the Savoy Quartet had recorded Irving Berlin's *Nobody Knows and Nobody Seems to Care*, a title which summed up the attitude of the more affluent to the problems of the majority.

The Depression quickly led to widespread unemployment and grinding poverty on both sides of the Atlantic. In 1932 it would be Yip Harburg and Jay Gorney's *Brother, Can You Spare a Dime?* which reflected the despair of a generation facing a bleak future, increasingly menaced by the shadow of the swastika.

Chapter Eight

1930

'Dancing
On The Ceiling'

'Of time's passage none can be unaware this morning; even the letters we date remind us that for good or bad the Nineteen-Twenties are over, while the one indisputable fact about the Thirties is that they must be different.' Thus commented *The Times* on January 1, 1930, ponderously overstating the obvious. Different the Thirties undoubtedly were: an economic collapse saw to that.

But the grim Thirties had their lighter moments, popular entertainment bringing some relief to many desperately needing an antidote to acute Depression. Stage and screen offered a brief escape from reality for those who could afford to go; the wireless was a rich and varied source of pleasure; and the British dance bands aroused the admiration of discerning Americans. If the dark clouds lacked a silver lining, at least they drew aside occasionally to permit a few sunny gleams.

In 1930 song-plugging was still rife; both the BBC and the *Melody Maker* expressed concern. Music publishers, well aware of the value of radio publicity, offered considerable inducements to bandleaders. BBC payment rates being what they were, bribes were taken and mediocre songs unscrupulously pushed. Many new songs, of course, did well on their own merits, the Thirties being singularly rich in good ballads as band vocalists began to achieve greater – but not too great – prominence.

July saw the ignominious demise of Dominion, which was ordered to be wound up, but Jay Wilbur left before the end to become Crystalate's Musical Director. Over the years he assembled some interesting session bands for Imperial, Eclipse, Crown and Rex. He became Harry Bidgood's boss when Crystalate took over Vocalion, but in the early Thirties they were rivals. Wilbur died in South Africa in 1968.

Jay Wilbur and his Orchestra were much featured by Imperial, with arrangements and performance of equally high standard. Good singers were always used. *Dancing on the Ceiling*, a typical recording by this 'house' band, featured Les Allen. An imaginative song by Rodgers and Hart, it came from C. B. Cochran's *Ever Green*, which opened at the Adelphi in December, with Jessie Matthews and Sonnie Hale sharing the lead. Gaumont's screen version of 1934 amended the title to *Evergreen*.

Records by the 'house' Blue River Band appeared on Piccadilly and included two songs by Al Dubin and Joe Burke, *When Love Comes* and *Highway to Heaven*, taken from Warner's *Oh! Sailor, Behave!* which first introduced filmgoers to the zany antics of Ole Olsen and Chic Johnson. The vocalist on both was Jimmy Allen.

Jessie Matthews: A brilliant international star with an unhappy private life.

Although one of the lesser record manufacturers, Piccadilly issued some enjoyable dance music, not exclusively by session bands. Jock McDermott and his New Carlton Players first recorded for this label in the autumn, continuing to do so until January, 1931. Led by McDermott on trombone, this was the resident band at the Carlton Danse Salon in Tottenham Court Road.

McDermott recorded *Oh! Donna Clara!* a European tango by J. Petersburski, transformed on this occasion into a fox-trot. It was an immensely popular song in 1930, despite a lyric of little merit by Jimmy Kennedy. The vocalist was Fred Douglas.

McDermott's band also recorded *The Kiss Waltz*, a Dubin and Burke contribution to Warner's *Dancing Sweeties*, co-starring Grant Withers and Sue Carol. Although it basked awhile in the sun of popular esteem, the song had no lasting qualities. Fred Douglas was again the vocalist.

Born in Zurich on June 10, 1891, and among America's most original lyricists, Dubin was already a veteran, one of his earliest collaborations being with Ernest R. Ball, of *Mother Machree* fame. Back in 1917 they had joined forces to create *All the World will be Jealous of Me*. Al Dubin, who wrote many good songs with Joe Burke, followed by others equally pleasurable with Harry Warren, died in New York in 1945.

Dancing Sweeties also featured a number by the very experienced partnership of Alfred Bryan and George W. Meyer, *I Love You, I Hate You*. Jennie Howard's Piccadilly recording was backed by *The Things You Want Most are Hard to Get*, a fair summary of life during a Depression. For this song, Bryan and Meyer were aided by J. McLaughlin. It came from First National's *Hard to Get*, starring Dorothy Mackaill, Louise Fazenda and Jack Oakie. Jennie Howard's accompanist was Ian Stewart.

In his youth a church organist in Somerset, Stewart's big moment came in 1935 when Carroll Gibbons engaged him as assistant pianist for the Savoy Hotel Orpheans. After Gibbons' death in 1954 he assumed leadership, becoming an institution at the Savoy, just as Gibby had been. Dignified and rather reserved; an outstanding but never flamboyant pianist, Ian Stewart, M.B.E., retired in July, 1978, being then in his seventieth year, and died on July 30, 1989.

Percival Mackey had left Columbia in May, 1927, flitting from label to label until, in September, 1930, he returned to the fold. The following month he recorded *I Have No Words*, a Desmond Carter and Arthur Schwartz song from *Little*

Tommy Tucker, with Gene Gerrard and Ivy Tresmand in the cast, a resounding flop at Daly's. Mackey's vocalist was Maurice Elwin.

Bristol-born Carter, a distinguished lyricist who worked with Schwartz on several occasions, frequently collaborated with Vivian Ellis, who also composed some songs for the luckless *Little Tommy Tucker*.

Schwartz was born in Newark, New Jersey, on November 25, 1900, and went to the local Central High School and Billings Polytechnic, Montana. He got his B.A. at New York University in 1920, and his M.A. at Columbia in 1921, but although for some years in law practice, gave it up to compose songs for New York revues. He became internationally famous, his career extending well into the Forties.

At the same Columbia session, Mackey and Elwin recorded *Your Sunny Disposition and Mine*, one of many songs composed by pianist and conductor Billy Mayerl, or Joseph William Mayerl, as he was born in London on May 31, 1902. His lyricist on this occasion was Frank Eyton.

Mayerl studied at Trinity College of Music, making a provincial debut in Variety in 1920. His London debut occurred in January, 1923, when he appeared in *You'd be Surprised* at the Covent Garden Theatre. A prolific stage composer, who also wrote a wealth of individual piano pieces, he founded the Billy Mayerl School of Pianoforte Tuition. Less well-known is his interest in aquaria: he became a Fellow of the Zoological Society.

At this time, Percival Mackey's band included Jack Jackson on lead trumpet; other distinguished players being Ben Oakley (trombone), George Smith (tenor saxophone), Pat Dodd (piano) – he joined the ex-R.A.F. Skyrockets in the immediate post-war period – and Bill Harty (drums). Early in 1931, Mackey lost all four when his line-up changed almost completely. His new band brought in Len Shevill (banjo), Spike Hughes (bass), and Dan Ingman (drums).

Shevill's articles on banjo playing were a regular feature of the *Melody Maker*, for which Ingman was then Technical Editor. As for Patrick Cairns 'Spike' Hughes, a Londoner born on October 19, 1908, he was a thoroughly trained musician and an authoritative writer who in 1933 became the *Daily Herald's* Music Critic.

Spike Hughes' serious compositions included a ballet, *High Yellow*, performed at the Savoy Theatre in 1932, with Alicia Markova, and an opera, *Cinderella*, seen on BBC Television in 1938. But it is for his contributions to British

Top – *Billy Mayerl: Pianist, composer, songwriter and Fellow of the Zoological Society.*

Above – *Pianist Pat Dodd: After World War Two he joined the Skyrockets.*

NEW "RHYTHM-STYLE" RECORDS

JOE VENUTI'S BLUE FOUR.

LOUIS ARMSTRONG AND HIS ORCHESTRA.
With Vocal Refrain.

R778 { No. 45 Raggin' the Scale, Fox-Trot.
LOUIS ARMSTRONG AND HIS ORCHESTRA.
With Vocal Refrain.
No. 46 I'm in the Market for You, Fox-Trot.

R753 { No. 43. I Can't give You Anything but Love, Fox-Trot.
SEGER ELLIS. Piano Solo.
No. 44. Sentimental Blues.

EDDIE LANG'S ORCHESTRA.

R740 { No. 41. Walkin' the Dog, Fox-Trot.
LUIS RUSSELL AND HIS ORCHESTRA
No. 42. Jersey Lightning, Fox-Trot.

*Ask your dealer for Special Booklets giving full particulars of
previously issued New "Rhythm-Style" Recordings—Now Ready.*

OTHER AMERICAN DANCE BAND SUCCESSES

SAM LANIN'S FAMOUS PLAYERS AND SINGERS.

R766 { I wonder how it feels, Fox-Trot.
Lonely, Fox-Trot (" Singer of Seville.")

R756 { When Hearts are Young, Fox-Trot ("The Lady of the Rose.")
Under the Sun, it's Anyone, under the Moon, it's You.
Fox-Trot.

ED LOYD AND HIS ORCHESTRA.
With Vocal Refrain.

R755 { Just a Little Closer, Fox-Trot (" Remote Control.")
This is Love, Waltz (" Madam Satan.")

ROOF GARDEN ORCHESTRA.
With Vocal Refrain.

R757 { It Seems to be Spring, Fox-Trot (" Let's go Native.")
My Mad Moment, Fox-Trot (" Let's go Native.")

R765 { Don't tell Her (what's happened to me), Fox-Trot.
So Beats My Heart for You, Fox-Trot ("Rah Rah Daze.")

TAMPA BLUE ORCHESTRA.
With Vocal Refrain.

R754 { Old New England Moon, Waltz.
You're the Sweetest Girl this side of Heaven, Fox-Trot.

A Great Novelty Record
CABARET DANCE ORCHESTRA.
With Accordeon Specialty and Vocal Refrain.

R758 { Accordeon Joe, Fox-Trot.
With Whistling Specialty and Vocal Refrain.
That's a Drop in the Bucket, Fox-Trot.

ALL 10 in. DOUBLE-SIDED RECORDS 3/- each.

PARLOPHONE

THE PARLOPHONE CO. LTD.   81, CITY ROAD, E.C.1.

Above – *H. Leonard Shevill
played banjo for Percival Mackey
and taught others how to play the
instrument.*

Left – *For those who liked it hot:
a Parlophone advertisement of
1930.*

jazz that he will always be remembered. Apart from his skill
as a bass player, he was a superb arranger; and as a composer
in the jazz idiom created music of a haunting beauty.

Nocturne, Arabesque, Pastorale and *Donegal Cradle Song*
were among his compositions recorded at Brunswick's New
York studio in 1933, when Hughes directed Benny Carter's
loss-making but unbelievably starry band.

Apart from Carter himself, the sidemen included such
near-legendary figures as Red Allen, Dicky Wells, Wilbur de
Paris, Coleman Hawkins, Choo Berry, Luis Russell and
Sidney Catlett. It says sufficient about Hughes' stature that
such superlative players were happy to use his arrangements
and accept his direction.

Radio records in 1930: 'In a class by themselves.'

The records were issued here by Decca, labelled as by Spike Hughes and his American Negro Orchestra. In addition, Spike Hughes and his Dance Orchestra were much featured in Decca supplements, but this British 'house' band played jazz, rather than commercial dance music. Although Hughes confined his bandleading expertise to session recordings, his niche in the annals of British hot music is a secure one. He died on February 2, 1987.

In September, 1931, Percival Mackey was relegated to Regal, and two months later recorded Archie Gottler and Horatio Nicholls', *Kiss Me Goodnight*, with a vocal by Val Rosing, before dropping out of the supplements. Save for his direction later of a few HMV 'house' sessions, his recording career was over.

Decca had some way to go before justifiably claiming to be on an equal footing with HMV and Columbia, but it was an ambitious and well-managed company. The rather too ornate blue and gold label first began to spin early in 1929, and the original catalogue was decidedly slim. Recording, too, left something to be desired in early years.

But Decca had money to spend and knew where it wanted to go. Before long it was pulling some very big fish into its net, and there came a time when Decca reproduction led the way. It is sad to think that a truly great name among record manufacturers was finally lost, by virtue of a takeover, in January, 1980.

One of the earliest bandleaders to sign a Decca contract was American violinist Jack Harris, who did so in 1930. Harris, whose bands blew very hot at times, and could certainly swing, came to London in 1927; the following year he was at the Embassy Club, and in 1930 he went to Grosvenor House.

He remained in the forefront throughout the Thirties, recording much of interest, and in 1937 bought and refurbished Ciro's Club in partnership with Bert Ambrose. The latter soon withdrew and Ciro's closed in March, 1939. Harris was still very active when war was declared, but in May, 1940, went back to America for a visit. The acceleration of hostilities made his return impossible and he began to play in the States, but whatever the quality of his band there, it made no musical headlines.

In 1930 one could dance at Grosvenor House until 2 am. Despite its zestful approach to popular music, the Harris band never encountered there the sort of hostility which drove Fred Elizalde from the Savoy. But then Harris was astute enough to suit his style to his surroundings. On a concert platform, of course, the band could blow its heart out and confidently expect applause.

Harris' early Decca recordings included two Walter Donaldson fox-trots. *My Baby Just Cares for Me*, with a Gus Kahn lyric, came from Sam Goldwyn's *Whoopee*, in which Eddie Cantor starred and Betty Grable led the chorus. It also marked the debut of Busby Berkeley, whose incredibly imaginative choreography has never been surpassed. Cavan O'Connor was Harris' vocalist on that occasion.

Little White Lies was entirely Donaldson's work, and for this recording O'Connor duetted with Tom Barratt. However, he was again sole vocalist for Bert Kalmar and Harry Ruby's *Three Little Words*, created for RKO's *Check and Double Check*, in which Sue Carol and comics Amos 'n' Andy were joined by Duke Ellington and his Orchestra.

Kalmar, an accomplished lyricist, librettist and composer, was born in 1884. At one time a magician in vaudeville, he contributed to many New York productions, particularly in the second half of the Twenties, and died in 1947.

His partnership with Harry Ruby (actually Rubinstein), began in 1918. Ruby, a New Yorker, born on January 27, 1895, became a renowned song and revue composer who, in 1930, began to create songs for the movies. He was still busy in the mid-Forties.

Unlike Elizalde, Jack Harris was quite willing to play and record waltzes, such as Harry Carlton and Horatio Nicholls' *Gypsy Melody* and *Dancing With Tears in My Eyes*, which Dubin and Burke wrote for *Dancing Sweeties*. It was cut from the film but did very well on its own.

In October, 1930, three months after Jack Harris made his first sides for Decca, another American bandleader was lured to their recording microphone. His name was Roy Fox, and because of his soft, very sweet style he became known as 'the whispering cornetist'. Although originally intending only to fulfill an eight-week engagement, the tall, immaculately dressed American with the quiet, pleasant manner, stayed to direct bands as fondly remembered as any that graced the dancing Thirties.

Roy Clifton Fox was born in Denver, Colorado, on October 25, 1901, but became a Californian before his first birthday. As a young man he played in the bands of Abe Lyman, Henry Halstead, Earl Burtnett and Gus Arnheim; he led his own at the Club Royale in Culver City until the place was totally

Jack Harris once played violin with Ross Gorman's Earl Carroll Orchestra. He settled in nicely at the Embassy Club, Grosvenor House and Ciro's.

Roy Fox, the 'whispering cornetist' who gave Harlean Carpenter a new name.

destroyed by fire; and was with Fox Films (the name is coincidental) as Musical Director when he was wired by the Cafe de Paris to bring over a small band and play there for two months.

Located in Coventry Street, near Piccadilly Circus, Martin Poulsen's Cafe de Paris was actually a large restaurant. Top stars performed in its cabarets and it was patronised by the Prince of Wales. One of its hostesses, Nora Turner, later became Lady Docker. Just why Roy Fox was chosen remains a mystery. He was hardly a 'name' in America and quite unknown over here.

Fox's engagement began on September 29, 1930, and was not extended beyond the prearranged termination date, after which his fellow players went home. The band apparently had no outstanding qualities, only its leader's distinctive solos attracting interest. Eight recordings were issued, all with vocals by Kenneth Allen.

Of these, perhaps the most appealing were two waltzes, *Song of the Islands*, an enduring work by the Hawaiian composer Charles King, first heard in 1915, and *Someday I'll Find You*, the famous Noel Coward song from *Private Lives*.

The career of Roy Fox, although much interrupted by ill-health, was an impressive one. Decca quickly appointed him their musical adviser, and he recorded for them until the end of 1935, then switching to HMV, for whom he made his last records in August, 1938. That year he went to Australia, where he made little impact. Unable to come back when war broke out, he directed bands of no particular importance in New York until 1946, then returned to London.

He found the musical scene changed out of all recognition, and not for the better. Stale Miller, blaring brass and over-emphasised vocalists were hardly his style, and in any case the public had long ago found new idols. In 1951 he was declared bankrupt, eventually becoming a theatrical agent. Roy Fox, one of the most charming of all pre-war bandleaders, died in London on March 22, 1982.

While Harris and Fox were just beginning to attract public attention, a key figure of the Twenties was no longer involved in the London scene. At the start of 1930, Cyril Ramon Newton was leading his own band at Tilley's Grand Assembly Rooms at Newcastle upon Tyne. Hardly in the Joe Venuti class as a violinist; an adequate vocalist at best; he had nevertheless helped to make the Savoy bands the legends they became. Today, he is almost forgotten.

Jimmy Campbell (above) *and Reg Connelly* (far right): *Music publishers and lyricists.*

Rarely interesting, occasionally exasperating, the Debroy Somers Band was surprisingly popular with the general public and recorded at frequent intervals for Columbia. Tom Barratt was the vocalist for *'t Ain't No Sin*, a mildly surrealist novelty by Edgar Leslie and Walter Donaldson suggesting it was quite acceptable to shed one's skin and dance around in one's bones.

On May 5, Amy Johnson set off in a tiny De Havilland Moth biplane for a solo flight to Australia. She was home again on August 4, to receive a civic reception at Croydon, no doubt much amused by *Amy, Wonderful Amy*, then very popular. Written by Joe Gilbert and composed by Horatio Nicholls, it was recorded by the Debroy Somers Band, with Tom Barratt, and by Jack Hylton, with his new singer Pat O'Malley. Hylton also featured the song in a band show at the Piccadilly Theatre.

Bill Somers' band also appeared on stage in 1930, supporting Binnie Hale and Clifford Mollison in *Nippy*, which opened in October at the Prince Edward Theatre, with music by Billy Mayerl. Somers recorded a selection from this musical comedy, featuring the Welsh singer Dan Donovan, an equally capable saxophone player, who later had his own band at the Lansdowne Restaurant.

Dan Donovan: After playing and singing for Henry Hall from 1934 to 1937, he assembled his own band for the Lansdowne Restaurant.

Jack Hylton probably looked back on 1930 with great satisfaction. Early in the year he took his band on a strenuous tour, visiting Belgium, Denmark, France, Germany, Italy and Sweden. The French made him a member of the Légion d'Honneur for his services to entertainment, and in 1931 a Chevalier of the same order.

Sam Browne, wanting no more tours, made his last sides for Hylton on January 30. Mid-way through the month he had sung with the band at Madame Tussaud's Cinema, the Wurlitzer of resident organist Edward O'Henry helping things along. Appropriately, the session included *When the Organ Played at Twilight*, a waltz by Raymond Wallace, with a Jimmy Campbell and Reg Connelly lyric. Browne was succeeded by Pat O'Malley.

Campbell and Connelly wrote lyrics for Ray Noble and were very successful song publishers. Campbell, who married the film actress Betty Balfour, was born at Newcastle in 1903; his partner at Buckhurst Hill, Essex, in 1895.

Just as Jack Hylton had given Sam Browne his big break, so the signing-up of O'Malley brought another little-known singer to the fore. Patrick James O'Malley had been

Reg Connelly.

drummer and vocalist with the Cambridge Nightwatchmen, a hot semi-pro band, his place being taken by Val Rosing, actually an Oxford undergraduate, who later sang for Jack Payne and Henry Hall.

Hylton featured O'Malley on scores of records, but there was a blandness about his singing sometimes verging upon monotony, reminding one of Ray Eberle, who joined Glenn Miller eight years later and grew wearisome with over-familiarity.

Pat O'Malley also recorded with Hylton's American band in Chicago at the start of 1936, and decided to try his luck in the States. He left Hylton that December to become a cabaret artist and film actor, later providing Walt Disney with animal voices for some of his feature-length cartoons, such as *The Jungle Book*. He died in America in March, 1985.

Jack Hylton, although content to let O'Malley handle the ballads, liked to sing an occasional comedy number. He added his own touch of humour to *Maggie's Cold*, by Harry Tilsley, Robert Hargreaves and Stanley J. Damerell, his Lancashire accent being quite noticeable.

Moanin' Low, quite unsuitable for O'Malley, was allocated to Ella Logan, then a teenager, who was not only a delightful singer but an excellent mimic. She later sang for Ambrose and Roy Fox before going to America. Ella had a leading role in *Finian's Rainbow* at New York's 46th Street Theatre in 1947, her lovely rendering of Yip Harburg and and Burton Lane's *How are Things in Glocca Morra?* being one of the high-spots of the show.

Created by Howard Dietz and Ralph Rainger, *Moanin' Low* was a highly effective torch song in the blues idiom, first heard in April, 1929, at New York's Music Box Theatre in *The Little Show*,where it was sung by Libby Holman.

Lyricist and librettist Howard Dietz was born in New York on September 8, 1896, and went to Columbia University. A successful journalist who served in the U.S. Navy during World War One, he became MGM's Director of Publicity, as well as writing lyrics for stage productions for over 20 years, beginning in the mid-Twenties.

Composer Ralph Rainger, a fellow New Yorker, was born on October 7, 1901, his real name being Reichenthal. Having found a law career unappealing, he played in a small dance band and tried his hand at song writing, *Moanin' Low* being his first hit. In the Thirties he established himself as a film composer, many of his songs created with Leo Robin being particularly charming. He died in an aeroplane crash in California on October 23, 1942.

With a Song in My Heart was a smoothly romantic ballad which quite suited Pat O'Malley. It was written by Rodgers and Hart for *Spring is Here*, an Alvin Theatre, New York Production of 1929. *When You're Smiling, the Whole World Smiles with You* expressed Mark Fisher, Joe Goodwin and Larry Shay's attitude to the Depression, and this song too was right for O'Malley's style.

On the Sunny Side of the Street will always recall Tommy Dorsey's classic RCA Victor recording, made in Hollywood in 1944, with its crisp Sy Oliver arrangement and close harmony vocal by the Sentimentalists. It would be unfair to disparage the Hylton – O'Malley version which, after all, pre-dated the swing era. Dorothy Fields and Jimmy McHugh created this optimistic song and it was featured in Lew Leslie's *International Revue* at New York's Royale Theatre in October, 1930.

Pat O'Malley, Jack Hylton and an unknown singer formed a vocal trio on one occasion to perform *Meet Me in My Dreams Tonight*, a winner by Joe Gilbert and Horatio Nicholls in waltz-time. It was recorded (in June) in Kingsway Hall.

The graceful music of Vivian Ellis, usually composed for the stage, frequently appealed to bandleaders. *The Wind in the Willows*, a real charmer with a Desmond Carter lyric, was written for Cochran's 1930 Revue at the London Pavilion. As usual, the Hylton band gave an impeccable performance, but O'Malley's vocal was somewhat perfunctory.

That was also true of *The First Week-End in June*, a beautiful song by Douglas Furber and Ellis, one of several quite outstanding numbers in *Follow a Star*, which opened in September at the Winter Garden Theatre. O'Malley had a pleasant voice, but seemed to lack the feeling which Browne, Plant, O'Connor and Bowlly usually projected.

Thoroughly modern, *Follow a Star* re-introduced London to Sophie Tucker, who had been here in 1922, 1925 and 1928. She was well received, but her show only enjoyed a brief run. She brought over Ted Shapiro, her regular accompanist, and Jack Yellen, who was no longer squabbling with Milton Ager.

Instead of the major labels, it was Broadcast Twelve which stepped in smartly to record Sophie Tucker. The big, blonde Red Hot Momma smote us with the full force of her considerable personality in Furber and Ellis' *If Your Kisses*

Sophie Tucker, Broadway's 'Red Hot Momma'. The photograph was probably taken in the Twenties.

Sydney Baynes: Bandleader, theatre conductor and composer of pretty waltzes.

Can't Hold the Man You Love, Your Tears Won't Bring Him Back, a masterpiece of cynicism, partly sung and partly spoken.

She was equally effective singing *Follow a Star* and *I Never Can Think of the Words*, both by Yellen and Ellis, and *That's Where the South Begins*, a more conventional song by Yellen and Shapiro. Sophie was accompanied by pianist Shapiro and the Winter Garden Theatre Orchestra, conducted by Sydney Baynes, composer of the lovely waltz *Destiny*.

Among the bands that recorded *That's Where the South Begins* was Alfredo's, which did so for Radio in October. The same session produced *Californian Serenade*, a typically inconsequential ditty, fleetingly popular, by Gilbert and Nicholls. Each had an Eddie Gross-Bart vocal. A month later, Alfredo's Band recorded a quartet of tunes for Winner, with vocals by Les Allen and Al Bowlly as a duet, before breaking up. An above average violinist, Alfredo soon began to tour with his new Gypsy Orchestra, sporting a wide-brimmed hat and ear-rings.

Paramount's *The Love Parade*, starring Maurice Chevalier and Jeanette MacDonald, had songs by Clifford Grey and Victor Schertzinger. *My Love Parade* and the beautiful waltz *Dream Lover* were recorded for Radio by Alfredo's Band earlier in the year, with vocals by Harry Jacobson and Hal Swain respectively.

The March of the Grenadiers, reminiscent of operetta, also came from *The Love Parade*, recorded for Sterno by Vincent Howard's Dance Orchestra (in reality a studio band assembled by Nat Star), with a vocal duet by Tom Barratt and Cavan O'Connor.

Born in 1883, Charles 'Nat' Star played clarinet and alto saxophone with Ciro's Club Orchestra in 1928. During his tenure as British Homophone's Musical Director, he also recorded as André Astan, Bernie Blake, Bert Maddison and Louis Ramel. His 'house' bands made easy listening, but were hardly sensational. Indeed, the term 'commercial', used derisively by hot music devotees, was particularly applicable to Sterno's session recordings. Star died in 1950.

Jeanette MacDonald: Her Hollywood musicals are frequently shown on television.

The lyrics of Clifford Grey were among the best of their kind, and he had an international reputation. Born in Birmingham on January 5, 1887, he was the son of George and Emma Davis. Educated at King Edward's School, Camp Hill, Birmingham, he was an actor from 1907 to 1913. Achieving no particular recognition, he wisely turned to lyric writing, contributing prolifically to revues, musical comedies and films. He died on September 26, 1941.

Victor Schertzinger's music had grace and charm. Born at Mahanoy City, Pennsylvania, in 1889, he went to Philadelphia High School and Brussels University. After touring Europe as a concert violinist he became orchestral leader for various New York musical comedies.

His lilting waltz song *Marcheta* appeared in 1913; three years later he wrote a score for Thomas Ince's *Civilization*, believed to be the first film to have one. A distinguished Hollywood director, Schertzinger died on October 26, 1941.

Sir Robert Peel was probably the only hereditary peer who led a dance band. In September, 1930, it was heard four times in one week over the BBC London Regional or National Programmes, relayed from Tony's Ballroom, Birmingham.

Peel, a direct descendant of the founder of the Police Force, was born on April 7, 1898, and went to Harrow. In 1920 he married Beatrice Lillie, and five years later succeeded his father as fifth baronet.

A former cowboy and West of England fisherman, Peel

assembled a band after the General Strike of 1926, using unemployed miners. At Lady Peel's suggestion he turned professional, obtaining a contract from Sir Oswald Stoll. A 14-man band, it made a handful of records for Sterno in the summer and autumn of 1930.

Sam Coslow's *Sweeping the Clouds Away* was one of these, and had a Tom Barratt vocal. The song came from Paramount's very starry revue *Paramount on Parade*, featuring, among many others, Maurice Chevalier, Dennis King, Fay Wray (of *King Kong* fame), Clara Bow (the 'It' Girl), Helen Kane and Abe Lyman's band. It was produced by Elsie Janis.

It is uncertain how long Peel's band lasted, and it appears to have made no other records. Peel himself died on April 6, 1934, and his son in 1942, killed on active service. Beatrice Lillie, Lady Peel, died at Henley-on-Thames on January 20, 1989, in her 95th year.

Although Bert Ambrose disliked his players making extra money on session dates, he apparently had no objection to his vocalists doing the same. Sam Browne was always in demand for both session bands and regular ones. With Ray

Abe Lyman's band, based in California, appeared in several movies. It is seen here in Warner's Hold Everything (1930).

Starita's Ambassadors' Club Band he recorded *Gee, It Must be Love*, a fox-trot by Lee Richards; but for *The Sunshine of Marseilles*, another fox-trot by the Gilbert and Nicholls team, Starita used Lou Abelardo, a velvety-voiced cabaret artist discovered by Van Phillips.

Phillips was another who never had his own band, but the 'house' one he assembled for Columbia, whose Musical Director he was from 1929 to 1931, made many contemporaries sound effete. Born Alexander van Cleve Phillips Jr. at Boston, Massachusetts, in 1905, he played with the Savoy Havana Band for four years, produced commercial broadcasts for Universal Programmes Corporation Ltd., composed film scores and conducted the Carlton Theatre orchestra in 1928 during the run of *Good News*.

Two sides he made for Columbia in 1930 were especially good. Not only was the band's performance quite exciting, but Maurice Elwin revealed how at home he was with up-tempo material. *I'm Doing That Thing* and *Go Home and Tell Your Mother* were marvellous songs by Dorothy Fields and Jimmy McHugh, heard in MGM's *Love in the Rough*, duetted by Robert Montgomery and Dorothy Jordan.

Happy Days are Here Again, Yellen and Ager had claimed in 1929, just before Wall Street brutally dispelled such optimism. Among the last songs they wrote together, it was breezily performed in January, 1930, by the Ambrose band, with Lou Abelardo and heard in MGM's *Chasing Rainbows*, starring Bessie Love and Charles King.

Decca soon lost Ambrose, for a time anyway. By then a very 'hot property', he cut one farewell side at Chelsea in February, and the following month was back at Hayes. HMV had learned a lesson. The May Fair Hotel Orchestra was regularly featured in the supplements, recording many of the finest songs available.

This time, Ambrose stayed with the Gramophone Company until early in 1933, switching to Brunswick a few months later, before Warner Brothers sold the label to Decca. By the autumn of 1934 he was on Decca itself, remaining until April, 1947, by which time dance music sounded very different.

His swan-song for Decca in 1930 was *Body and Soul*, a distinctive ballad for which Edward Heyman, Robert Sauer and Frank Eyton wrote the lyric, and Johnny Green the music. Sam Browne was the vocalist, having joined Ambrose in February.

Body and Soul was sung in *Three's a Crowd* at the Selwyn Theatre by Libby Holman. The later famous tenor Allan

Clara Bow was dubbed the 'It' girl after starring in Paramount's 1927 silent film of that name. With a screenplay by Elinor Glyn, it was a box-office 'smash'. 'It' became synonymous with sex-appeal.

Jones was in this revue. Heyman, Sauer and composer-pianist-bandleader Johnny Green were Americans, but Frank Eyton was English. Born in London on August 30, 1894, he became a well-known author and lyricist, making notable contributions to the West End during the Thirties and Forties.

So many satisfying records were waxed by Ambrose and Browne in 1930 that one can only select a few personal favourites. *Crying for the Carolines* was an odd but appealing song by Sam Lewis, Joe Young and Harry Warren, heard in First National's *Spring is Here*, with Bernice Claire and Frank Albertson, while *Moanin' for You* was created by Dan Dougherty and Edmund Goulding.

Goulding, a Londoner, was born on March 20, 1891, and made his debut at the Holborn Empire in 1909. He appeared regularly on the London stage until 1915, then went to New York. Later, Hollywood called, and he became a well-known director, also writing screen plays. He appears to have been quite a capable composer, and a minor novelist.

Just Like in a Story Book and *I'm in the Market for You* came from Fox's *High Society Blues*, co-starring Janet Gaynor and Charles Farrell. They were bright little songs by Joseph McCarthy and James F. Hanley.

Equally peppy and tuneful was *Living in the Sunlight, Loving in the Moonlight*, an Al Sherman and Al Lewis contribution to Paramount's *The Big Pond*, teaming Maurice Chevalier and delightful Claudette Colbert. *You Brought a New Kind of Love to Me*, by Irving Kahal, Pierre Norman and Sammy Fain, also came from this movie.

Sammy Fain, a New Yorker, was born on June 17, 1902, and Irving Kahal in Houtzdale, Pennsylvania, on March 5, 1903. Fain's first hit, *Nobody knows what a Redheaded Mama Can Do*, had a lyric by Irving Mills and Al Dubin; it appeared in 1925. Two years later, Fain began a remarkably productive partnership with Kahal which was to last until the latter's death in New York, on February 17, 1942. Active into the Seventies, Fain died in Los Angeles on December 7, 1989.

Blue, Turning Grey, Over You was a pleasant little song by Andy Razaf and Fats Waller; but perhaps the prettiest song recorded by Ambrose and Browne in 1930 was *A Japanese Dream*, with Dorothy Fields' ethereal lyric well-matched by Jimmy McHugh's delicate melody.

These songs, typical of the early Thirties, were never better performed than by the Ambrose band, but it is

Edmund Goulding: London-born Hollywood director and occasional song composer.

regrettable that so capable a singer as Sam Browne should have received no label recognition. It was, of course, the custom; and Lew Stone is known to have told Decca that Al Bowlly's name was not to be shown on his band recordings. A foolish policy, really: vocalists had a considerable following among the public.

Considering his long career as a bandleader, it is surprising how few records Marius B. Winter made. He became well known on the Continent for his commercial radio programmes and in 1930 directed his Black Cats for Sunday evening shows over Radio Paris. But he did record here sometimes, and between September, 1930, and May, 1931, made fourteen sides for the Broadcast label.

They included *My Future Just Passed*, a charming song by George Marion Jr. and Richard Whiting, which 20-year-old Annette Hanshaw recorded so touchingly; and *My Heart Belongs to the Girl Who belongs to Somebody Else*, a waltz by Al Sherman and Al Lewis, which was a hit for Rudy Vallee.

In September the Marius B. Winter band broadcast over BBC London Regional; and in October it entertained nightly at Romano's Restaurant in the Strand, along with the famous West Indian singer and pianist Leslie Hutchinson, better known as "Hutch".

Leslie Arthur Hutchinson forsook law studies for popular music. 'Hutch' was still going strong long after the Second World War had ended.

Hal Swain formed a new band early in 1930, and in October left Regal for Broadcast. At his first session for the latter he recorded two songs from *Great Day*, Vincent Youmans' latest show, which had opened the previous year in New York. *Great Day* and *Without a Song*, both fox-trots, had lyrics by William Rose and Edward Eliscu. Swain handled the vocals himself, forming one of a vocal trio on *Great Day*.

Harry Bidgood was always ready to challenge the leading record manufacturers. Getting Sophie Tucker to record for Broadcast had been a remarkable achievement for a minor label. Some months earlier, however, he presented a novelty song in a manner so original as to make Jack Hylton's version look ridiculous.

For Ben Black's *The Punch and Judy Show*, Tom Barratt was joined by a professional Punch and Judy showman, one 'Professor' Smith, who arrived at the studio with his frock coat, brown boots and long, flowing hair. The *Melody Maker* hailed this most entertaining disc rapturously.

Bidgood's little gem was credited to the 'house' Manhattan Melody Makers and issued in the Super Dance Series. Jack Hylton's recording, made for HMV a month later, was non-vocal and featured a long rather pointless xylophone solo by Harry Robbins.

Julius Kantrovitch is a very shadowy figure who, during the spring and summer of 1930 made about a dozen sides for Piccadilly, mostly waltzes. He appears to have made no more records, but was still around in January, 1939, when he could be heard on the BBC Regional programme.

William Kernell and Charles W. Cadman's *My Lonely Heart* and S. Winstrom, Huntley Trevor and Werner R. Heymann's *The Love Waltz* came from *Double Cross Roads*, an obscure and possibly German film. The arrangements were pleasing and the music tastefully performed, but these recordings by Kantrovitch were hardly memorable. For *My Lonely Heart*, Jimmy Allen was the vocalist.

It is interesting to encounter Charles Wakefield Cadman, a distinguished American serious composer, and creator of the ballads *At Dawning*, *I Hear a Thrush at Eve* and *From the Land of the Sky-Blue Water* in such an environment.

With Hylton and Ambrose taking the lions' share of the best songs, it was up to Ray Noble to do his best for the New Mayfair Dance Orchestra with what remained. He succeeded in making his 'house' band a constant best-seller.

Noble liked comedy, and recorded many humorous songs,

such as *Airman! Airman! Don't Put the Wind Up Me!* another Harry Tilsley, Robert Hargreaves and Stanley J. Damerell collaboration. Noble gave the vocal spot to Leonard Henry, popular comedian, whose stage and radio partner was 'Blossom'.

Elizabeth, with a witty lyric by Rowland Leigh, came from Robert Katscher's *Wonder Bar*, which brought Dorothy Dickson and Carl Brisson to the Savoy Theatre in December. Noble's recording featured Jack Plant, a widely-used vocalist with a very high, clear tenor and faultless diction. Anonymous on band recordings, he sang as Jack Gordon on Imperial, and as Carol Porter on Eclipse. He died in 1977.

Jack Payne's visits to Columbia produced some attractive recordings in 1930. He was sole vocalist for *Exactly Like You*, another Fields and McHugh song from Lew Leslie's *International Revue*, and Fred Fisher's *Blue is the Night*, but duetted with Jack Plant – two very high voices in harmony! – for *When It's Springtime in the Rockies*, a harbinger, by Mary Hale Woolsey and Robert Sauer, of the cowboy songs soon to make grass skirts and ukuleles démodé in Tin Pan Alley.

Plant had the solo spot to himself for Friedrich Holländer's waltz song *Falling in Love Again*, given an English lyric by Reg Connelly. It was heard in the German U.F.A. film *The Blue Angel*, which rocketed Marlene Dietrich to international stardom in 1930.

Jack Plant: Widely used band vocalist, who became 'Carol Porter' for Eclipse and 'Jack Gordon' for Imperial.

Left – *Marlene Dietrich:* The Blue Angel *made her an international star.*

Billy Cotton and his Ciro's Club Band. Although now remembered for knock-about comedy, Cotton once recorded much tasteful dance music and some surprisingly hot numbers.

Val Rosing, son of the famous Russian operatic tenor Vladimir Rosing, recorded with Payne's BBC Dance Orchestra in 1930 and 1931. His voice was most suitable for sweeter songs, such as Rose, Eliscu and Youmans' *More Than You Know*, another fox-trot from *Great Day*.

Nat Shilkret was Victor's Light Music Director first and a song composer second, but his music always had a light touch and his waltzes were particularly graceful. *Down the River of Golden Dreams*, with a lyric by John Klenner, was recorded by Billy Cotton and his Band; in 1930 on Regal and playing at Ciro's Club.

Naturally, Shilkret made his own Victor recording, using the Hilo Hawaiian Orchestra, increased to eighteen players for the occasion. Johnny Marvin sang and played the steel guitar.

In the early Thirties most American bands seemed to be running out of steam. Perhaps the horrific Depression shocked their leaders out of any desire for innovation, so they played safe with a bland and spiritless style at a time when the London bands were both stylish and exciting.

Only among American vocalists could one detect a star or two of the immediate future, Bing Crosby being the most talented of all. Things would change within a few years, of course, as America began to hear from Perry Como, Doris Day, Lena Horne, Dinah Shore, Frank Sinatra, Jo Stafford and Kay Starr, all of whom began with bands.

We had gifted young singers too, such as Eve Becke, Al Bowlly, Denny Dennis, Anne Lenner, Vera Lynn, Phyllis Robins and Judy Shirley, comparable with any in the States but, with the exception of Bowlly and later on Dennis, little known across the Atlantic.

Britain was particularly rich in arrangers. Men like Paul Fenoulhet, Leighton Lucas, Ray Noble, Sid Phillips, Bert Read, Lew Stone, Billy Ternent and Peter Yorke were eager to show their transatlantic counterparts just what could be done with dance music.

Our bandleaders were justifiably proud of their magnificent bands, and they had a tremendous following. Bert Ambrose, Billy Cotton, Roy Fox, Geraldo, Henry Hall, Jack Harris, Jack Hylton, Sydney Lipton, Jack Payne, Harry Roy and Lew Stone helped to bring a glitter to the music of the Thirties that only faded when swing ousted melody, introducing a different kind of band with which we could not compete.

Typical of American bands dispensing unrefined schmaltz at the start of the Thirties were those directed by Harry Reser, Lou Gold and Smith Ballew, some of whose recordings were issued here by Imperial, a label notorious for its poor sound quality.

Harry Reser's Clicquot Club Eskimos offered us Gus Kahn and Harry Archer's *Where the Golden Daffodils Grow*. A thoughtful arrangement would have vastly improved this routine ballad, but banjoist Reser, although very popular in the States, produced a record of only minor interest.

New York Society bandleader Lou Gold was no better. *Cheer Up, Good Times are Coming* may have been an attempt by Ray Klages and Jesse Greer to inject a little optimism into a drab year, but their song received a lacklustre treatment.

The sole redeeming feature of most recordings by Smith Ballew and his Orchestra was the pleasant singing voice of its Texan leader. Otherwise, songs like Harry Link, Bert Lown (a bandleader too) and Chauncey Gray's *You're the One I Care*

For were given a very ho-hum rendition. Imperial was inclined to over-indulge in pseudonyms, labelling Ballew as Buddy Blue and his Texans.

Ordinarily, the same critical brickbats could be hurled at Rudy Vallee and his comatose Connecticut Yankees, but young Mr Vallee did pull one rabbit out of his hat in 1930, albeit a somewhat archaic one. *The Stein Song* had begun in 1910 as *The Maine Stein Song*, an affectionate tribute to the University of Maine by Lincoln Colcord and E. A. Fenstad. Vallee simplified the title and gave an uncharacteristically rousing performance, joining Joe Miller, Ray Toland and Jules de Vorzon for the vocal. Recorded in February, it made a lot of money for Victor.

The Stein Song with its irresistible march tune, inevitably crossed the Atlantic. Jack Payne recorded it in April and Jack Hylton in June. Virtually inescapable, it finally provoked American bandleader Johnny Johnson and his singer Harry McDaniel to write *I'd Like to Meet the Guy that Wrote the Stein Song*.

Johnson's Post Lodge Orchestra recorded the latter for Victor in July; three months later, Jack Payne waxed it for Columbia. But before the year ended both the original song and its sequel were fading away, as catchy new melodies came dancing along.

It was Vallee's only sprightly record in 1930. Walter Donaldson's new fox-trot *You're Driving Me Crazy* received the usual lackadaisical treatment; and in his autobiography, published that year, 29-year-old Vallee revealed an unsurprising aversion to hot music. He called his book *Vagabond Dreams Come True*. What people had begun to call *The Stein Song* is best left unrecorded.

Sam Coslow, who became a music publisher and film producer, helped to create many hits, and in 1930 collaborated with W. Franke Harling, usually a more serious composer, to write two fox-trots for Paramount's *Honey*, starring Nancy Carroll, with the tragic singer Lillian Roth in a supporting role. Coslow was born in New York on December 27, 1902.

Both songs were recorded by the High Hatters, directed by Leonard Joy. Dependable Frank Luther was the vocalist for *Sing, You Sinners*, but for *In My Little Hope Chest* Joy used the impressively named Olga Medolago Albani, a concert-trained soprano, who died, aged 36, in 1936.

Ben Selvin's sweet but beautifully arranged music was the kind that swing later swept away, but in 1930 it still had a

Nancy Carroll, a Paramount star, began in silents. Her real name was Ann la Hiff.

Lillian Roth, bright star of Broadway and Hollywood, turned to drink and drugs. Her downfall was portrayed by Susan Hayward in MGM's I'll Cry Tomorrow (1955).

following. Typical of his style was *Moonlight on the Colorado*, recorded for Columbia; a waltz by Billy Moll and Bob King. It was ideal for soothing the day's cares away.

Vincent Lopez favoured a more flamboyant approach. *There's Danger in Your Eyes, Cherie*, he announced on a record issued here by Imperial, adding, as usual, 'Lopez speaking!' A fox-trot by Harry Richman, Jack Meskill and Pete Wendling, it was created for United Artists' *Puttin' on the Ritz*, starring Richman, a pleasant singer but no great shakes as an actor, and Joan Bennett, who was quite delightful.

Harry Richman (real name Reichman) was born in Cincinnati, Ohio, on August 10, 1895, and from his early youth toured widely in vaudeville. He appeared in many top-flight New York revues, including George White's *Scandals*

Harry Richman, a revue artiste who went to Hollywood, was better as a lyricist and song composer than as an actor.

(1927-8), Lew Leslie's *International Revue* (1930), and the *Ziegfeld Follies* (1931), making his film debut in 1929. Richman was quite a competent lyricist and song composer. He died on November 3, 1972.

Most American bandleaders might be marking time, but Paul Whiteman was still *King of Jazz,* or so United Artists proclaimed him in their 100-minute Technicolored extravaganza, built around Pops and his show band. John Boles and Laura La Plante ostensibly starred, but it was the Whiteman band and the Rhythm Boys who pulled in the crowds.

Three good songs from *The King of Jazz* were recorded for Columbia; but on wax the Whiteman band lacked the sparkle of its early years, although still worth hearing. *Happy Feet* and *A Bench in the Park* were good, but hardly vintage Yellen and Ager. Fox-trots both, they had vocals by the Rhythm Boys, joined on the second song by the Brox Sisters. *It Happened in Monterey*, a Mabel Wayne waltz, had a lyric by Billy Rose.

Not long after *The King of Jazz* was filmed , the Rhythm Boys left Pops to sing for Gus Arnheim's band at the Coconut Grove, making a few sides with Arnheim for Victor. The following year, Bing Crosby branched out on his own, recorded *Where the Blue of the Night*, and was well-launched on a career that would make him one of the best-loved singers of all time.

It meant the end of the Rhythm Boys, of course. Al Rinker's name soon faded from public memory, but Harry Barris established himself as a song composer with a number of hits to his credit.

Chapter Nine

1931

'Dancing In The Dark'

'The music of dance orchestras, whether from the studio or from restaurants, night clubs and dance halls outside, remains one of the most popular features of the (Vaudeville) programme', observed the *1932 BBC Year Book*, commenting on the previous year. It went on to state that 'the most popular dance orchestra broadcasting is that directed by Jack Payne,' adding, rather naively, 'it is also heard far more often than any other'.

In fairness to Payne, it was as much his varied and lively repertoire as his 'most favoured band' status which won him his great following; and he remained among the really big names for years after he had severed his 'official' ties with Broadcasting House.

An advertisement of July, 1931. Nine months later, Piccadilly records were off the market.

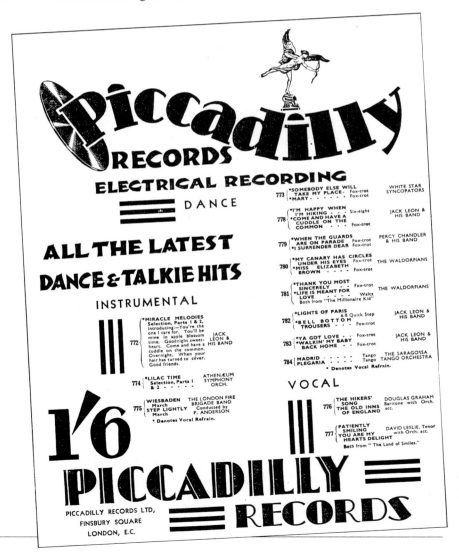

The Year Book listed nine bands contributing most to outside broadcasts in 1931. They were those of Ambrose (May Fair Hotel); Billy Mason (Cafe de Paris); Bertini (Winter Gardens, Blackpool); Henry Hall (Gleneagles Hotel and Midland Hotel, Manchester); Jack Harris (Grosvenor House); Maurice Winnick (Piccadilly Hotel); Howard Jacobs (Claridges and the Savoy Hotel); Roy Fox (Monseigneur Restaurant); and Melville Gideon (Dorchester House).

Of these, Melville Gideon and the Dorchester Dance Band are the most intriguing, for Gideon had only recently taken up the baton, and he made no records as a bandleader. His first venture began late in 1930 when he fronted his short-lived Symphonic Dance Orchestra at the Dominion Theatre. The *Melody Maker* found it 'ragged and unwieldy'.

But Gideon learned from his mistakes and assembled a new band which made an April, 1931, debut at the brand-new Dorchester House Hotel in Park Lane. It made its maiden broadcast from there in August and remained resident band until October. Popular alike with dancers and listeners, it was regarded by the *Melody Maker* as 'a first-class band'. It is curious that no record company signed up Melville Gideon's band, considering his reputation as an entertainer.

Gideon did record in 1931, of course, but only as a crooner. Irving Berlin's *Reaching for the Moon* was made for Parlophone at the start of the year, the accompanying orchestra including pianist and composer Clifford Hellier, a graduate of the Royal Academy of Music, Tich Poster (saxophone) and Percy Martin (guitar).

Jack Payne and his BBC Dance Orchestra kept the Columbia recording engineers busy throughout 1931, but the comedy numbers are best forgotten. Humour has always been a poor time-traveller, and songs like *Why is the Milk of a Red Cow White, When It Always Eats Green Grass?* would be coldly received nowadays.

In December, Garry Allighan, writing a radio feature for the Sunday Referee, stated confidently that Payne, whose contract was due to end in March, 1932, would not renew. The *Melody Maker* derided his prophesy, saying that Payne was more likely to be with the BBC for three more years. 'We'll see who's right!' said staff writer 'Detector'.

Jack Payne' proportion of tunes broadcast was claimed by the BBC to be roughly 50% British, 40% American and 10% Continental, and one can only speculate how much freedom of choice he had in the selection of his material.

The Melody Maker derided journalist Garry Allighan's statement that Jack Payne would not renew his BBC contract in 1932. But Allighan was right!

Pardon Me, Pretty Baby was an American fox-trot, written by Ray Klages and Jack Meskill, with a melody by Vincent Rose. Vocal trios were still very popular, and Payne's, on this occasion included Billy Scott-Coomber.

Non-vocal recordings were comparatively rare for all bands, and usually of interest. The *Melody Maker* considered Payne's version of *Love for Sale* one of his most successful records so far. An unusual song by Cole Porter, it came from *The New Yorkers*, which had opened at the Broadway Theatre in December, 1930.

Songs by Yellen and Ager were still around, and Payne contributed his own vocal to *I Like a Little Girl Like That*, as he did to Billy Moll and Harry Woods' *Hang Out the Stars in Indiana*. However, for *Live, Laugh and Love* and *Just Once For All Time*, two happy songs by Rowland Leigh and Werner R. Heymann, from the German film *Congress Dances*, starring London-born Lillian Harvey, he again used his new vocalist, Billy Scott-Coomber, in the first instance as part of a trio.

A classically trained singer, born at Rawalpindi in 1905, Scott-Coomber had won the Irish Feis Ceoil Award for Singing, just as John McCormack had once done. A minor song composer too, he stayed for years with Payne, but did make records elsewhere, usually under an assumed name. In 1931, for example, he appeared on Eclipse as Malcolm Desmond, singing Ray Noble's *I Found You*, which had a Campbell and Connelly lyric.

Born on May 16, 1902, Rowland Leigh was a distinguished author and lyricist whose first play was produced in 1925. His many contributions to the theatre included lyrics for Charlot revues and English adaptations of *Wonder Bar* (1930), *The Dubarry* (1932), and *A Gift for the Bride* (1945).

Eclipse, in an eight-inch format, was launched by Crystalate in April to challenge Broadcast and Radio. It sold for sixpence (2½p) at Woolworth counters until July, 1935, being then replaced by Crown. Recording was good, but the surface subject to rapid wear, in common with most cheap discs. Eclipse's pseudonyms often hid well-known artists, the label offering inexpensive entertainment at a time of high unemployment.

By this time, the name of Jimmy Kennedy had begun to appear on sheet music covers. Born in Omagh, County Tyrone, on July 20, 1902, he got his B.A. at Trinity College, Dublin, and married the song composer Margaret Galpin. From 1931-1935 he was Feldman's Lyric Editor. A prolific lyricist and occasional composer, Kennedy became a wealthy man, but preferred to avoid publicity. He died on April 6, 1984.

The Twilight Waltz had an early Kennedy lyric, and a tune by Walter Dobson. It was recorded for Regal by the San Marino Piano-Accordion Syncopators, a 'house' ensemble foreshadowing the very popular piano-accordion bands soon to come.

It is amusing to note, in passing, that although record labels in the Thirties referred to 'piano-accordeons', the word should correctly have been shown as 'accordion'.

Pasadena Rose had another Kennedy lyric, and a simple, pretty melody by Ted Renard. It was recorded for Columbia by the Debroy Somers Band, with a vocal by Dan Donovan. However, Somers' version of *Betty Co-Ed*, a campus ditty by Paul Fogarty and Rudy Vallee, was allocated to Regal and a vocal quartet used. 'Nippy' having closed, the Somers band began a London and provincial Variety tour early in 1931.

Significantly, as it turned out, Billy Cotton also decided to try his luck on the Halls. His band had been well-liked during its sojourn at Ciro's Club and broadcast frequently, but Cotton felt his future lay with a showband, rather than one catering for dancers. In February he ended his Ciro's engagement; the following month he made his Variety debut at the Holborn Empire.

Cotton continued to record profusely, appearing on both Regal and Columbia in 1931. For the latter he recorded Billy Moll, Eddie Dowling and James F. Hanley's *Honeymoon Lane*, a pretty song but soon forgotten, and *Walkin' My Baby Back Home,* by Roy Turk, Fred Ahlert and Harry Richman, which was enthusiastically revived some years after the war.

Mention is somewhat overdue of Harry Roy, a small bundle of noisy energy who became known as the 'king of hotcha'. He had been directing his New Lyricals, a quintet at the Bat Club, but during the summer of 1931 formed his first big band, the RKOlians, which opened at RKO's new Leicester Square Theatre in August.

His new band included Nat Temple and (briefly) Sid Millward among the reeds, the latter later famous for his stage and radio act, Sid Millward and his Nitwits. Ivor Moreton and Dave Kaye at two pianos became a celebrated duo, with or without the band, and the drummer was Joe Daniels.

The RKOlians cut eight sides for Broadcast in the latter part of the year, and four more in January, 1932, but Roy

Small and noisy 'King of Hotcha', Harry Roy married a daughter of the White Rajah of Sarawak.

Elizabeth Brooke, who married
Harry Roy and sang with his
band as 'Princess Pearl'. The
marriage ended in divorce.

Russian-born violinist Joseph
Muscant recorded for Winner;
Broadcast Super Twelve; Regal-
Zonophone and Decca as
conductor of the Grand Orchestra
at the Commodore Theatre,
Hammersmith, providing a
veritable feast of lovely light
music.

later began an association with Parlophone which lasted for eight years.

The little man with the enormous eyes, raucous singing voice and quasi-Dixieland clarinet style, was just as much a showman as a bandleader, but must be included among the truly great names or the Thirties. Born Harry Lipman in London on January 12, 1900, he created a sensation in 1935 by marrying Elizabeth, daughter of Sir Charles Vyner Brooke, White Rajah of Sarawak. She sang briefly with the band, calling herself Princess Pearl, but the marriage ended in divorce. Harry Roy continued to direct bands throughout the Forties, and died in Marylebone on February 1, 1971.

Although Percival Mackey ceased to record in 1931, he remained extremely busy, but found time to get married. After directing the London Pavilion Orchestra for Cochran's unsuccessful 1931 Revue, he became Musical Director for Paramount Sound Film Studios at Elstree.

The magnificent Commodore Grand Orchestra, which used to broadcast from the Commodore Theatre, Hammersmith, played a rich variety of music, but never attempted to be a dance band. However, it occasionally recorded a dance tune for Winner, one such being Clive Greer's charming little novelty, *Granny's Photo Album*. Sam Browne took the vocal spot. In its heyday this remarkable orchestra was directed by Russian-born Joseph Muscant; later, Harry Davidson took over, having previously been the Commodore Theatre's resident organist.

Hoagy Carmichael's unforgettable *Star Dust* was composed in 1929 and received its wistful Mitchell Parish lyric the following year. Carmichael's mother had been a ragtime pianist, and *Star Dust* actually began as a ragtime piano piece. This classic ballad really took off in 1931, but the recording made in January by Ambrose was non-vocal.

Nevertheless, Sam Browne was kept busy recording with the May Fair Hotel band throughout 1931. Saul Klein, Jack LeSoir and Ray Doll's *On a Little Balcony in Spain* suited his unflamboyant style. The *Melody Maker* liked this recording: 'The band is practically perfect throughout'.

Half-Caste Woman, a haunting song by Noel Coward from Cochran's 1931 Revue, was beautifully performed by the band, using a Lew Stone arrangement. Browne's sensitive, rather subdued vocal was excellent – but not for the *Melody Maker*, which suggested he might just as well have been singing about a cricket match.

A Lew Stone arrangement also graced *Blue Again*, an amusing little song by Dorothy Fields and Jimmy McHugh. Sam Browne's nonchalant approach was perfect for the rather rueful lyric, but the band got the praise: 'Stylish and agreeable!'

Just One More Chance, a yearning torch song by Sam Coslow and Arthur Johnston, was probably too intense for Sam Browne, but it had made a superb vehicle for Bing Crosby's rich and throbbing baritone, helping to make people realise that here was a great new star in the ascendancy.

Arthur James Johnston, yet another New Yorker, was born on January 10, 1898, and directed some of Irving Berlin's early Music Box Revues. In 1929 he went to Hollywood, doing orchestration for Berlin. He died at Corona del Mar, California, on May 1, 1954.

Bing Crosby in 1931, the year in which his career really took off.

Smile, Darn Ya, Smile! was more in Browne's line. The work of Jack Meskill and Charles O'Flynn, it added a cheery note to dreary Depression days. For this Ambrose recording, Browne was joined by the Carlyle Cousins, a newly formed vocal trio, which became very popular, making its first broadcast that year.

At this time, the Carlyle Cousins (who weren't) consisted of Cecile Thornton (better known as Cecile Petrie), who was born at Nairn in 1910; Lilian Taylor, born in Edinburgh the same year; and Pauline Lister. In 1933, Pauline left to be married in India, her place being taken by Cecile's sister Helen, who was born at Nairn in 1914.

Cecile, Lilian and Helen had studied operatic singing at the Royal Academy of Music, were accomplished pianists, and shared the same address in Highgate. Cecile, who made solo recordings as a band vocalist, had a particularly

The Carlyle Cousins: Cecile and Helen Thornton with Lilian Taylor.

WILL'S'S CIGARETTES

THE CARLYLE COUSINS

Below – They Didn't
Believe Me, *M. E. Rourke
and Jerome Kern's
enchanting song, appeared
on a set of 'song cards'
during the Great War,
published by Bamforth &
Co., of Holmfirth.*

*Sidney Kyte: In 1931, his
became the resident band at
the Piccadilly Hotel.*

attractive voice, deserving wider recognition than it actually received.

In October, Bert Ambrose took his May Fair Orchestra to the London Palladium for a two-week show with an emphasis on well-orchestrated popular music, increasing his players from 11 to 23 for the occasion. Sam Browne was sometimes discreetly supported by the Carlyle Cousins, but this gifted trio rarely had a chance to sing by themselves.

A good example of Sam Browne and the Carlyle Cousins harmonising together was *They Didn't Believe Me,* created by M. E. Rourke and Jerome Kern in 1914 for the Broadway edition of *The Girl from Utah,* in which it was sung by Julia Sanderson, who married Frank Crumit. Ambrose's recording found favour: *This side is a gem,* enthused the *Melody Maker.*

One can readily understand why the Ambrose band was so greatly admired, for even quite simple ballads were given a polish that transformed them into things of beauty. Two instances, both with Sam Browne vocals, were Walter Hirsch, Frank Magine and Phil Spitalny's *Save the Last Dance for Me* and Nick and Charles Kenny and J. Fred Coots' *Love Letters in the Sand.* A hackneyed arrangement and a routine performance could so easily have made either seem trite.

Love Letters in the Sand, pleasantly sentimental but hardly outstanding, went to the top of the American hit parade in 1957, sung by Pat Boone, who had forsaken rock 'n' roll for ballads. In this country it reached second place. But sweet songs were on their way out by then, and have yet to return.

Occasionally a song by de Sylva, Brown and Henderson still surfaced, to remind us how fruitful that partnership had been. *Come to Me* was tastefully recorded for Imperial by 35-year-old Margaret Bannerman, a Canadian actress who had made her London debut at the Adelphi back in 1915 and remained much in demand.

Lew Brown and Ray Henderson still collaborated, but their songs lacked that essential ingredient supplied by Buddy de Sylva. *This is the Missus,* briefly popular, was featured in the eleventh edition of George White's *Scandals* at New York's Apollo Theatre, which opened in September. The following month it was recorded for Regal by Sidney Kyte's band, settling in for a five-year stay at the Piccadilly Hotel.

This is the Missus was Kyte's first recording, his vocalists being the Three Ginx, who sang with him until July, 1933. All were bandsmen, Ivor Robinson playing alto saxophone, Jack Joy second piano, and Eric Hanley drums. Later they went on the Halls, as well as recording elsewhere.

The Kyte band had some good men in its ranks. Canadian Alfie Noakes was sole trumpeter; Lionel Clapper played alto saxophone and Billy Thorburn was principal pianist. Billy Thorburn and his Music, formed in 1936, included Clapper as a multi-instrumentalist. Two years later, Thorburn, an ex-Savoy Orphean, became popular with his *The Organ, the Dance Band and Me,* featuring himself and organist H. Robinson Cleaver.

Below – *Lionel Clapper, alto sax player for Kyte, joined Billy Thorburn in 1936.*

Left – *The Three Ginx began as sidemen in the Kyte band, but later went on the Halls.*

In 1925, Billy Thorburn was a Savoy Orphean. He formed 'The Organ, the Dance Band and Me' in 1938.

Roy Fox's Cafe de Paris band had been unkindly criticised by those unaware that it had only been engaged to support his 'whispering cornet'. He received better notices when he formed a fine British band to make 'house' records for Decca until he established himself in London. Lew Stone was pianist and Spike Hughes on bass; both men contributing arrangements; the singers were Betty Bolton and Al Bowlly.

The new Fox band made its recording debut on January 5, opening with Rodgers and Hart's *Ten Cents a Dance,* a marvellous song from *Simple Simon*, a Ziegfeld Theatre production which had begun in February, 1930. The following month Ruth Etting made her beautiful recording. Fox allocated it to Betty Bolton, and the arranger was Spike Hughes.

Roy Fox's big opportunity came in May when he became resident bandleader at the new Monseigneur Restaurant, close to Piccadilly Circus. He made some personnel changes, taking on Nat Gonella and Sid Buckman for his trumpets, and Joe Ferrie as sole trombonist; his guitarist was Al Bowlly. It was a band of top players and sounded good; but the 'whispering cornet' fell silent at the end of October, when Fox decided to leave the playing to others.

Because the band was only a few feet away from the dancers, on a slightly raised stage, the music had to be restrained. Fox knew exactly what was required of him, and his band made an excellent impression, as did its leader, with his faultless tails, soft voice and good manners. The Monseigneur band became a broadcasting favourite, but Fox was taken ill and from October, 1931, to the end of March, 1932, Lew Stone had to deputise.

The Fox band made records for Decca during every month of 1931, his Monseigneur band beginning to do so in June. Many had vocals by Al Bowlly, who had a fine sense of rhythm and a most distinctive voice, but whose diction at times bordered on the slovenly. At his best, however (and that was often), he was beyond doubt one of the most talented vocalists in Britain.

Albert Alick Bowlly, of Greek and Lebanese parentage, was born on January 7, 1899, at Lourenço Marques, in Portuguese East Africa. He moved to Johannesburg, where he had his own barbershop, but having become a proficient banjoist (and later guitarist), and aware that he had a pleasant singing voice, decided to try his luck with the bands.

For a time he worked with the rather obscure outfits of Edgar Adeler and Jimmy Lequime in India; later he joined Arthur Briggs and his Savoy Syncopators in Germany. In 1928 he came to London and sang for Fred Elizalde; but Elizalde being too hot for his time, Bowlly ended up singing on the streets.

It was his engagement by Fox that put Bowlly in the big time, although he had been singing with Ray Noble's 'house' band since November, 1930. His dark good looks and velvety voice commanded attention; his career blossomed; and the time he spent in New York with Noble gave him international stature.

In January, 1937, he returned to England, toured in Variety, and began to record with various bands. His voice had become singularly rich, particularly after an operation on his vocal chords. He made his last recording on April 2, 1941, singing Irving Berlin's *When That Man is Dead and Gone,* an allusion to Adolf Hitler. Fifteen days later, while in his Jermyn Street flat during an air-raid, a bomb blast blew him out of bed, killing him instantly.

Among the many recordings Bowlly made with Fox's Monseigneur band in 1931 were two particularly pleasing songs. *Lazy Day*, a languorous ballad suiting his sometimes rather drawling style to perfection, had an Earl Martin lyric and a tune by George Posford, who made some useful contributions to British popular music.

The Savoy Hotel Orpheans in 1931, showing both directors.

Born Benjamin George Ashwell Posford in Folkestone on March 23, 1906, he was educated at Downside and Christ's College, Cambridge. Like so many successful songwriters, he began by studying law, but in 1930 started to compose music for BBC productions, and later for such films as Associated British's *The Good Companions* (1932), in which Jessie Matthews gave a sparkling performance.

Bowlly actually recorded *Lazy Day* twice, his version for Fox being waxed five days after he had appeared with Ray Noble's New Mayfair Dance Orchestra. It was not uncommon for vocalists to record the same song more than once, and it made for some interesting comparisons.

You Forgot Your Gloves, an equally attractive ballad, written by Edward Eliscu and composed by Ned Lehak, had been featured in the *Third Little Show* at New York's Music Box Theatre, which opened in June. Bowlly recorded it in October, just prior to Roy Fox's illness.

In September a new band began to play at the Savoy Hotel under the joint direction of alto sax player Howard Jacobs and pianist Carroll Gibbons. The Savoy Hotel Orpheans bore little resemblance to their illustrious predecessors, styles having greatly changed in the intervening years. A rather bland style prevailed, probably bringing sighs of relief from a management with uncherished memories of Elizalde's short but stormy residence. Obviously the newcomers fitted in well, for the Orpheans remained at the Savoy for the rest of the Thirties, throughout the war years, and into the early post-war period.

The band cut its first Columbia side in October, with Al Bowlly as guest vocalist. *There's a Time and Place for Everything,* a ballad by Roy Turk and Fred Ahlert, got a rather lukewarm reception from the *Melody Maker,* which referred to 'some florid piano work by Carroll Gibbons'. Bowlly was merely 'the vocalist', and considered 'only just right'.

The Savoy Hotel Orpheans had some accomplished instrumentalists apart from Carroll Gibbons. His co-director, Howard Jacobs, liked to play solos in a rather restrained Rudy Wiedoeft manner; both Reginald Leopold and Hugo Rignold, the violinists, became famous, Leopold for his tasteful 'Palm Court' music and Rignold as conductor of the Liverpool Philharmonic Orchestra. Rudy Starita presided over the drums and xylophone.

Sweet and Lovely, recorded ten days later, had been a Gus Arnheim, Harry Tobias and Jules Lemare hit for Bing Crosby, but Bowlly's version did him no discredit. The *Melody Maker* unbent very little, deciding that the record was 'indeed sweet and nearly lovely', but 'the vocalist' seemed 'a bit uncertain'.

Columbia obviously thought highly of the band, which never recorded for any other label; it became a regular visitor to their studios.

Although the Orpheans soon became popular at the Savoy, they faced competition from a band that had been there since August, 1930, the colourful Gaucho Tango Orchestra, directed by Geraldo. Neither its costumes nor its tipica-style music were authentic, much of the latter originating in Europe.

Born in London in August, 1904, Gerald Bright was an accomplished pianist who had studied at the Royal Academy of Music. For five years he led a broadcasting band at the Hotel Majestic, St. Annes-on-Sea, before assembling his Gauchos and transforming himself into Geraldo.

Geraldo's Gaucho Tango Orchestra lasted for about seven years, although long before its demise he had become increasingly involved with 'straight' dance music, much of it very lush and sweet. When swing arrived, Geraldo's bands sometimes gave a fiery performance, and later even a creditable impression of Stan Kenton. Too frequently, however, his battery of excellent singers were permitted to reduce the

Gerald Bright became Geraldo when he formed his Gaucho Tango Orchestra, which began to record for Columbia in November, 1930.

band to an accompanying role. 'Gerry' died at Vevey, Switzerland, on May 5, 1974.

A typical Gaucho Tango Orchestra recording of 1931 was *An Old Spanish Tango,* a German song by Fritz Rotter and Walter Jurmann, with an English lyric by Frank Eyton. The band had an unvarying style and was probably more entertaining visually than on the air or records.

The Thirties never had anything like the rich cavalcade of stage musicals that added charm to the Twenties, but the West End did offer something appealing from time to time. *Stand Up and Sing* opened at the London Hippodrome in March, 1931, with lyrics by Douglas Furber and music by Vivian Ellis and Philip Charig. *It's Not You* and *There's Always Tomorrow* were duets by Jack Buchanan and Elsie Randolph. Both were recorded for Columbia by Ray Starita's band, still in residence at the Ambassadors' Club, with vocals by Maurice Elwin.

Bandleaders moved from label to label as frequently as they changed the places at which they played. Jack Harris stayed at Grosvenor House throughout 1931, but left Decca for the new, ten-inch Broadcast Super-Twelve label, resplendent in gold and bright red.

At this time, Harris' vocalist was Harry Bentley, a well above average singer. Sadly, he died on March 3, 1935, aged only 36. Among the records he made with Harris were *Moonlight Saving Time*, a novel idea expressed by Irving Kahal and Harry Richman, and *When I Take My Sugar to Tea*, an Irving Kahal, Pierre Norman and Sammy Fain song which the band swung blithely.

Later in the year, the Harris band and Bentley recorded *That's My Desire*, a ballad by Carroll Loveday and Helmy Kresa which came and went without much comment in 1931 but shot to the top of the American hit parade 16 years later.

Apart from his many records with 'house' and regular bands, Jack Plant appeared on various labels as solo artist, although often in disguise. Among his 'Jack Gordon' sides for Imperial was *You'll be Mine in Apple Blossom Time*, a fair example of Tin Pan Alley pastorale, with a Charles Tobias lyric and a good tune by Peter de Rose.

Columbia issued Plant under his real name, although whoever labelled him as a baritone had never heard him sing. He always treated a song with respect, and in the case of *I Surrender, Dear* tackled a recent hit by Bing Crosby. One of the current crop of very soulful effusions, it had a lyric by

Gordon Clifford and music by Bing's old partner Harry Barris, already showing his mettle as a songwriter.

In February, 1931, the Paris Opera House opened its doors to Jack Hylton and his Orchestra, a singular honour, for it ws the first time a variety show had been staged there. Afterwards the director personally congratulated Hylton. Among the highlights of the show were excerpts from Stravinsky's operetta *Mavra*, arranged by Billy Ternent, which won praise from both the composer and the press.

The Hylton showband recorded two charming light orchestral pieces in 1931, and did so with faultless taste. *The Grasshoppers' Dance* had first appeared in 1907, the work of composer and musical director Ernest Bucalossi, who died, aged 69, on April 15, 1933. This recording was backed by Léon Jessel's beautiful intermezzo *The Wedding of the Rose*, originally called *Der Rose Hochzeitzug*. It was first published in 1911.

Born in Stettin (now Szczecin) on January 22, 1871, Léon Jessel composed operettas which were soon forgotten, but his intermezzo *The Wedding of the Rose* and his novelty *The Parade of the Tin Soldiers,* also published in 1911, remained popular for years. Jessel died in Berlin in 1942.

Versatile entertainer and songwriter Leslie Fry took his mother's maiden name to become Leslie Sarony. He is seen here on his wedding day in 1939.

Oddly enough, Hylton made fresh recordings of these melodies in 1933, this time for Decca. Over the years, Hylton recorded quite a lot of light music, on at least one occasion his band being conducted by Eric Coates.

Diminutive Leslie Sarony never became a Guards drummer, his boyhood dream, but in 1931 saluted the men he admired by writing *When the Guards are on Parade*. With a melody by Horatio Nicholls it became a hit. Baritone George Baker added a virile vocal to Jack Hylton's recording.

Stuart Robertson, who went to Chigwell School, Essex, and the Royal College of Music, recorded the concert ballad *Trees* for Hylton in 1931, a setting by Otto Rasbach of a poem by Joyce Kilmer. At 19 he was solo bass at St. Paul's Cathedral, and he went with Dame Nellie Melba on her farewell tour of Australia. He made his first broadcast in 1924 and his first record two years later.

In 1927 he married the soprano Alice Moxon, with whom he recorded several duets for HMV. He had a small singing part in the 1933 film version of *Bitter Sweet*, starring his sister Marjorie, better known as Anna Neagle. Much overshadowed by Peter Dawson, he recorded rather less for HMV than he might otherwise have done, but his splendid voice sometimes graced 'house' band recordings, albeit anonymously.

However, Baker was again the vocalist when Hylton recorded *The Changing of the Guard*, a hit by Flotsam and Jetsam, played as a 6/8 one-step. At the same HMV session, Hylton also recorded *Time Alone Will Tell*, one of several ballads for which Horatio Nicholls collaborated with famous American lyricist Archie Gottler. Not only was it a good song, but both the band performance and Pat O'Malley's vocal were quite outstanding.

Ironically, Hylton provided the Gramophone Company with a best-seller just before he bade them adieu. *Rhymes*, a collection of mildly naughty limericks with the last lines prudently omitted, gave Leslie Sarony a splendid chance to demonstrate his bubbling personality, well supported vocally and instrumentally by the band. It occupied two sides of a Zonophone record. Decca wanted more of the same, so the following month further *Rhymes* were recorded, this time sung by Sarony, Hylton and others.

Just why Hylton decided not to renew his HMV contract at the end of October has never been disclosed. One can only assume that financial inducement overrode any feeling of loyalty, for he had been a mainstay of the HMV catalogue, and to a lesser degree that of Zonophone, for over ten years. It came as a great shock to the Gramophone Company, but

Entertainers and songwriters Mr Flotsam (B. C. Hilliam) and Mr Jetsam (Malcolm McEachern). Hilliam was a Yorkshireman who had lived in Canada; McEachern, a concert bass from Australia, made some serious records for Vocalion.

Jack Hylton

WHY I RECORD ONLY FOR "His Master's Voice"

By JACK HYLTON

"I choose to record exclusively for "His Master's Voice" because I am firmly convinced that *only* "His Master's Voice" can record my performance with the realism that is necessary to maintain my reputation.

Listening to my recordings I am continually delighted to hear the 'tone colour,' the faultless reproduction of the minutest detail and the subtle manner in which every shade of expression is faithfully caught."

Jack Hylton

Sorry, I've changed my mind! *An HMV advertisement of July, and a Decca one of December, vividly illustrate what a surprise Jack Hylton must have given the recording industry in 1931.*

"HIS MASTER'S VOICE" NEW DANCE RECORDS

Jack Hylton and His Orchestra
When the Guards are on Parade (*six-eight with Vocal Refrain*)—*Oh, Rosalita*
B6015
*By the River Sainte Marie —
*When I take my sugar to tea
B6016

Ambrose and His Orchestra
*Thank you most sincerely ("*The Millionaire Kid*")—*Out of nowhere
B6017
*It must be true—*It looks like love
B6018
*When your lover has gone—
*One little raindrop
B6014

New Mayfair Dance Orchestra
*Come and have a cuddle on the common—*I'm happy when I'm hiking
B6019
Lights of Paris (*nine-eight one-step with Vocal Refrain*)—*June time is love time
B6023

JACK HYLTON and DECCA

EVERYONE else has whooped 'sensational,' 'phenomenal,' 'staggering,' so all we have to do is to confirm the news. Jack Hylton and his orchestra will, in future, record *exclusively* for Decca.

There is no need to press home the importance of the news to readers of the 'Melody Maker.' Especially in view of the fact that Jack's records will be sold at the usual low Decca prices, 10" 1/6, 12" 2/6, it means something really BIG in gramophone history.

Here are the first numbers. Look to Decca each month for a new batch of Hyltonisms, full of originality, pep and popular appeal.

★ ★ ★ ★ ★ ★

JACK'S FLYING START

JACK HYLTON AND HIS ORCHESTRA
Cavalcade—Selections Parts 1 and 2 (12-inch) K619, 2/6
Time alone will tell—Just one more chance (12-inch) K618, 2/6
Goodnight, sweetheart—My sunshine is you (12-inch) K622, 2/6
Nevertheless I'm in love with you (fox-trot)—You're my decline and fall (fox-trot) F2664, 1/6

THE BIG 8 FOR XMAS

Rhymes (Novelty Record) Parts 1 and 2 F2679, 1/6
Heartaches (fox-trot)—Close your eyes (fox-trot) F2665, 1/6
Tom Thumb's drum (quick one-step)—Oh! What a night! (fox-trot) F2672, 1/6
When it's sleepy time down south (fox-trot)—Three littl: times (fox-trot) F2681, 1/6

All the above records have vocal refrains

JACK HYLTON
the world's biggest seller
NOW RECORDS EXCLUSIVELY for DECCA

Complete Catalogue and latest lists from :—
DECCA RECORD CO., LTD.,
Dept. 232, 1-3, Brixton Road, London, S.W.9

ROY FOX
and his band record
exclusively for DECCA

This is the Missus—Life is just a Bowl of Cherries F2682, 1/6
Over the Blue—'Neath the Spell of Monte Carlo F2683, 1/6
Sweet & Lovely—Sing another chorus, please F2514, 1/6
Kiss me, Goodnight—That's what I like about you F2581, 1/6
You forgot your gloves—Take it from me F2582, 1/6
Smile, Darn ya, Smile—Just one more chance F2580, 1/6

HENRY HALL
and his Gleneagles Hotel Band
record **exclusively for DECCA**

A Musical Comedy Switch (12-inch) K581, 2/6
Sylvia Waltz : Hieland Laddie F2357, 1/6
Goodnight—The King's Navee F2464, 1/6
Cheery Song Memories F2615, 1/6

ARTHUR LALLY
and the Million - Airs record
exclusively for DECCA

I idolize my Baby's eyes—Down Sunnyside Lane F2647, 1/6
To-day I feel so happy—Lover of my dreams F2648, 1/6
The Wooden Rocking Horse—On a cold and frosty morning F2655, 1/6
Mausie—The King's Navee F2595, 1/6
Sing a little jingle—Got a date with an angel F2612, 1/6
I'm loving you still—Life's Desire F2596, 1/6

SPIKE HUGHES
and his dance orchestra
record **exclusively for DECCA**

Witness—Is there a place up there for me ? F.2649, 1/6
The Darktown Strutters Ball — Blues in my Heart F.2611, 1/6
Roll Jordan—Joshua fit de battle ob Jericho F.2373 1/6

An advertisement of January, 1931. Regal lost its separate identity at the end of 1932.

Decca were understandably jubilant. To lure an internationally famous bandleader away from Britain's most prestigious record label was a remarkable achievement. It also provided a tremendous boost to Decca's sales, and from then onwards they presented a serious challenge to the leaders.

Hylton only stayed with Decca for two years, however, and from December, 1933, to February, 1935, made no records at all, which is most intriguing. Why was Decca unable to hold him any longer, and why did no other record manufacturer snap him up? Whatever the reason, he was back on HMV in March, 1935, remaining with them until he cut his last side on March 6, 1940. The following month he disbanded.

Jack Hylton's defection (as HMV must have regarded it) was not the only exciting event of 1931 for the record industry. On March 20, the Gramophone Company and the Columbia Graphophone Company merged to form Electric and Musical Industries, thus bringing under a single management His Master's Voice and Zonophone on the one hand, and Columbia, Parlophone and Regal on the other.

The merger spelled the approaching end of Zonophone and Regal as separate entities. Zonophone had been HMV's cheaper label for 28 years, and Regal had held a similar position for Columbia since April, 1914. They continued to function independently until the end of 1932, but the following year saw the emergence of Regal-Zonophone, initially sporting a distinctive livery of matt red and green. Regrettably, this beautiful colour scheme was discontinued in 1935, and for the remainder of its existence Regal-Zonophone glittered less appealingly in bright red and gold.

Throughout 1931, Broadcast records, increased to a nine-inch format, were as busy as ever, as Harry Bidgood continued to create unpretentiously pleasant dance music with his 'session' men. Bidgood's Good Boys recorded the fox-trot *Faithfully Yours*, combining the talents of Ted Snyder, James Brockman and Abe Lyman, and *The Springtime Reminds Me of You*, a pretty waltz by Fritz Rotter and Walter Jurmann, for which Desmond Carter wrote an English lyric. The vocalists were Bob Pearson and Cavan O'Connor respectively.

John Thorne had two numbers better suited to his concert style than the more usual fox-trots. *Lights of Paris*, a quick-step, had a lyric by Erell Reaves and a typically lilting Tolchard Evans melody. *Sally*, a waltz by Harry Leon, Leo Towers and Will Haines, was an important number for 33-year-old Gracie Fields, making her screen debut for Associated Radio Pictures in *Sally in Our Alley*. Bidgood allocated both songs to his Riverside Dance Band.

William George Haines, a Londoner born in 1876, not only helped to write many songs but had been a music hall artist for over 20 years when, in 1931, he was appointed London Consul for Haiti.

By an odd coincidence, two songs called *Between the Devil and the Deep Blue Sea* appeared in 1931. Fortunately, titles cannot be copyrighted, or a lawsuit might have resulted. In America, Ted Koehler and Harold Arlen's version was featured in the obscure film *Rhythmania*, but the more striking of the two was Ray Benson's ditty, with its unusual melody and wryly humorous lyric. It was given a punchy performance for Imperial by Jay Wilbur and his Band, with Les Allen nonchalantly handling the vocal.

Exactly who played in Imperial's San Remo Rumba Orchestra will probably never be known, but this session band gave a most exuberant rendition of *The Peanut Vendor*, a son, although usually performed as a rumba, by the Cuban composer Moises Simons. *El Manisero* – which means the same thing – received its English language lyric from Marion Sunshine and L. Wolfe Gilbert.

Gracie Fields' first film was Sally in our Alley, *released in 1931. From it came her great hit* Sally, *which became her theme song.*

Marion Sunshine's brother-in-law was Don Azpiazu, who recorded the song in New York, in May, 1930, for Victor with his Havana Casino Orchestra, featuring vocalist Antonio Machin. This authentic Cuban version swept across America like wildfire.

Many people will associate *The Peanut Vendor* with the 1947 Capitol recording (also made in New York) by Stan Kenton and his Orchestra, augmented by Machito's pounding rhythm section. That terrific beat, some rather frantic brass passages and Milt Bernhart's marvellous trombone solo gave Kenton a best-seller in the days before his music became so 'progressive' as to be well-nigh incomprehensible.

The Rhythmic Eight may have suggested a jazz group to the uninitiated, but was actually a sweet and swingy 'house' combo playing dance music from 1927-28 under the direction of Bert Firman, and from 1928-1932 under that of his brother John. It was the demise of Zonophone that put an end to the Rhythmic Eight, rather than any diminution of popularity.

Some of London's finest players took part in these sessions, and a vocal trio was employed, often including Maurice Elwin. For years recordings were made at Hayes, Kingsway Hall or Small Queen's Hall, but from August, 1931, the new Abbey Road studios in St. John's Wood were employed.

Cliff Friend's *If It's Good Enough for the Birds and Bees* and Richard Whiting's *Maybe it's the Moon* were recorded at the band's first Abbey Road session. One could detect the voice of Maurice Elwin in the vocal trio, and the piano-accordion of George Scott-Wood was also on hand.

Other recordings included two big hits of 1931, *Wrap Your Troubles in Dreams and Dream Your Troubles Away,* a piece of good advice by Ted Koehler, Billy Moll and Harry Barris, and *Whistling in the Dark*, with a lyric by Allen Boretz and music by Dana Suesse.

There was no reason why women composers should not have been as successful as men in Tin Pan Alley, but very few did make any impact. This is somewhat surprising when one considers how many women had turned out best-sellers when the concert and salon ballad reigned supreme. Among those who made significant contributions were Mabel Wayne, Ann Ronell, Bernice Petkere and Dana Suesse.

Paul Abraham's *Viktoria and her Hussar* opened at the Palace Theatre in September, with Harry Welchman and Margaret Carlisle sharing the lead, the theatre orchestra being under the direction of Franz Steininger. A Hungarian operetta, with some lilting music, it had been adapted by Captain Harry Graham, who also wrote the English lyrics.

Harry Jocelyn Clive Graham, ex-Eton, Sandhurst and the Coldstream Guards, had served in the Boer War and the Great War. Born in London on December 23, 1874, he came from a military family. A journalist who also wrote a lot of bitingly witty verse, Graham contributed lyrics and libretti to many famous West End shows, among them *The Maid of the Mountains, A Southern Maid, Katja the Dancer, Land of Smiles* and *White Horse Inn.* He died on October 30, 1936.

The most popular songs from *Viktoria and her Hussar* were *Goodnight* and *Pardon, Madame*, both waltzes. To record them for Sterno, Nat Star became André Astan and his Orchestra, performing them in a very sweet and relaxed style, but as dance music rather than in the Marek Weber light orchestral manner. His vocalist was Tom Barratt.

Born at Apatin, in Yugoslavia, close to the Hungarian border, on November 2, 1892, Paul Abraham was a serious composer who turned to operetta, *Viktoria and her Hussar* being his first real success. *Die Blume von Hawaii* (1931), and *Ball at the Savoy* (1933), were others.

After living successively in Berlin, Vienna and Paris, he made the mistake of going to America, where there was no interest in his kind of music. The world had forgotten Abraham when he died in Hamburg on May 9, 1960.

The crème de la crème of 'house' bands was undeniably Ray Noble's New Mayfair Dance Orchestra, which had the pick of the top London players and its director's superlative arrangements. All the tunes to which reference is now made had vocals by Al Bowlly.

Much that was recorded was forgettable trivia, but a lot of good music was waxed too. Noble's own song, *Goodnight, Sweetheart* was among the latter. With a lyric by Campbell and Connelly, it was an early hit for Bing Crosby, and also featured in the ninth (1932) edition of the *Earl Carroll Vanities*, at New York's Earl Carroll Theatre.

Erell Reaves and Tolchard Evans had a rip-roaring success in 1931 with the much-recorded one-step *Lady of Spain.* So much of Tolchard Evans' music had a Spanish flavour that one suspects he would have been quite at home there, composing paso dobles for corridas.

Noel Coward's *Twentieth Century Blues* was in more sombre mood, an expression of discontent with the way things were going. It was written for the very successful *Cavalcade,* which began at Drury Lane in October.

Guilty was a mournful ballad by Gus Kahn, Harry Akst and Richard A. Whiting. People seemed to enjoy sad songs – the Country and Western hit parade has always been full of them – and *Guilty* lingered on.

Hold My Hand, a sparkling musical comedy, opened at the Gaiety Theatre in December, starring author Lupino Lane, Jessie Matthews and Sonnie Hale. The title song, by Maurice Elwin, Harry Graham and Noel Gay, was recorded by Noble, who surprisingly disregarded Gay's equally attractive *Turn on the Music and Dance,* with its Desmond Carter lyric, although it too would have been a good number for Al Bowlly.

Noel Gay was a Yorkshireman, even if he did compose *The Lambeth Walk*. Born in Wakefield on July 15, 1898, he went to Christ's College, Cambridge, and for some years was a church organist until he turned to stage music and popular songs, eventually forming his own publishing company. In private life Richard Moxon Armitage M.A., Mus. Bac., Cantab., he died in London on March 4, 1954.

Having lost his Rhythm Boys, Paul Whiteman engaged a new male voice trio, the King's Jesters, from Cincinnati. Mildred Bailey, who was Al Rinker's sister, also began to sing with the band. They all came together at Victor's Chicago studios in October to record *When It's Sleepy-Time Down South*, a song by Leon and Otis René and Clarence Muse, which became a standard.

1931 was a good year for Whiteman. Having shed a lot of weight at her insistence, he married screen actress Margaret Livingston. He began to direct a 30-piece band at Chicago's Edgewater Beach Hotel, and to broadcast exclusively over NBC. No doubt, Victor were delighted to have him back after his brief flirtation with Columbia. The record industry was having a lean time on both sides of the Atlantic, and the Whiteman band could still sell a lot of records.

A CBS contract took Bing Crosby to New York, where he was heard nightly as a highly publicised radio star. He also began to record at frequent intervals, being issued over here on Brunswick. He had a much more intense style in those days; the lazy-voiced 'Old Groaner' had yet to materialise.

Those early records are still pure magic. Among many others they include Phil Baxter's *A Faded Summer Love;* Sam M. Lewis and Victor Young's *Too Late;* Gus Kahn, Jay Livingston and Matty Malneck's *I'm Through with Love;*

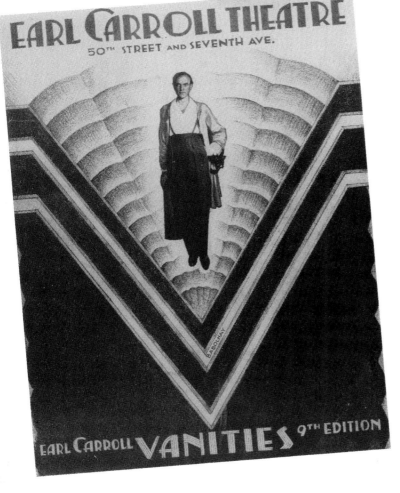

The 9th Earl Carroll Vanities: The 11th Scene was built around Ray Noble's Goodnight, Sweetheart, *sung by Milton Watson and Woods Miller.*

Edward Heyman and John W. Green's *Out of Nowhere*, and, perhaps best of all, *Dancing in the Dark*, a gem by Howard Dietz and Arthur Schwartz.

From the Broadway revue *Crazy Quilt* came Billy Rose, Mort Dixon and Harry Warren's *I Found a Million-Dollar Baby*, and there was *At Your Command*, composed by Harry Barris, who was singing for West Coast bandleader Jimmie Grier. Bing helped Harry Tobias to write the lyric.

But the song that really swept the country was *Where the Blue of the Night Meets the Gold of the Day*, with Crosby's golden voice soaring in an ecstasy of romantic yearning. He had lent a hand with that song too, although Roy Turk and Fred Ahlert probably deserved most of the credit. Recorded in November, it was a wonderful ballad, and after that Bing never looked back.

Johnny Hamp took his Kentucky Serenaders to Victor's Chicago studios for the last time in November, 1929. He did not return there until February, 1931, by which time he had become plain Johnny Hamp and his Orchestra. Not that he sounded much different. Two months later, by then in New York, he recorded *Nevertheless I'm in Love with You*, with Andrew Freeman, Carl Graub and Cliff Gamet as his vocal trio.

A fox-trot by Bert Kalmar and Harry Ruby, it had no remarkable qualities as a ballad but refused to go away, and was successfully revived on several occasions in future years.

It would seem that not everyone loved Rudy Vallee. At a band show in Boston two ripe grapefruits were hurled at him. They missed, and Vallee continued singing while his assailants were ejected. To his untold admirers, the sighing bobby-soxers, such an attack must have seemed like the ultimate in sacrilege and, perhaps mindful of his image, Vallee declined to prosecute.

Chapter Ten

1932

'It's Just The Time For Dancing'

The World's Finest
RECORD VALUE

EdisonBell
Winner

Red Label   1/6
Gold Label   2/-

June (1932) Supplement
No. 645

revival of "THE LAND OF SMILES"
Records on page 3.

EDISON BELL LIMITED.   LONDON, S.E.15

COMPLETE CATALOGUE

ZONO'S

Zonophone
Electrical
Recordings

ZONOPHONE

1932
1933

Top – *A Winner supplement of June, 1932. The following January, the Receiver sold the company to Decca.*

Above – *Cover of the 1932/3 (and almost certainly last) Zonophone catalogue.*

On March 11, 1932, at 4pm, Stuart Hibberd, the BBC's 'golden voice', had a special announcement for listeners to the National Programme: 'Mr. Jack Payne has been with the BBC for four years, and this is the last time that listeners will hear him conducting his BBC Dance Orchestra'.

Despite all the rumour and innuendo which began in January, when the news of Payne's impending departure first broke, there seems to have been no rift. Indeed, Sir John Reith came to the studio for the farewell performance to wish Payne good luck.

Payne's decision to leave arose from a desire to challenge Jack Hylton on his own territory as a touring showband, and for that he needed mobility. He had already experienced some heady success in Variety, including a week at the Palladium in April, 1930, followed by a Royal Command performance there not long afterwards. As plain Jack Payne and his Orchestra he began a long and fruitful career away from the shelter of Broadcasting House, but despite some European engagements never managed to dent Hylton's awesome international reputation.

Payne had enjoyed an unbroken association with the Columbia Graphophone Company since February, 1927. He had first appeared on Regal, and it was for Regal that his BBC Dance Orchestra made its last sides on March 8, 1932.

He had already signed a Crystalate contract, and a few days later began to record for Imperial, among his early sides being Al Sherman and Al Lewis' *Now's the Time to Fall in Love*. The vivid red label carried a portrait of its new star attraction. When Imperial was phased out in 1934 he went over to Rex which, like Crystalate itself, became part of Decca.

Meanwhile, much of what Jack Hylton was recording for Decca lacked the sparkle of earlier years. The band had become so smooth that it sometimes seemed to be playing mechanically; and an apparently endless succession of unanimated Pat O'Malley vocals did nothing to dispel the monotony.

Nevertheless, a few enjoyable sides were waxed that year by a band that, for a time, seemed to have lapsed into the same uninspired pattern as so many across the Atlantic. *The Younger Generation* had a good tune and a slice of Noel Coward's keen-edged wit. For once, both singer and band really did come alive. *Paradise* was another little gem, becoming O'Malley's favourite song; it certainly suited his style.

Above – *Andrew Stuart Hibberd, who announced the last broadcast by Jack Payne's BBC Dance Orchestra. He joined the BBC in 1924 at Savoy Hill, and retired in 1951. He was the Corporation's 'golden voice', but at his funeral in November, 1983, not one executive came to show respect.*

Left – *Broadcasting House was officially opened by King George V and Queen Mary on July 7, 1932. This photograph was probably taken the same year.*

Phyllis Robins of the distinctive voice, who recorded for Henry Hall (Columbia), Jack Hylton (Decca) and solo for Rex.

Paradise got Gordon Clifford and Nacio Herb Brown into trouble. A waltz with a most seductive tune, it had humming passages in the vocal which the Americans considered so suggestive that they banned the song from the air. The usually hypersensitive BBC did not, to my knowledge, follow suit.

Probably Hylton's most outstanding record of 1932 was *Mad About the Boy*, sung by Phyllis Robins in her husky, quite unmistakable voice. Coward's lyric, polished and cynical, was enhanced by a typically graceful melody.

Phyllis Robins, a petite blonde, good-natured and friendly, came from Sheffield. From August, 1933, to June, 1934, she sang for Henry Hall. Later, having become a bill-topper in Variety, she appeared on his Guest Nights. She died, aged 70, on March 25, 1982.

Throughout 1932, Ambrose continued to demonstrate why his May Fair Hotel Orchestra was one of the best around. Joe Young and Bernice Petkere's *Lullaby of the Leaves*, Edward Heyman and Dana Suesse's *My Silent Love,* and Ann Ronell's *Rain on the Roof* were all winners for their respective lady composers, and sung by Sam Browne.

Browne had other top-notch songs to sing with Ambrose that year, including Irving Berlin's *How Deep is the Ocean?* and *Soft Lights and Sweet Music*, the latter title summing up the whole concept of Society dance music at this time. Louis Rey's waltz *My Mystery Girl,* a hit for Layton and Johnstone was recorded in January, and John Jacob Loeb's *Masquerade*, another waltz, was waxed during an August visit to Monte Carlo; *You Try Somebody Else,* a reminder of departed magic, was one of the last songs by de Sylva, Brown and Henderson.

Elsie Carlisle's misguided recording of *My Man o' War* may have helped to put Dominion on the rocks. In 1932 she began to sing for Ambrose. Her drawling voice and fine sense of rhythm had earned her a singular compliment in 1927 when the *Melody Maker* decided she was about the only English female artist with both style and refinement.

She managed to make *Pu-leeze, Mr. Hemingway!* sound very naughty, but got away with it. A witty song by Milton Drake, Walter Kent and Abner Silver, it appeared on Regal-Zonophone.

A Lancashire girl, born in 1900, Elsie Carlisle often made records under her own name, and for Ambrose sometimes duetted amusingly with Sam Browne. Later they toured together. She died on September 5, 1978.

Herman Hupfeld's *Let's Put out the Lights and Go to Sleep* was clever and harmless, but in 1932 considered quite daring. It made a delightful duet for Sam Browne and Elsie Carlisle, but the Ambrose HMV recording had competition from Lew Stone on Decca, with Al Bowlly and Mary Charles.

Stone's able direction at the Monseigneur during Roy Fox's absence had reaped its reward. When Fox departed for the Cafe Anglais in October, 1932, the Monseigneur management insisted he take over. It was his first band.

A fine pianist and a brilliant arranger, Lewis (actually Louis) Stone was born on May 28, 1898. With neither Harry

Lew Stone: He would not permit Decca to show Al Bowlly's name as band vocalist.

Roy's brashness nor Roy Fox's studied elegance, he was genuinely liked and respected by those who played for him.

He remained at the Monseigneur until November, 1933, then he too tried the Cafe Anglais. In March, 1934, he returned to the Monseigneur, but later that year it became a cinema. From 1931-34 he was also Musical Director for British and Dominion Films.

Stone recorded for Decca until November, 1934, then switched to Regal-Zonophone. After a year he returned to Decca, for whom he then recorded until 1949. He died on February 13, 1969.

Al Bowlly rarely received more sympathetic accompaniment than he did from Lew Stone, who actually rated him no higher than any other proficient vocalist. Two songs they recorded together in 1932, *Brighter than the Sun* and *What More Can I Ask?* were by Anona Winn and Ray Noble.

Georgia on My Mind was recorded by Roy Fox for Decca with the Monseigneur Band, prior to his disagreement with the management. It had a nostalgic lyric by Stuart Gorrell of the Miami Herald and a mildly jazz-flavoured tune by Hoagy Carmichael.

Fox gave the vocal to Nat Gonella, whose singing and hot trumpet were influenced by Louis Armstrong. The song made such an impression on Gonella that he called his own group the Georgians and made it his signature tune.

Most Hoagy Carmichael ballads had the stamp of quality, coming as they did from a man with a diversity of talents. Born Howard Hoagland Carmichael in Bloomington, Indiana, on November 22, 1899, he had a degree in law and practised for a time until he turned songwriter. Early bandleader, pianist, lyricist, composer, singer and character actor, he added his own individual touch to all. He died in Palm Springs, California, on December 27, 1981.

Another popular song classic recorded during Fox's stay at the Monseigneur was the Gershwins' *I Got Rhythm!* It had been sung by Ethel Merman (whose surname was actually Zimmerman), making her New York debut in *Girl Crazy* at the Alvin Theatre in October, 1930. No doubt, Al Bowlly's vocal was more restrained than that by the boisterous Miss Merman.

Ira and George Gershwin were the sons of Rose and Morris Gershvin, a Russian Jewish couple who emigrated to America. Ira, the elder brother, was born on New York's tough Lower East Side on December 6, 1896. Apart from his brilliant

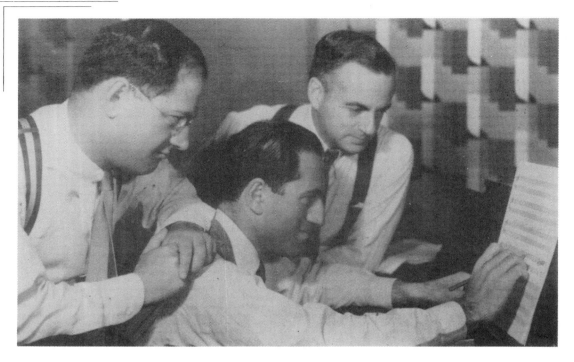

Ira and George Gershwin, with librettist Guy Bolton.

lyrics, many for George, he wrote the libretto for *Porgy and Bess,* in collaboration with Du Bose Heyward. He died in Beverly Hills, California, on August 17, 1983.

During his tragically curtailed life, George (actually Jacob) Gershwin composed a remarkably diverse amount of music, from simple dance tunes to *Rhapsody in Blue* and *An American in Paris*. Born in Brooklyn on September 26, 1898, he had his first song published when he was 18. In 1931 his musical comedy *Of Thee I Sing* received the Pulitzer Prize. His death from a brain tumour in Hollywood on July 11, 1937, ended a career that had shown no signs of flagging.

Fox opened at the Cafe Anglais in Leicester Square on October 24, and stayed there until January 16, 1933. Having lost Al Bowlly, he used Jack Plant for many recordings, including Rodgers and Hart's *Isn't It Romantic?* He formed a vocal trio, appropriately called the Cubs, drawn from his sidemen. They were trumpeter Les Lambert, tenor sax player Harry Gold (later famous for his Pieces of Eight, a 'commercial' Dixieland band), and guitarist Ivor Mairants. The Cubs sang a Rodgers and Hart ballad too, *Mimi,* from Paramount's *Love Me Tonight*, starring Maurice Chevalier and Jeanette MacDonald.

Admirers of Jack Harris were in for a disappointment. In

April he cut his last sides for Broadcast and made no more records for four years. *Cuban Love Song*, a waltz by Dorothy Fields, Jimmy McHugh and Herbert Stothart, *That's Why Darkies were Born,* another Lew Brown and Ray Henderson contribution to the eleventh George White's *Scandals*, and *Auf Weidersehen, My Dear*, by Al Goodman, Ed Nelson, Al Hoffman and Milton Ager, were among his farewell offerings.

Geraldo's Gaucho Tango Orchestra recorded two striking tunes in 1932, with vocalist Gino Berni. *Let Me Be Your Carmen for Tonight* was by Friedrich Holländer, with a Reg Connelly lyric added. Jacob Gade's *Jealousy*, first heard in 1926, was due to languish again until 1935, when Arthur Fiedler found the sheet music in a junkshop, recorded the melody with his Boston Pops Orchestra, and created a light orchestral classic. The lyricist on Geraldo's version was Patience Strong, calling herself Winifred May.

According to Dr. Sigmund Spaeth, from 1929 to 1931 Irving Berlin seemed to lose inspiration, an assertion hotly disputed by Brian Rust, who sites *Let Me Sing and be Happy*, *Putting on the Ritz* and other songs as evidence of continued creativety. Berlin was undeniably in top form in 1932, when *Let's Have Another Cup of Coffee, Soft Lights and Sweet Music, How Deep is the Ocean?* and *Say it isn't So* proved that his incredible genius was very far from being burned out.

Say it isn't So, a hit for Rudy Vallee, was recorded here by Billy Cotton and his Band, actually during the last days of Regal, and thus issued on Regal-Zonophone. For all its success, this particular song rather lacked the sparkle of Berlin at his best.

Among the most inventive and tasteful of British song composers, Ray Noble differed from Berlin in providing his own arrangements. He had begun to write a succession of hits, his music being equally suitable for dance band or concert orchestra. *Love is the Sweetest Thing* was recorded by Harry Roy, now on Parlophone. The brassy bounce of the RKOlians was heard at the Palladium that year, but Roy's biggest break-through would come in 1933.

In August, British Homophone launched their ten-inch, blue-labelled 4-in-1 records, probably the first extended-play, double-sided discs to be manufactured. Two full-length performances appeared on each side, much of the material being issued simultaneously on Sterno. They were excellent value at 1s 6d (7½p) each, but discontinued in March, 1934. Many of the bands heard on 4-in-1 were 'house', but the

Top – *Arthur Lally, multi-reedsman, heard with the Blue Lyres and Bert Ambrose. Brilliant but eccentric, he took his own life.*

Above – *Sydney Lipton: As much a part of the scene at Dorchester House as Carroll Gibbons was at the Savoy Hotel.*

Twelve Rhythm Monarchs were actually Ray Starita and his Ambassadors. *The Song of the Harp* and *On a Dreamy Afternoon*, both by Stanley Damerell, Robert Hargreaves and Tolchard Evans, and *Gosh Darn!* a novelty by Joe Young and J. Fred Coots, were all recorded by Starita in disguise

Gosh Darn! had a duet in Carlisle and Browne manner. The girl singer undoubtedly was Elsie Carlisle, but her companion on this occasion is believed to have been Les Allen.

When Melville Gideon left the Dorchester midway through October, 1931, the vacancy was filled by an Ambrose band directed by Arthur Lally, but it too only stayed briefly. In July, 1932, Lally was replaced by Sydney Lipton, a concert-trained violinist, whose daughter Celia became a well-known actress, although for a time she sang with her father's band. Born in London on January 4, 1906, Lipton was the ideal hotel bandleader, favouring a sweet, rather lushly orchestrated style, with no hot licks or brassy blares. He left the Dorchester in 1941 for the Royal Corps of Signals, seeing active service in Europe and Africa. After demobilisation he returned, and was still at the Dorchester in the early Seventies.

Lipton's Grosvenor House Band made its first records for Zonophone in July, 1932. They included *The Sun Has Got His Hat On,* a novelty by Ralph Butler and Noel Gay. In February, 1933, Lipton formed a new band and began to record for Sterno and occasionally 4-in-1.

Reports in contemporary *Melody Makers* implied that Howard Jacobs was really in charge of the Savoy Hotel Orpheans, even if Carroll Gibbons was co-director. Certainly, Jacobs was spokesman where policy was concerned.

'I do not think there is much call for hot music . . . in such an establishment as the Savoy,' he observed, shortly after the band was formed, going on to advocate beautifully played melodies and artistic blending of tone colour, although the Orpheans' arrangements were fairly simple, with an emphasis on sweet music. Just what the Savoy wanted, of course.

Early in 1932 the Orpheans recorded *A Prisoner of Love*, with a lyric by Leo Robin and a melody by composer, crooner and New York bandleader Russ Columbo. At one time offering strong competition to Bing Crosby, Columbo accidentally killed himself in 1934 with a revolver from a friend's gun collection.

The Orpheans' recording featured Jack Plant, also the vocalist for Herman Hupfeld's dreamy *As Time Goes By*, which was dramatically revived in 1942 when Dooley Wilson sang and played it for Humphrey Bogart and Ingrid Bergman in Warner's *Casablanca*.

In contrast, *When We're Alone* had Al Bowlly. This enchanting ballad by Will Jason and Val Burton became famous as the *Penthouse Serenade*. It was recorded at the last session before Jacobs went to the Berkeley, leaving Gibbons on his own. At this point a few changes occurred: George Melachrino was brought in to replace Jacobs, and Sid Bright (Geraldo's brother) took over the piano stool from Harry Jacobson.

The Voice in the Old Village Choir was recorded in June, shortly after Jacobs' departure. A waltz by Gus Kahn and Harry Woods, it sounded like something from Victorian times, but was surprisingly popular. It was ideal for Plant's high tenor. The Orpheans also recorded another nostalgic song, *Cabin in the Cotton*, by Mitchell Parish and Frank Perkins, this time with a vocal by Les Allen and the Carlyle Cousins.

Harry Jacobson: Pianist for the Savoy Hotel Orpheans from the autumn of 1931 to the spring of 1932. He was replaced by Sid Bright, brother of Geraldo.

Jack Payne's imminent departure left the BBC with the problem of finding a successor capable of winning over the allegiance of a host of listeners loyal to the Payne brand of music and humour. A big-name bandleader was unlikely to be suitable, and in any case the BBC had no intention of being caught twice.

The BBC had no control over Payne's band once its leader had given notice to quit. The next BBC Dance Orchestra was therefore to be a 'house' organisation, and its director a BBC employee. In addition, it was felt that the previous knockabout comedy should give way to good music, not all of it intended for dancing. First, however, the BBC must find its man.

An approach was made to Henry R. Hall, Musical Director of the L.M.S. Railway hotel chain, who had been broadcasting from the Gleneagles Hotel in Perthshire, and later from the Midland Hotels in Manchester or Liverpool, since 1924. Ambitious, well-spoken; a good-mannered man who stood no nonsense; above all, a fine organiser: he seemed the ideal choice.

Arthur Towle, boss of Midland Hotels, agreed to his release, and Henry Hall began the formidable task of assembling a suitable orchestra (which underwent some changes in its early days) and winning over listeners. The New BBC Dance Orchestra, as it was initially styled, made its maiden broadcast on March 15, 1932. Reactions were

Val Rosing: Son of a distinguished Russian operatic tenor. He eventually went to Hollywood, but success there presumably eluded him.

Arthur Tracy, who called himself the Street Singer, was an American of Russian parentage. His recorded output for Decca and Panachord was prodigious, and his career a very long one.

understandably mixed, but its popularity grew, and before long its director had become a household name.

Henry Robert Hall was born in Peckham, of Salvationist parents, on May 2, 1898. He attended Trinity College of Music, studying piano and composition under George Aitken (composer of the well-known ballad *Maire My Girl*). He also had trumpet tuition from the very famous John Solomon.

At 16 he began work in the Salvation Army music department, later composing several marches. During the war he served with the Band of the Royal Field Artillery. He was demobilised in 1919, and began to play piano at a Notting Hill Gate 'kinema'. His appointment as director of the Gleneagles Hotel band, which followed, was a major break-through; he made his first broadcast on June 4, 1924, the hotel's opening night.

Records made by the Gleneagles band were rarely of much interest, and hardline bandsmen were sometimes contemptuous of the BBC Dance Orchestra. 'Insipid, spineless schmaltz,' according to Sid Colin. But, as Colin acknowledged, the public loved their showband, and that to the BBC was all-important.

Such criticism was in any case unduly harsh. Hall had to cater for an audience of diverse tastes, not just for dancers. Indeed, he was required to amuse the children during his 5.15pm broadcasts, doing so with well-chosen songs, such as those about *Rusty and Dusty*.

Payne had always opened with with *Say it with Music*, but Hall went one better. He began with *It's Just the Time for Dancing*, but signed-off with *Here's to the Next Time*, an adaptation of his Salvationist *Sunshine March*, with a lyric by Margery Lawrence added.

The BBC Dance Orchestra only recorded for Columbia. Beginning in March, it made an enormous number of records, a battery of distinguished arrangers being employed. For the first six months Val Rosing sang with the band, but in October Hall made considerable changes, and Les Allen was brought in. Only a few of the songs recorded by Rosing with the band can be mentioned here.

Marta, Rambling Rose of the Wildwood was arranged by Sid Phillips. A Cuban song by Moises Simons, with an L. Wolfe Gilbert lyric, it became the signature song of Arthur Tracy, the internationally famous Street Singer.

A Londoner, born in 1907, Phillips went to London University. For five years he arranged for Lawrence Wright, followed by a year with Campbell-Connelly, and from 1930 to

Above – *Henry Hall and his Gleneagles Hotel Band in 1931. When Hall left to join the BBC, Orlando took his place.*

Left – *This* is *Henry Hall!*

Les Allen: Singer and alto sax player, who formed his own 'Canadian Bachelors', a vocal group.

1939 he supplied a great many arrangements to Ambrose. A highly proficient alto sax player and clarinettist, he recorded much Dixieland jazz in a style that was unmistakeably his own. He died in 1973.

An Old Violin and *Speak to Me of Love* were arranged by Tony Lowry. The former, a concert ballad composed by Howard Fisher, had a lyric by Helen Taylor. Born at Little Dunmow, Essex, in 1876, she collaborated with Sir Landon Ronald, Julius Harrison, Easthope Martin and May Hanna Brahe. She died in Chelsea on April 19, 1943.

Parlez-vous d'Amour, a Jean Lenoir hit in France before it crossed the Channel, received an English lyric from Bruce Sievier. Born Robert Brudenell-Bruce Sievier in Paris in 1894, he went to Uppingham. He was associated with many songs, among them *Her Name is Mary, Love's Last Word is Spoken* and *The Silver Patrol.*

A really big hit to which Val Rosing contributed was *The Teddy Bears' Picnic*, which Henry Hall and Burton Gillis arranged. For years it was the BBC engineers' test record. It had begun in 1907 as an intermezzo by John W. Bratton, a tribute to President Theodore Roosevelt, and was long a favourite with military bands and light orchestras.

It got its lyric from Jimmy Kennedy in 1930, but then waited two years until Henry Hall's stylish record made it a fantastic success. John Bratton died in 1947.

Les Allen remained with Hall until 1934, then formed his Canadian Bachelors and began to tour. They recorded for Columbia, and sometimes broadcast with Big Bill Campbell's Rocky Mountaineers. Eventually, Allen returned home, but in 1954 paid us a visit and appeared on Henry Hall's Guest Night.

Phil Cardew arranged two of the popular ballads recorded by Allen in 1932, *Just an Echo in the Valley*, a rather wistful song by Campbell and Connelly, with Harry Woods, and *A Shanty in Old Shanty Town*, love in the slums escapism by Joe Young, John Siros and Little Jack Little, redeemed by a flowing melody.

The Rhythm Rascals was just another session band assembled by Harry Bidgood for Broadcast. His bands differed from those directed by Jay Wilbur in that they rarely, if ever, attempted to play hot music. *Same Old Moon*, a waltz by Ed Rose and Billy Baskette, was typical of the fleetingly popular songs that Bidgood arranged so competently.

Eclipse issued many records by Hardy and Hudson, but

the identity of the singers (never disclosed) varied considerably. *Underneath the Arches*, a Depression classic by Reg Connelly and Bud Flanagan, was actually duetted by Cavan O'Connor and Harry Hudson, whereas *Why Don't You Say that You're Sorry?* a minor ballad by Margaret Galpin, teamed O'Connor with Sam Browne.

A new novelty appeared in April, when Durium Products (G.B.) Ltd., of Slough, introduced a single-sided, cardboard disc in a ten-inch format. Both the silver-lettered label and the shellac were dark-brown. Recording was surprisingly good, and for dance band issues two tunes were played.

An early Durium disc had *Just Humming Along,* by Stanley Damerell, Robert Hargreaves and Montague Ewing, and *Can't We Talk it Over?* by Ned Washington and Victor Young, played by the 'house' Durium Dance Band, directed by Lew Stone. The vocalist was Al Bowlly.

Ewing, who also wrote as Sherman Myers, was born at Forest Gate in 1890. Back in 1911 he had composed the famous one-step *The Policeman's Holiday.* Much of his output was light orchestral, but he had some hits as a songwriter. He died on March 6, 1957.

The Durium Revellers, another session band directed by Lew Stone, had Sam Browne, who actually announced the tunes to be played. On one occasion they were *Too Many Tears*, a melancholy ditty by Al Dubin and Harry Warren, and *When Yuba Plays the Rumba on the Tuba*, a bit of lively nonsense by Herman Hupfeld from the *Third Little Show.*

Most labels only showed a composer's surname, but Durium quoted the full names of lyricist and composer. Easily bent or cracked, few still survive. These unusual records went off the market in the autumn of 1933.

One of Ray Noble's most evocative songs was *By the Fireside*, with a cosily romantic Campbell and Connelly lyric. It was recorded by the New Mayfair Dance Orchestra, with a very satisfying vocal by Al Bowlly.

Bowlly was Noble's vocalist when *Good-Night, Vienna* was recorded. A haunting tango by Holt Marvell and George Posford, it came from their wireless operetta of that name, broadcast in January and filmed later in the year by Herbert Wilcox, with Jack Buchanan and Anna Neagle co-starring.

Holt Marwell was actually Eric Maschwitz, editor of the Radio Times from 1927-1933. Born in Birmingham on June 10, 1901, he went to Repton, and then Gonville and Caius College, Cambridge. He joined the BBC in 1926, and from

Eric Maschwitz: In 1940, Judy Campbell launched his great hit A Nightingale Sang in Berkeley Square.

Dick Powell's cinematic career changed from likeable singer to tough guy roles.

Ginger Rogers once won the Texas State Championship in a Charleston contest. Her first film was Paramount's Young Man of Manhattan *in 1930.*

1933-1937 was Director of Variety. Novelist, playwright, screenplay writer and lyricist, he died on October 27, 1969.

Leo Robin and Ralph Rainger created some quite sophisticated songs. *Here Lies Love* was heard in Paramount's *The Big Broadcast*, starring Bing Crosby, with the Mills Brothers, the Boswell Sisters and Cab Calloway and his Orchestra. It was recorded by Bowlly in December, by which time HMV were calling their 'house' ensemble Ray Noble and his Orchestra.

Warner's *42nd Street*, with Dick Powell, Ruby Keeler, Bebe Daniels and Ginger Rogers, had songs by Dubin and Warren. *You're Getting to be a Habit with Me* was recorded by Waring's Pennsylvanians. In addition to the standard '78', Victor waxed it at 33⅓ rpm. The Depression was no time to think about entirely new record players, and the idea was dropped. The L.P. had to wait for almost another 20 years before making the 78 rpm disc obsolescent. Now it is in turn being supplanted by the Compact Disc.

Ann Ronell's *Willow, Weep for Me* was a pretty song which Paul Whiteman recorded with his new singer, Irene Taylor. Years later, Stan Kenton resurrected this sad ballad, providing a brassy accompaniment for June Christie.

Broadway was reeling from an onslaught of Hollywood musicals, but by no means vanquished. *The Gay Divorce,* opening at the Ethel Barrymore Theatre in November, had songs by Cole Porter. *Night and Day* and *I've Got You on My Mind* were recorded by Leo Reisman and his Orchestra, with guest singer Fred Astaire.

Good songs in plenty were coming from the Americans, but their bands were in the doldrums, and would remain becalmed until swing blew up a wind of change. It took the inspired arrangements and superb playing of British bands to bring out the best in the music of Broadway, Hollywood and Tin Pan Alley.

Chapter Eleven

1933

'We'll All Go Riding On A Rainbow'

By 1933 British bands were well into a so-called golden age that only began to fade when the Thirties themselves were drawing to their close. Conversely, for two more years the American scene remained one of musical stagnation, despite the adulation accorded to many bandleaders by the uncritical.

In 1935, however, things there started to change dramatically, given impetus by the extraordinary occurrence at New York's Paramount Theatre, when at a Benny Goodman concert the audience left its seats to jitterbug wildly in the aisles.

The United States has always reacted (or over-reacted) to change more swiftly than here in Britain. Before long, swing had dealt a savage blow to the majority of sweet bands, and new names and new styles began to make news. Paul Whiteman, so-called *King of Jazz*, was overthrown by Benny Goodman, *King of Swing*, as well-orchestrated jazz, and popular music arranged in the same manner, became the essential library of most big bands.

Here, change came about more gradually, but the pervasive influence of swing music, and particularly the sweet-swing of Glenn Miller, dominated the British band scene during and after the Second World War, until such time, indeed, as the big bands began to disappear.

Meanwhile, in 1933, the more established British bandleaders continued to delight their followers in ballrooms, hotels, night clubs and restaurants, at the theatre and, for the majority as the Depression tightened its grip, over the air and on gramophone records. There were no startling musical events, and few sensational hits; just a cavalcade of pleasant songs, stylishly arranged and melodiously performed.

Jack Hylton was tremendously busy in 1933; too much so for his doctor, who made him take a holiday. Band concerts and broadcasts in Paris; a show at the Palladium; and the pleasurable task of introducing Duke Ellington and his Orchestra to London, were the high-spots of his year.

He made a lot of records too, the majority with Pat O'Malley. The waltz *A Boy and a Girl were Dancing*, treacly sentiment by Mack Gordon and Harry Revel, was an early hit that year. Revel was born in London on December 21, 1905. After gaining composing experience in Europe, he went to America when he was 24 and there met Mack Gordon, his partner until 1942. Revel died in New York on November 3, 1958.

I've Told Every Little Star, sheer magic by Oscar Hammerstein II and Jerome Kern, was from *Music in the Air*, which had opened at the Alvin Theatre in November, 1932. The show became a Fox film in 1934, starring Gloria Swanson and John Boles.

Born in New York on January 27, 1885, Kern was 48 in 1933, with years of imaginative work before him. Not until November 12, 1945, would he collapse in a New York street, unidentified by those who rushed him to a hospital where he died not long after admission.

Harold Ramsay wrote several ballads with lyricist Bruce Sievier. *Her Name is Mary,* charming but rather old-fashioned, quite suited O'Malley's smooth style. Harold Fairbrother Ramsay, L.R.A.M., organist, conductor and composer, was born at Wandsworth in 1889.

A very popular organist of the Thirties, Harold Ramsay joined Bruce Sievier to write Her Name is Mary. *It sounded rather old-fashioned for 1933, but Jack Hylton made a Decca recording with Pat O'Malley.*

Warner's *Gold Diggers of 1933,* the second of a series, had a wonderful cast, including Dick Powell, Ruby Keeler and Ginger Rogers. The songs of Dubin and Warren make it still worth watching. *The Shadow Waltz* was one of them. Hylton and O'Malley recorded this and other numbers from the film.

The sagebrush serenaders had arrived, and cowboys began to round up the dogies to the fox-trot or the waltz. *There's a Home in Wyoming,* Billy Hill and Peter de Rose informed us; and they certainly made the West a money-spinner.

Warner's *Footlight Parade* starred James Cagney, Joan Blondell, Dick Powell and Ruby Keeler. It also had Dubin and Warren's *Honeymoon Hotel,* which Hylton for a change gave to his vocal trio, and *By a Waterfall,* a little charmer by Irving Kahal and Sammy Fain, sung very well by O'Malley.

These two songs were recorded in November at Hylton's penultimate session before he bade Decca a permanent farewell. In 1934 he took a trip to the States, and on his return temporarily disbanded.

It was *The Last Round-Up* which really catapulted both sides of the Atlantic into the singing cowboy era. A rather haunting slow fox-trot by Billy Hill, it caught on like a stampede, and over here the Billy Cotton band recorded a beautiful version, with vocalist Alan Breeze.

Until then, Hill had been an obscure lyricist and composer, with several unperformed songs which his publisher hastily trotted out. He quickly became famous, frequently working with the very talented Peter de Rose.

Hill was no Westerner. Born in Boston on July 14, 1899, he studied at the New England Conservatory and later played

*Joan Blondell, a proficient
swimmer, saved two boys from
drowning in August, 1932. She
sparkled in Warner films
throughout the Depression years.*

JOAN BLONDELL.

violin for the Boston Symphony Orchestra. He married
Dedette Lee, who helped him write *Put on an Old Pair of
Shoes*. Billy Hill died in New York on December 24, 1940, the
year his *Call of the Canyon* was recorded by Tony Martin;
Guy Lombardo; and Glenn Miller, with Ray Eberle.

Johnny Mercer and Hoagy Carmichael's rather insensitive
Snowball was another song recorded in 1933 by Billy Cotton
and his Band, as well as the delightful *Louisiana Hayride*, by
Howard Dietz and Arthur Schwartz, from *Flying Colours*,
which had not done well at New York's Imperial Theatre in
1932. Both had vocals by Alan Breeze.

Billy Hill's *The Old Spinning Wheel* typified his simple, charming, but occasionally almost corny style. It was recorded by Bertini and the Tower Ballroom, Blackpool, Band, with a vocal by Brian Lawrance.

Bertini, actually a Londoner named Bert Gutsell, had been playing in Blackpool for at least four years. His band had been on various labels, including eighteen months with Sterno. Early in 1933 he signed-up with Eclipse, for two years pouring out sides, many of excellent quality, sometimes accompanied by the Tower organ of 'Mr. Blackpool' himself, Reg Dixon.

In 1935, Bertini left his safe haven at the Tower to go on tour. It proved an unwise decision: he made no more records and gradually faded from sight. He died in 1957.

One of the most appealing Bertini recordings of 1933 was *I Cover the Waterfront*, on which was heard the lovely voice of Cecile Petrie. Edward Heyman's lyric actually made little sense – the title came from a totally irrelevant book – but such was the beauty of John W. Green's music that a memorable song resulted.

It was simply impossible to escape from Billy Hill in 1933. Partnered by de Rose, he had another winner with *There's a Cabin in the Pines*, recorded by Ambrose and the ever reliable Sam Browne in March for Brunswick, to which they had transferred after a short spell on Regal-Zonophone.

By autumn, Ambrose had a new band and was back at the Embassy Club. Not long after the move, he and Browne recorded *Who's Afraid of the Big, Bad Wolf?* written by Ann Ronell and Frank E. Churchill for Disney's *Three Little Pigs.*

Roy Fox's stay at the Cafe Anglais was fairly brief. Early in January, 1933, he took his band to the Kit-Cat Club; and in May appeared in the Royal Command Performance at the Palladium.

His Decca recordings included a rather unusual song by Harry Woods, *The Wind's in the West*, with a vocal by Jack Plant, Peggy Dell and the Cubs. In December, Fox engaged Derby-born Dennis Pountain, changing his name to Denny Dennis. (He had earlier changed Harlean Carpenter into Jean Harlow). It proved a popular appointment, and Dennis remained with Fox until he disbanded in 1938, after which he sang first for Ambrose and then for Jack Hylton.

Denny Dennis' rich baritone has been compared to Bing Crosby's, but the resemblance was only superficial. He was a fine singer, and among the few Britons to work for a famous

Top – *Would Bertini have been as popular under his real name of Bert Gutsell? His decision to leave Blackpool Tower in 1935 may have been an error of judgement.*

Above – *Brian Lawrance played at Quaglino's and Lansdowne House before breaking up his band to concentrate on singing. He appeared on Decca (1934–37) and Rex (1937–1940).*

*Denny Dennis made his name
with Roy Fox, and in 1948 sang
for Tommy Dorsey.*

*Collie Knox: Without him, the
BBC might have got away with it!*

American bandleader. In 1948 he began to sing for Tommy Dorsey.

His first recording with Roy Fox was *Did You Ever See a Dream Walking?* a very big hit for Mack Gordon and Harry Revel, heard in Paramount's *Sitting Pretty*, in which Ginger Rogers appeared.

In August the public flocked to see the BBC Dance Orchestra helping to boost the Radio Exhibition at Olympia. Afterwards, Henry Hall left for a part-holiday, part-business trip to the States, meeting Rudy Vallee (a devout Anglophile), Vincent Lopez, Ben Bernie and Wayne King, among others, and understandably gaining an impression that Americans only liked sweet music.

He went back in 1934, and during his absence the BBC introduced the orchestra as though it were still under his personal direction. An announcer with a similar voice was used. Collie Knox discovered the deception, denouncing it in the *Daily Mail*. On his return, Hall began his broadcasts with 'This *is* Henry Hall speaking', which caught on, and he continued to do so for over 20 years, long after his bandleading days were over.

Not every song recorded by the BBC Dance Orchestra was a current hit. Clare Kummer's *Egypt*, played as a fox-trot, had been interpolated into *The Girl from Kay's* during its 1903-4 run at New York's Herald Square Theatre; and Princess Lydie Kamakaeha Liliuokalani's *Aloha Oe*, transformed into a slow fox-trot, had been composed in 1878. She later became Queen of Hawaii, but in January, 1893, was compelled to abdicate when revolution broke out. Both songs had vocals by Les Allen.

For Dewey Bergman and Lou Handman's *On a Steamer Coming Over*, Les Allen duetted with Phyllis Robins; and she was sole vocalist for *It's the Talk of the Town*, a melancholy masterpiece by Marty Symes, Al J. Neiburg and Jerry Levinson. A good band performance and Miss Robins' unusual voice added touches of distinction to a record that was by no means 'insipid, spineless schmaltz'.

Old Father Thames, with Raymond Wallace's philosophical verse and a rollicking tune by Lawrence Wright as Betsy O'Hogan, made a smash-hit for Peter Dawson, but the bands played it too. Sterno's version was credited to Syd Raymond and his Commanders; it was simultaneously issued on 4-in-1 as by the Silver Serenaders. Sydney Lipton's Grosvenor House Band was actually responsible, together with vocalist Sam Browne.

The same band and vocalist also recorded *Butterflies in the Rain*, with an Erell Reaves lyric and a Sherman Myers tune nearly as fluttery as the theme. At least it was a welcome change from the 'moon-June-croon' banality of too many Alley potboilers of its period.

Unashamed romanticism, tastefully handled, was the mood of *In the Valley of the Moon,* a new waltz by Charles Tobias and Joe Burke. It appeared on Winner, recorded by Sidney Kyte and his Piccadilly Hotel Band, with Norman Phillips' vocal.

Yvonne, another waltz, was composed by the old master Horatio Nicholls, and recorded by Jack Jackson, who had left Jack Payne to lead his own band, taking with him Chappie d'Amato and the brilliant multi-reedsman Edward O. 'Poggy' Pogson (who died at Crewkerne, aged 75, on February 7, 1980). The vocal was by Sam Costa.

Jackson cut his first records for HMV very early in the year, and was at first labelled John Jackson and his Orchestra. In August he began to play at the Dorchester, where he would remain until April, 1939, although he ceased to record early the previous year. He remained faithful to HMV until 1937, but then switched to Decca.

Ned Washington and George Bassman's *I'm Getting Sentimental Over You* was recorded shortly after Jackson opened at the Dorchester. In 1935 it became the signature tune of Tommy Dorsey, a 'sentimental gentleman' with a hot Irish temper. Jackson's version featured Denny Dennis, four months before he became Roy Fox's new songbird.

Jackson, who composed his own signature tune, *Make Those People Sway*, and recorded it in September, 1933, had played hot trumpet in earlier years, but at the Dorchester he prudently confined himself to directing music that was restrained but hardly schmaltzy.

Oscar Rabin and his Romany Band offered no competition to Alfredo, despite the name. Formed about 1925, it was a decidedly unadventurous octet which in 1930 had left the Royal Palace Hotel, Kensington, to replace Billy Cotton at the Astoria Ballroom. It was still there in 1933, with the reputation of an ideal palais band.

Rabin, born at Riga in 1899, doubled, rather oddly, bass saxophone and violin. His band, co-directed by Harry Davis, a close friend who made all the announcements, cut its first sides for Sterno at the end of 1932. Nearly everything was issued on 4-in-1 too, an example being *Shuffle Off to Buffalo,*

'Poggy' Pogson: A real asset to the reed section of any band.

Oscar Rabin and his Romany Band: The ideal Palais band, but no threat to Alfredo's Gypsy Orchestra.

Charlie Kunz: Arthritis ended his long career.

another Dubin and Warren hit from *42nd Street*, with a vocal by Harry Bentley.

Many people who recall the piano selections recorded in profusion by Charlie Kunz are probably unaware that he was a bandleader for at least nine years. In 1928-9 he had directed the Chez Henri Club Band, and in 1933 he took charge of the Casani Club Orchestra.

Born at Allentown, Pennsylvania, in 1896, he came to England in 1922, his rhythmic but in no sense jazz-influenced piano style becoming very popular. Santos Casani, a former Royal Flying Corps pilot, had run the Casani School of Dancing at Hyde Park Corner. In March, 1933, he opened the Casani Club in Regent Street, on the mezzanine floor of Imperial House, engaging Kunz to direct the band. It recorded for Sterno until early in 1935, and thence for Rex until 1937, in which year he disbanded.

Vera Lynn, who sang with the band from 1935 to 1937, recalls Charlie Kunz as a kindly, rather shy man. Although his piano selections had tremendous mass appeal for years after he ceased to direct a band, arthritis eventually ended his career. He died in 1961.

Reflections in the Water, a waltz by Paul Francis Webster and John Jacob Loeb, based on a piano composition by Debussy (just as *In the Valley of the Moon* owed much to the Violin Concerto by Mendelssohn), and *Lazy Bones,* an exercise in tranquility by Johnny Mercer and Hoagy Carmichael, were made at the Casani Club Orchestra's first recording session, appearing on both Sterno and 4-in-1. Vocals were by Harry Bentley and Phyllis Robins respectively. *Learn to Croon,* by Sam Coslow and Arthur Johnston, recorded around the same time, was allocated to Plaza and also had a vocal by Harry Bentley. On this occasion, Kunz became Al Bertram and his Dance Band.

Learn to Croon was sung by Bing Crosby in his new Paramount film *College Humour.* The lyric gently guyed his own style, but Crosby probably enjoyed the joke. In any case, the song became a hit.

Plaza, an eight-inch disc introduced by British Homophone in 1933, only lasted until July, 1935. Most artists were, like Kunz, heavily disguised. Recording quality was unexceptional and surface wear rapid.

Harry Woods, a prolific songwriter, came up with *You Ought to See Sally on Sunday,* which the Debroy Somers Band recorded. By all accounts something of an eccentric, Woods was well-known for his ability to go missing for days on end; but he had a deft touch as lyricist and composer.

Ball at the Savoy opened at Drury Lane in September, a German operetta, adapted by Oscar Hammerstein II, with music by Paul Abraham. The cast was led by Oskar Denes, Rosy Barsony and Valerie Hobson. One of the prettiest songs was *A Girl Like Nina*, a tango, recorded by Geraldo and his Gaucho Tango Orchestra.

Jack Payne had a new and likeable singer by the autumn, the Scottish Ronnie Genarder. At his first record session with the band, Genarder sang *Dinner at Eight*, the title song (by Dorothy Fields and Jimmy McHugh) from an MGM film starring John and Lionel Barrymore, Marie Dressler and Jean Harlow.

Stormy Weather was one of the most distinctive songs of the year. Ted Koehler wrote the lyric and Harold Arlen the

Top – *George Barclay, a popular vocalist who sang with Charlie Kunz, Mantovani, and Felix Mendelssohn's Hawaiian Serenaders. He joined Kunz after Harry Bentley died.*

Above – *Ronnie Genarder, from Clydebank, who joined Jack Payne in 1933.*

faintly blues-tinted melody. Harry Roy recorded it for Parlophone, with a vocal by Ivor Moreton.

The son of a cantor, Arlen was born Hyman Arluck in Buffalo, New York, on February 15, 1905. In his youth a pianist and singer, he began to write songs at the start of the Thirties. He had a string of hits, and in 1954 joined Ira Gershwin to create songs for Warner's *A Star is Born*, starring Judy Garland and James Mason. He died in New York on April 23, 1986.

Very few records were made in this country of *Brother, Can You Spare a Dime?* in which E. Y. Harburg and Jay Gorney expressed all the despair of the Depression. Those in work preferred to ignore the miseries of the unemployed; those out of work wanted no songs on the subject.

Born in Bialystok, then in Russia and now Poland, on December 12, 1896, Gorney probably arrived in America as a child. He studied at the University of Michigan and dabbled in law, changing course after his first song was published in 1923. From the Twenties through the Forties he contributed to stage productions, *Brother, Can You Spare a Dime?* being in the 1932 version of *Americana*.

Bing Crosby recorded this poignant song in 1932, and so, surprisingly, did Rudy Vallee and that doyen of Society band-leaders Leo Reisman. Here it was waxed by Harry Roy, who went to the Cafe Anglais in January, and in the summer replaced Ambrose at the May Fair Hotel. Roy's vocalist was Bill Currie.

A title like *Have You Even Been Lonely?* suggested another grim song of its time, but this was merely a tale of unrequited love. George Brown wrote the self-pitying lyric; the brisk tune, reminiscent of the Twenties in style, was by the very busy Peter de Rose. It was recorded by Ray Noble and his Orchestra, and, like others mentioned below, had a vocal by Al Bowlly.

Pettin' in the Park and *I've Got to Sing a Torch Song* came from *Gold Diggers of 1933*. Al Dubin and Harry Warren seemed determined to prove that very bright songs could still be written, despite the break-up of de Sylva, Brown and Henderson.

Bernice Petkere's *Close Your Eyes*, a rather slumbrous serenade, was marred by Bowlly's careless diction. He did better when *Love Locked Out* was recorded. A ballad by Max Kester and Ray Noble, it may have been inspired by a once famous painting.

It is hard to believe that Joe Loss formed his first band in 1930 to play at the Astoria Ballroom in Charing Cross Road. Born Joshua Alexander Loss, in or near Liverpool Street,

Joe Loss: He left the 'Make-Believe Ballroom' to be 'In the Mood'.

London, on June 22, 1910, he studied at Trinity College of Music. In 1933 he was at the Kit-Cat Restaurant, and made his first records for Winner, one being *Under a Blanket of Blue,* by the team of Marty Symes, Al J. Neiburg and Jerry Levinson. His singer was Jimmy Messini.

Later both a ballroom and a Society bandleader, Loss recorded everything from strict tempo dance music to swing; and his many long-playing albums reveal how closely he kept abreast of changing trends in popular music. In 1937 he recorded Andy Razaf and Joe Garland's *Let's Dance at the Make-Believe Ballroom,* then his signature tune, although he later settled for *In the Mood.*

Loss has maintained a high standard throughout his incredibly long career, but his 78 rpm records are inclined to be rather disappointing, being too much devoted to the singer instead of the band. Certainly, many he made in the Thirties were less than exciting, although those with vocals by Chick Henderson are examples of fine singing by a remarkably good baritone.

There was often a touch of originality about Harry Woods' songs, despite their simplicity. *We'll All Go Riding on a Rainbow* helped to spread a little sunshine in the grey days of 1933. It was recorded by Layton and Johnstone, to whom every Society door was then open.

In the early Thirties two white Americans, songwriters as well as entertainers, tried to challenge Layton and Johnstone, making a lot of records for HMV. Charles Derickson and Burton Brown, the latter a fine pianist, recorded Charles Tobias and Joe Burke's *Goodnight, Little Girl of My Dreams.*

Derickson & Brown: No real hope of dislodging Layton & Johnstone.

*Joe Loss died on June 6, 1990.

It is doubtful they could have achieved anything like the success of the two gifted black singers, but tragedy soon ended the partnership. Derickson died young in 1935, and Brown eventually returned to the States.

Perhaps the most serious challenge came from another black entertainer, Leslie A. Hutchinson, who combined a splendid voice with the most exquisite piano playing. Born in Grenada, Hutch went to New York with the intention of studying the law, but was soon attracting attention as a night club entertainer.

Later he went to Paris, and there C. B. Cochran engaged him to appear in the 1927 London Pavilion production *One Dam' Thing After Another.* Hutch became a well-liked cabaret artist, making many Decca records. His career extended well into the post-war period, and he died, aged 69, on August 18, 1969.

There was a touch of real class about any recording made by Hutch. In 1933 he added his distinctive touch to Rodgers and Hart's *You are Too Beautiful,* from the Lewis Milestone film *Hallelujah, I'm a Bum!* which had a Depression theme and was thus box-office poison, even if it did star Al Jolson.

Hutch also recorded Brown and Henderson's *Let's Call it a Day*, from *Strike Me Pink*, then at New York's Majestic Theatre. Nobody else sang like Hutch. You either liked his style or you didn't. A lot of people did.

During his 1933 visit to New York, Henry Hall was taken to the Riviera, a fashionable night-spot, where Emile Coleman's band was in residence. A sweet Society band, no doubt splendid for dancing, it had little to offer the more critical listener, as demonstrated by its recordings of *Let's Begin* and *Smoke Gets in your Eyes*, from *Roberta*, which I have heard on Australian Regal-Zonophone.

Roberta, a play by Otto Harbach (also the lyricist), was based on Alice Duer Miller's novel *Gowns by Roberta*. Opening late in 1933 at New York's Ambassador Theatre, it became an RKO picture in 1935, starring Irene Dunne, Fred Astaire, Ginger Rogers and Randolph Scott. The entrancing music was by Jerome Kern, whose *Smoke Gets in Your Eyes* wins my accolade as the loveliest song of the decade.

Just for once, Rudy Vallee stepped right out of character. Perhaps he wanted something to rouse his somnolent Connecticut Yankees. He collaborated with Hoagy Carmichael to create *Old Man Harlem Gives Me Sunday Headaches*, and made his liveliest recording since *The Stein Song.* He had left

Victor, so Columbia got this unusual treat.

In September, Crystalate launched a new ten-inch record aimed, as ever, at the popular market. Its name, Rex, appeared in a shield, supported by two lions, with the motto: 'Hear what you like – when you like'. The colours were dark-blue and gold. Rex was acquired by Decca, but not discontinued until February, 1948.

Many American bands were heard on Rex, but too frequently disguised by the collective pseudonym of Ed Lloyd and his Band. In 1933 they included those led by Freddy Martin, Joe Venuti and Adrian Rollini.

Adorable, a waltz by George Marion Jr. and Richard A. Whiting, and *My Moonlight Madonna*, an adaption by Paul Francis Webster and William Scotti of Fibich's *Poème*, were recorded by Freddy Martin and his Orchestra.

Born at Cleveland, Ohio, in 1908, Martin was an expert with the rather unfashionable C-melody saxophone. In the mid-Thirties his band was at the Bossert Hotel in Brooklyn, and he was still active at the close of the Sixties.

Build a Little Home, recorded by Joe Venuti and his Orchestra, was an odd little song by Dubin and Warren from Samuel Goldwyn's *Roman Scandals*. Eddie Cantor was the star, but there was a treasurable appearance by Ruth Etting, singing a much better Dubin and Warren number, *No More Love*.

Ruth Etting, the bright star from Nebraska, whose records are a perfect reflection of Twenties and Thirties attitudes. She is seen here with Sam Goldwyn and Eddie Cantor.

Venuti, one of the few jazz violinists, is remembered more for the many different bands and groups with which he recorded than as a bandleader. Certainly, there was nothing of particular interest about this very commercial recording.

Good Morning, Glory, by Mack Gordon and Harry Revel, was an uninspired effort from *Sitting Pretty,* recorded in a manner no better than it deserved by Adrian Rollini and his Orchestra. A brilliant multi-instrumentalist, forever in demand for session work, Rollini favoured the bass saxophone, but also played the curious goofus and hot fountain pen, both his own inventions.

Not one of these recordings could hold a candle to anything played by Ambrose, Fox, Stone or Hylton. They exemplified the rut into which most American dance bands had settled too comfortably. But at least Rex was to be congratulated in issuing material less familiar than some to British record buyers, although the more discerning must have wondered why Ed Lloyd's band seemed to sound different with each record it made.

In March, 1933, a new American band cut its first sides for Victor, among them Little, Oppenheim and Schuster's *Hold Me,* a short-lived success. It was a small outfit, centred around the flashy, not always accurate piano solos of its leader, Eddy Duchin, soon to become a much esteemed Society performer. He had at one time played for Leo Reisman.

Duchin was born in 1910 and died in 1951, and four years later Columbia's Technicolored biopic went on general release, with Tyrone Power as the star of *The Eddy Duchin Story,* and Carmen Cavallero as the actual pianist. No more credible than any of its kind, it was nevertheless an entertaining movie.

Eddy Duchin was a Society bandleader whose piano solos were strictly for the uncritical.

Chapter Twelve

1934

'It's Time To Say Goodnight'

Throughout 1934 the jog-along rhythm and simple melodies of cowboy songs helped to brighten the long Depression months. Some were British, and by no means inferior to those coming over from the Wide Open Spaces of Manhattan.

Roll Along, Covered Wagon, a hit for Jimmy Kennedy, was recorded by Billy Cotton and his Band, with a vocal by Alan Breeze, as had *It's Only a Paper Moon,* a lilting fox-trot by Billy Rose, E. Y. 'Yip' Harburg and Harold Arlen, for years after its introduction the darling of the dance halls.

William Samuel Rosenberg, better known as Billy Rose, was born in New York on September 6, 1899, and for a time married to Fanny Brice. He began to write songs in 1920, continuing to do so for well over ten years, but became increasingly well-known as a producer. He also owned the Diamond Horseshoe Restaurant in New York.

Wagon Wheels, another lazy-paced cactus carol by Billy Hill and Peter de Rose, had a very pretty tune. Les Allen's Canadian accent added a touch of apparent authenticity to Henry Hall's record.

The BBC Dance Orchestra waxed some very good songs that year, among the best being Vernon Duke's *April in Paris*. Les Allen was again the vocalist. It was composed for *Walk a Little Faster*, which had opened at New York's St. James' Theatre in December, 1932. Yip Harburg wrote the lyrics for this show. Born in New York on April 8, 1898, he was the son of emigré Russian parents.

Duke, born Vladimir Dukelsky at Pskoff on October 10, 1903, had been a dancer in the Diaghilev Ballet and studied music at Kiev Conservatory. From the Twenties well into the Forties he composed for many New York shows, also writing serious music under his real name.

It's Time to Say Goodnight, a lullaby in waltz-time, was written by Kate Gibson and composed by Henry Hall for Richard Streeton, a friend's small son. Les Allen handled it sympathetically. In the early post-war period, Radio Luxembourg used the song to sign-off.

Learning, by Symes, Neiburg and Levinson, revealed what an attractive singing voice Kitty Masters possessed. Fair-haired and rather shy, she came from Salford, and in June replaced Phyllis Robins. It was her first major engagement, but she had made a Sterno record a few months earlier, duetting Reginald Foresythe's *Because it's Love* with Leslie Douglas for Teddy Joyce and his Kit-Cat Restaurant Orchestra.

Henry Hall's first Guest Night, broadcast in March,

Kitty Masters, the shy blonde from Salford who sang for Henry Hall.

featured Flanagan and Allen, Layton and Johnstone, Elsie and Doris Waters ('Gert & Daisy'), Ronald Frankau, Leslie Sarony, June, Anona Winn and Lupino Lane; a glittering array of bill-toppers.

Love in Bloom was Leo Robin and Ralph Rainger's notable contribution to Paramount's *She Loves Me Not,* starring Bing Crosby and Miriam Hopkins. It was recorded by Bertini and the Tower Blackpool Band, with Donald Peers, a Welsh singer later to become a Variety star.

Ole Faithful, the archetypal cowboy-and-horse ballad, was a little treasure by Michael Carr and Hamilton Kennedy, sung on Bertini's recording by Sam Browne. It was an early hit for Carr, born at Leeds in 1904, who legally changed his name from Cohen to Carr in 1933. A boxer's son, who spent some years in Dublin and America, he died in Maida Vale on September 16, 1968.

Born at Fivemile Town, County Tyrone, in 1908, Joseph Hamilton Kennedy was Jimmy's younger brother. He got his BA at Trinity College, Dublin, and later wrote many cowboy songs, as well as the very popular *Tina.*

Ole Faithful and *I Saw Stars,* the latter by Maurice Sigler, Al Goodhart and Al Hoffman, also with a Browne vocal, were recorded at Bertini's penultimate Eclipse session. Early in 1935 he made two more sides before leaving Blackpool for eventual obscurity.

Records by Ambrose included a song by Dick Smith and Felix Bernard, destined to take its place alongside *White Christmas* and *Rudolf the Red-nosed Reindeer* as a Yuletide classic. The lyric is trite; the tune unremarkable; but *Winter Wonderland* seems set fair to go on forever. Sam Browne sang it urbanely for Ambrose: everything was grist to his mill.

Arthur Freed and Nacio Herb Brown's *All I Do is Dream of You* was heard in MGM's *Sadie McKee,* starring Joan Crawford and Franchot Tone, and recorded for Rex by Jack Payne and his Band, with his own vocal. Unlike Imperial, his new label did not have his portrait.

Easy Come – Easy Go was hardly a suitable theme for the Depression, but songs by Edward Heyman and Johnny Green were always worth hearing. Carroll Gibbons knew Green well, and the Savoy Hotel Orpheans recorded this song, together with Sam M. Lewis and J. Fred Coots' *For All We Know.* On each occasion, Harry Bentley was the vocalist.

By this time another of the better palais bands had become well-established and was making a lot of records.

Donald Peers, popular singer from Ammanford who made his debut at Lowestoft in 1927.

BILLY MERRIN

Below – Billy Merrin: He helped to dispel an illusion that only London bands were worth hearing.

LONDON HIPPODROME

Proprietors . . . . MOSS' EMPIRES LTD
Managing Director . . . . R. H. Gillespie
Direction . . . . George Black
Manager . . . . Frank Boor

"YES. MADAM ?"

A MUSICAL COMEDY   PROGRAMME

Above – Yes, Madam? did very well at the London Hippodrome, proving that a good stage musical could still hold its own in the mid-Thirties against the powerful allure of the silver screen.

Right – Chick Henderson: From a song contest in West Hartlepool to fame with Joe Loss.

Born at Nottingham in February, 1900, Billy Merrin had been banjoist and arranger for Alan Green's band. In 1931 he formed his own Commanders and settled down at Nottingham Palais de Danse.

Merrin flitted from label to label: Decca, Panachord, Winner, Regal-Zonophone and, by July, 1934, Sterno, for which he recorded *Oh! Muki Muki Oh!* a piece of tuneful nonsense by Hill and de Rose. Merrin, who took the vocal spot, had a voice no worse than most. For some reason, many bandleaders had a compulsion to sing, often with deplorable results.

In November, 1984, fifty years after it was first seen, the Gaumont-British film *Evergreen* was shown on television. It was inferior to contemporary American musicals, particularly the Busby Berkeley extravaganzas by Warner, but Jessie Matthews made it memorable.

Harry Woods had written a new song for her: *When You've Got a Little Springtime in Your Heart,* which Harry Case sang for the Joe Loss recording. He was only briefly with the band, before Chick Henderson was engaged.

Charlie Kunz and the Casani Club Orchestra were disguised again by Plaza, becoming Ben Fields and his Band. One can only wonder how bandleaders felt about some of the aliases conferred upon them. Kunz's unmistakeable piano style graced *The Show is Over*, a new song by Al Dubin, Sam Coslow and Con Conrad, sung by Harry Bentley.

It was back to Spain – musically – for Tolchard Evans, with some help from Robert Hargreaves and Stanley Damerell. Their one-step *Lady of Madrid* was recorded by Geraldo and his Gaucho Tango Orchestra, with a vocal by Birrell O'Malley, as 'Don Carlos'.

Gauchos, tough South American cowboys, were hardly likely to have danced the rumba, not even one as enchanting as *The Carioca*, by Gus Kahn, Edward Eliscu and Vincent Youmans. It was a high-spot of RKO's *Flying Down to Rio*, starring Dolores del Rio, which teamed Fred Astaire and Ginger Rogers for the first time (in supporting roles), and made another lively recording for Geraldo and his ersatz Argentinians.

In March, Roy Fox turned full circle by going back to the Cafe de Paris, but the contract was terminated amicably after three months to enable him to begin a major Variety tour. Fox continued to broadcast; and to record, somewhat intermittently, for Decca.

Yes, Madam? opened at the Hippodrome in September, with Binnie Hale and Bobby Howes. Lyrics were by R. P. Weston and Bert Lee; music by Jack Waller and Joseph Tunbridge. Two of the songs, *Sitting Beside o' You* and *Dreaming a Dream*, were recorded by Fox, with vocals by Sid Buckman (his lead trumpeter) and Peggy Dell respectively. The latter, a Dubliner, began to sing for Fox in December, 1932.

June in January, a ballad by Robin and Rainger, came from Paramount's *Here is My Heart*, which partnered Bing Crosby and Kitty Carlisle. It was robustly sung by Denny Dennis; as was Stanley Adams and Maria Grever's *What a Difference a Day Made,* recorded only three days before Fox's busy year ended.

Lew Stone handed out the vocal spot to anyone with a passable voice, instead of confining himself to Al Bowlly and Nat Gonella. Some of the most amusing vocals were by Tiny Winters, whose string bass helped to power the rhythm section. He always sang in a curious, but not displeasing falsetto.

Out for No Good was a typical example, written by Dubin and Warren for First National's *Twenty Million Sweethearts,* in which Dick Powell, Ginger Rogers and Pat O'Brien were joined by Ted Fiorito and his Orchestra.

Bowlly had a rather wistful number by Desmond Carter and Vivian Ellis, *Faint Harmony*, from *Jack and Jill*, which had reached the West End, renamed *Jill, Darling!* after a try-out at the Glasgow Alhambra late in 1933. Arthur Riscoe, Frances Day, and John Mills shared the lead.

But in September, Ray Noble left HMV for New York, taking Stone's drummer Bill Harty and Al Bowlly with him.

Peggy Dell sang for Roy Fox from 1932 to 1935, and was then replaced by Mary Lee; in 1936 she joined Jack Hylton.

Tiny Winters: Bass and falsetto! Born at Hackney on January 24, 1909, he remains an active musician and is a Freeman of the City of London.

Frances Day, Teddie St Denis and Arthur Riscoe in a scene from Jill, Darling! *at the Saville Theatre.*

Bill Harty: Not a very swinging drummer?

Harty, later regarded by the American writer George T. Simon as 'a flashy but not very swinging drummer', was succeeded by Jock Jacobson; but who could replace Bowlly? Stone chose Alan Kane, a competent enough singer but hardly in the same class.

Among Kane's early recordings with Stone was *Stay as Sweet as You Are,* a serenade by Gordon and Revel, written for Paramount's *College Rhythm,* in which Joe Penner (a radio comic), Jack Oakie and Lyda Roberti starred. Stone's arranger on this occasion was Stanley Black, later to become a very distinguished bandleader.

Many sides made by Jack Jackson's Dorchester Hotel Orchestra in the autumn of 1934 had vocals by Alberta Hunter. A black singer who had made a few sides for Victor in 1927 with Fats Waller's pipe organ accompaniment, she had a part in *Show Boat* at Drury Lane.

Her singing appearance in Elstree's *Radio Parade of 1935,* actually released in 1934, was among the high-spots of a Will Hay movie remarkable only for its wealth of Variety talent. Teddy Joyce's band was in this film, as were vocalists Eve

Becke and the Carlyle Cousins. A surprisingly restrained Hay gently satirised Sir John Reith.

Alberta Hunter, although only briefly with Jack Jackson, left a legacy of pleasant ballads superbly performed. *Be Still, My Heart*, by Allan Flynn and Jack Egan; *Two Cigarettes in the Dark*, by Paul Francis Webster and Lew Pollack; and *Stars Fell on Alabama*, an unforgettable song by Mitchell Parish and Ray Perkins which became a standard, were among her best. HMV departed from their usual practice with vocalists and gave her label credit.

Vivian Ellis was greatly in demand during the Thirties, and Jackson's band recorded his pretty song *You Turned Your Head*, with its lyric by Ronald Jeans. It was a duet by Meg Lemonnier and Esmond Knight in Cochran's 1934 revue *Streamline*, at the Palace Theatre.

The Very Thought of You was vintage Ray Noble, and recorded by his 'house' band, with Al Bowlly, being the kind of dreamy ballad in which the latter excelled.

Noble, Harty and Bowlly were in the HMV studio for the last time in August, recording, among other songs, *Isle of Capri*, a tremendous hit for Jimmy Kennedy and Will Grosz. Its lilting melody was reminiscent of European folk tunes, not too surprising, perhaps, for the composer was Austrian.

Wilhelm Grosz was a Jew who had fled with his family from the menace of his rabid fellow countryman. Born at Vienna in 1894, he obtained a Ph.D. (Musicology) from the University. Later he began to conduct at the National Theatre, Mannheim. His serious works included songs, piano pieces and orchestral compositions, but Dr. Paul Stefan described him as having 'a marked tendency towards the grotesque'.

Shortly before the outbreak of war, Grosz followed Marek Weber's example and went to America, perhaps feeling more secure there from the Nazi threat. He collaborated with Mack Gordon on at least two occasions, *In an Old Dutch Garden* (1939), recorded by Glenn Miller, with Ray Eberle, becoming something of a hit, and *Let's Sing a Song About Susie,* just one more song of 1943. He had nothing like the success he knew over here, but *Along the Santa Fé Trail*, written with Al Dubin and Edwina Coolidge, did quite well, being recorded by both Miller and Crosby in 1940.

Almost midway through the decade, the piano-accordion bands began to challenge the conventional ones. As Brian Rust once pointed out, they were true dance bands, the 'squeeze boxes' replacing both brass and reeds. Top-line

Publicity for a major hit of 1934.

vocalists appeared with them; arrangements and performance were of a high standard.

George Scott-Wood did much to enhance their popularity. A virtuoso himself, he was born at Glasgow in 1903. He became Parlophone's Director of Light Music in 1930, transferring to Regal-Zonophone a few years later. During the summer of 1935 he directed a few sessions for HMV's 'house' band, which had promptly reverted to its old name of the New Mayfair Dance Orchestra after Noble's departure. Scott-Wood died on October 28, 1978.

The London Piano-Accordion Band, studio-based, was already making records for Regal-Zonophone at the start of 1934, and very sprightly they were too. Among the first was a two-year old tango from Czechoslovakia, *Du Schwartzer Zigeuner!* composed by Karel Vacek. The lyric was by Beda, author of the original verse for *Oh! Donna Clara!* and again the adaptation was by Jimmy Kennedy. *Play to Me, Gypsy* swept the country, and its tune was ideal for a piano-accordion band.

The Continental, an unusual number by Herb Magidson and Con Conrad, won a 1934 Oscar for the best film song of the year. It was added to RKO's screen version of *The Gay Divorce*, renamed, heaven and Hollywood alone knew why, *The Gay Divorcee. The Continental* made a splendid tune for the London Piano-Accordion Band, with a vocal duet by Sam Browne and George Scott-Wood.

The rising popularity of piano-accordion bands provided Harry Bidgood with a fresh outlet for his energy and inventiveness, to which he responded magnificently. By that time working under Jay Wilbur for Crystalate, he began with his Don Porto sides, some of which boosted sales of Eclipse records to a remarkable degree, but it was as Primo Scala and his Accordion Band that he gave Rex a series of best-sellers.

Primo Scala records began towards the end of 1933 and were discontinued at the close of the Forties. Primarily a 'house' ensemble, it eventually escaped from the studio to broadcast and appear in Variety. Its repertoire varied little, mostly consisting of popular songs and medleys.

Tina was an early recording, and a great success for Hamilton Kennedy and Will Grosz. It had a rather sad, 'lost love' lyric, but a tune to set every foot tapping. The London Piano-Accordion Band recorded it too, of course.

Al Bowlly sometimes escaped too – from 'vocal refrain' anonymity – and in the spring made some Decca records under his own name. They included *Little Dutch Mill*, by Arthur Freed and Harry Barris, and *You Oughta be in Pictures*, by Edward Heyman and Dana Suesse. He sounded very relaxed and in marvellous voice; furthermore, he had superb accompaniment by the Russian pianist Monia Liter, whom he had first met while playing for Jimmy Lequime.

Could Bowlly have become a serious threat to Bing Crosby? It is possible, given considerable promotional backing, but rather unlikely. He had a strong personality and was attractive to women, but in all probability had no acting ability, whereas Crosby, making film after film for Paramount, was star material. Bing became an institution; a well-loved figure internationally. Bowlly, for all his fine voice, was not really in Bing's league.

Songs about children have always been popular, although usually over-sentimental. *Little Man, You've Had a Busy Day* must have struck a responsive chord in many a fond mama's heart, and was a winner for Maurice Sigler, Al Hoffman and Mabel Wayne. For her Rex recording, Phyllis Robins pulled out all the emotional stops, including a few moments' bedtime conversation with the 'little man' himself. She had discreet instrumental backing from Fred Hartley's Quintet.

The best song in *Twenty Million Sweethearts* was undoubtedly Dubin and Warren's *I'll String Along with You*. It was among the last sides recorded by Derickson and Brown. The latter tried to struggle on alone, after his partner's untimely death, but not for long.

Carl Brisson's British film *Two Hearts in Waltz-Time* went on general release in 1934, giving audiences a chance to see as well as hear Jack Hylton and his Orchestra. From it came *Two Hearts that Beat in Waltz-Time*, with a soaring tune by Robert Stolz and a Reg Connelly lyric. It was recorded for Decca by Brisson himself.

Stolz, born in Graz on August 25, 1886, achieved international fame with his Viennese operettas, composing at least forty, but also wrote many individual songs and was an accomplished conductor. *Whirled into Happiness* (1922); *The Blue Train* (1927); *White Horse Inn*, with Ralph Benatzky (1930), and *Wild Violets* (1932), all came to London, as did *Two Hearts in Waltz-Time* (1931), on which Brisson's movie was based. In 1940, Stolz went to live in America. He died on June 27, 1975.

Brisson also starred in Paramount's *Murder at the Vanities*. Arthur Johnston and Sam Coslow's *Cocktails for Two* was

Fred Hartley, pianist and composer. He came from Dundee.

heard in this film, although hardly one of their best efforts. It was recorded by Nye Mayhew's Orchestra, with a vocal by Douglas Newman. Decca issued it here as by Harry Woods and his New Jersey Orchestra.

Nye Mayhew, who played tenor saxophone, led a very popular sweet band during the Thirties, but by the close of the decade it had faded away. On the evidence of this recording, it was inferior in every respect to the leading British bands of the time.

Eddy Duchin and his Orchestra had established themselves on Victor. The public loved that flashy piano technique, whatever the more discerning thought. Dubin and Warren's *I Only Have Eyes for You* added a distinctive touch to Warner's *Dames*, starring Joan Blondell, Dick Powell, and Ruby Keeler; it was recorded by Duchin in Chicago.

Bandleader Richard Himber at one time played violin with a group accompanying Sophie Tucker. He cut his first Victor sides in March, 1934, being then resident at New York's Ritz-Carlton Hotel. In December he recorded Vernon Duke's hauntingly lovely *Autumn in New York*, which made many contemporary songs sound tawdry.

Records by Ben Selvin and his Orchestra sometimes turned up in unexpected places. *The Prize Waltz*, a Maurice Sigler, Al Goodhart and Al Hoffman opus, made for Columbia, was released (by prior agreement) under the collective pseudonym of the Ariel Dance Orchestra.

Ariel, first encountered about 1910, belonged to J. G. Graves Ltd., a Sheffield mail-order store selling a range of goods from ladies' wear to its own wireless sets. The dull maroon label, gold-lettered, featured everything from concert tenors to hotel orchestras, almost invariably under concealing names. Much of the material was pressed by Zonophone, Columbia and Parlophone, being issued under licence. Odd, but rather interesting, Ariel rode out the Depression but foundered in 1937, by which time most of the independent labels had gone.

Chapter Thirteen

1935

'I Won't Dance'

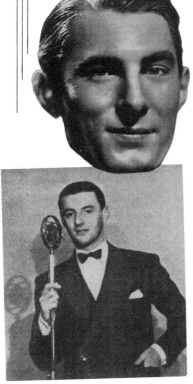

Top – *Jack Jackson:* Likeable
but lazy!

Above – *Fred Latham, who sang
and recorded with Jack Jackson,
1933–35.*

The year 1935 was the watershed between a sweet style of dance music becoming increasingly threadbare in America, and the louder, vibrant strains of swing, which Benny Goodman, Tommy Dorsey, Jimmie Lunceford and Count Basie, to name but a few, were beginning to unleash on a public growing weary of listless, cloying schmaltz.

It was very different in Britain, where dance music had reached its apogee as regards both arrangement and performance. The quality of singing had also greatly improved, although the band vocalist was still (rightly) in a subordinate role. Most leaders were using girls as well as the long-established males, thus adding charm and variety to broadcasts and records. The British bands were at the peak of their finest period, but, of course, nobody in those days realised that.

This was the year of the cowboy song; and among lesser examples may be mentioned *Goodbye, Broncho Bill, Goodbye! Moonlight on the Prairie, The Oregon Trail* and *Prairie Schooner;* with *Cowboy in Manhattan* as an interesting variation on an overworked theme.

Roll Along, Prairie Moon (Harvest and Kentucky moons had already rolled along), was by Harry Macpherson, Albert von Tilzer and Ted Fiorito. It could be heard in MGM's *Here Comes the Band*, with Harry Stockwell, Virginia Bruce and Ted Lewis and his Band. Simple and charming (like all the better cowboy ballads) it was among the last songs which Albert von Tilzer helped to compose.

One of three songwriting brothers (the others were Harry and Will), Albert von Tilzer was born in Indianapolis on March 29, 1878, his true surname being Gumm. He had an early hit in 1903 with *That's What the Daisy Said;* other musical landmarks in his long career including *Teasing* (1904); *Honey Boy* (1907); *Take Me Out to the Ball Game* (1908); *Put Your Arms Around Me, Honey* (1910); *Au Revoir, But Not Goodbye, Soldier Boy* (1917), published the year America went to war; and *I'll Be With You in Apple Blossom Time* (1920). He died in Los Angeles on October 1, 1956.

Roll Along, Prairie Moon was recorded by Jack Jackson and his Dorchester Hotel Orchestra, with regular vocalist Fred Latham; but for *Everything's in Rhythm with My Heart* Jackson joined the ranks of the singing bandleaders. This ballad, by the highly succesful team of Sigler, Goodhart and Hoffman, was sung by Jessie Matthews in her Gaumont-British movie *First a Girl.*

In 1935, Regal-Zonophone donned its resplendent new livery of red and gold, but Lew Stone, understandably displeased at being assigned to a cheaper label by the Gramophone Company, did not renew his contract at the end of October. Nevertheless, he made some excellent sides during his twelve-month absence from Decca.

My Old Dog, an unashamed weepie by Leslie Sarony, could so easily have been awful, but not as Stone arranged it, using a muted trumpet solo by Alfie Noakes to introduce the husky voice of Nat Gonella, who indulged in some soft whistling after his vocal. The effect was philosophical instead of maudlin.

The brilliant young composer Stanley Black began to arrange for Stone in 1933, being then only 20; the following year he succeeded Monia Liter as pianist. His arrangement of *Sidewalks of Cuba*, a rumba by Ben Oakland, Mitchell Parish and Irving Mills, was characteristically colourful, but Joe Crossman, an outstanding alto saxophonist but hardly a singer, had to do his best in an unsuitable role. Stone's insistence on giving non-singers the vocal spots occasionally had odd results.

For *It's Easy to Remember*, a good song by Rodgers and Hart heard in Paramount's *Mississippi,* teaming Bing Crosby and W. C. Fields, Stone sensibly allocated the vocal to Alan Kane. Stanley Black was again the arranger.

Stone was always varied in his choice of arrangers, but only used the best. For two outstanding songs by Cole Porter, *Anything Goes* and *I Get a Kick out of You*, he employed Stanley Black and Phil Cardew respectively. As vocalists he featured Ann Canning, Kay Cavendish and Joy Worth, who called themselves the Radio Three.

They were a stylish trio, their sweet, soft-voiced singing sometimes revealing an unanticipated astringency which was most effective in *Anything Goes*, the title song from an Alvin Theatre production opening in November, 1934.

Kay, a talented pianist, later formed the Cavendish Three, with her old co-singer Joy Worth, and a newcomer, Pat Rignold. They were doing quite well for themselves in 1938. Ann Canning was a solo artist by then: she was a fully trained singer. Joy Worth eventually became a BBC Announcer.

Lew Stone's odd vocalists included a visiting American; he roped in Al Hoffman to appear on a few records in the summer months. For once, Stone's judgement was unerring. The famous songwriter's pleasant voice and laconic delivery resulted in some minor gems.

Ann Canning, a concert-trained singer who left the Radio Three to go solo.

RKO's screen version of *Roberta* introduced the song *I Won't Dance*, by Oscar Hammerstein II, Otto Harbach and Jerome Kern, which had not been heard on Broadway. A clever lyric was wedded to a brisk tune. Al Hoffman's nonchalant rendition, supported by the Radio Three, brought out the best in a fine song. *Lovely to Look At*, another new song in *Roberta*, came from Dorothy Fields, Jimmy McHugh and Jerome Kern. On this occasion, Hoffman had the vocal spot all to himself.

Stanley Black had arranged both songs, as well as *She's a Latin from Manhattan*, with its deliciously ironic lyric by Al Dubin and almost staccato tune by Harry Warren. It was prominently featured in Warner's *Go Into Your Dance*, starring Al Jolson (who sang it) and Ruby Keeler, then still his wife. In my opinion, this was Al Hoffman's supreme performance as Stone's temporary vocalist.

Al Hoffman was born at Minsk on September 25, 1902, arriving in Seattle with his parents six years later. His first hit song was *Heartaches* (1931), with a lyric by John Klenner. In 1934 he came to England, composing for Gaumont-British Pictures. He remained here for three years, and died in New York on July 21, 1960.

Although Brooks Bowman, a Princeton University graduate, wrote other songs, he never had another hit like *East of the Sun*, with its delicate lyric and dainty melody. Its almost ethereal romanticism would have been destroyed by a poor singer, but it was awarded to trombonist Joe Ferrie who, fortunately, could sing quite well. The sensitive arrangement was by Monia Liter, born at Odessa in 1905, who died in January, 1989.

The General's Fast Asleep was another child (and his toy soldiers) ditty, created by Jimmy Kennedy and Michael Carr,

Michael Carr and Jimmy Kennedy told Hitler where we'd be hanging out the washing!
L to R: *Carr, film director Herbert Smith, Kennedy.*

who wrote some splendid songs together. It was more whimsical than sentimental, the kind which Stone always arranged very well. Alfie Noakes was landed with the vocal, although his voice was too weak to be effective.

This song and *Dinner for One, Please, James* were recorded at Stone's last session for Regal-Zonophone, after which he began an unbroken association with Decca lasting 14 years. The latter ballad, of the self-pitying kind, was entirely by Carr, and crossed the Atlantic successfully. For once, Stone used a top-line singer, the ever reliable Sam Browne.

Billy Cotton remained with Regal-Zonophone until the autumn of 1936, then moved to Rex. Meanwhile, he gave a polished rendition of another cowboy song of transitory fame, *Take Me Back to My Boots and Saddle,* by Walter G. Samuels, Leonard Whitcup and Teddy Powell, with Alan Breeze's vocal.

Curiously enough, Bob Nolan's *Tumbling Tumbleweeds* was disregarded by the bands, although it was a beautiful song, evoking the windswept loneliness of open country. Actually published in 1934, and recorded in 1941 by Ambrose, Cotton and Harry Roy, it became a hit again in 1946, recorded by Nolan with the Sons of the Pioneers, being issued here on Regal-Zonophone.

A good song which could have been even better with more careful rhyming was *The Wheel of the Wagon is Broken*, by John 'Paddy' Roberts, Elton Box and Sonny Cox. The theme was novel: a cowboy hanging up his gun and saddle and moving to the city. The tune was quite irresistible, and the public loved it. Desmond 'Sonny' Cox, a Londoner, and Harold Elton Box, from Leigh, Lancashire, were both born in 1903.

Sam Costa: Not yet at Much-Binding-in-the-Marsh.

Cabaret at the Cafe de Paris in July, 1935.

This kind of gently rhythmic tune was ideal for the piano-accordion bands, and recorded by Rossini's for Crown. A 'house' band, directed by Harry Bidgood, it actively, if fairly briefly, competed with his Primo Scala records on Rex. On this occasion the vocalist was Sam Costa.

Crystalate's nine-inch Crown records went on sale at Woolworth's for the first time in September, 1935, the month in which this Rossini recording was made. The tiny label was navy-blue; the lettering microscopic; the playing surface wore rapidly, but reproduction was good. Decca bought Crystalate in 1937, and Crown records were discontinued in March of that year.

At the same session, again with Sam Costa, Rossini's Accordion Band recorded another big British hit of 1935, *Red Sails in the Sunset,* by Jimmy Kennedy and Will Grosz, who had started to call himself Hugh Williams. There were competing versions by Lew Stone on Decca, with Joe Ferrie, and Henry Hall on Columbia, with Dan Donovan. Over in New York, Al Bowlly recorded it for Victor, with orchestral accompaniment directed by Ray Noble.

Geraldo was still directing his Gaucho Tango Orchestra, although diversifying into other aspects of band and orchestral music. The Gauchos recorded Jacob Gade's lovely tango *Romanesca*, less familiar than *Jealousy,* in January for Columbia, but midway through October Geraldo switched to Decca, with whom he remained for over two years.

Still active throughout the Thirties (and into the war years), Lawrence Wright seemed to have lost the sparkle found in so many of his earlier Horatio Nicholls tunes. *Rose of Italy* was a good enough song, but no better than many others heard at that time. It was recorded by Primo Scala and his Accordion Band.

Primo Scala also provided a fine performance of *When I Grow Too Old to Dream*, a lovely, wistful song by Oscar Hammerstein II and Sigmund Romberg, for their MGM operetta *The Night is Young,* starring Evelyn Laye and Ramon Novarro. After this film was made, Novarro took a 14-year vacation from the screen, eventually returning for supporting roles only.

The first sides to be issued on Crown were made by Mrs. Jack Hylton and her Band, actually recorded in August. She stayed with Crown until September, 1936, but never appeared elsewhere. Formed by Jack Hylton, but probably not under his direct control, it was a 15-man ensemble which toured the

Halls, pursuing a musically unadventurous course.

It first began to play early in 1933, and lasted until the summer of 1937, but was not Ennis Parkes' first experience as a leader. At some period in the Twenties she had directed the Metro-Gnomes, until forced by illness to retire. That band too had been assembled by Jack Hylton, then her husband.

Her first Crown recording was *In a Little Gypsy Tea Room*, a hit for Edgar Leslie and Joe Burke. Readers familiar with Romany ways may express surprise that they should become involved in the catering trade. It was a good song, anyway, and Mrs. Hylton supplied the vocal, being one of the few bandleaders with a trained voice. Her signature tune was Brown and Henderson's four-year old *This is the Missus*, which she did not record.

1935 was another important year for Jack Hylton, who took his band to Twickenham film studios to appear in *She Shall Have Music*. The star was Brian Lawrance, a good-looking Australian violinist, with a well above average singing voice. Born at Adelaide on August 13, 1909, he fronted various small units, first at Quaglino's and then at Lansdowne House from 1934 to 1940, then disbanded to concentrate on singing.

Life Begins at Oxford Circus, a vaudeville entertainment, opened at the Palladium in March, featuring the Hylton band. Horatio Nicholls composed a rather staccato and uninspired title song, which was Hylton's first recording when he returned to the HMV fold after an absence of four years.

Put On an Old Pair of Shoes, a Depression-inspired fox-trot by Dedette and Billy Hill, had the charm of unforced simplicity, and was Hylton's second recording. His vocal trio consisted of Sonny Farrar, Brian Lee and Ken Tucker.

Jack was back, as HMV delightedly proclaimed, but of the four dozen sides waxed in 1935, few had any distinctive qualities. Among the best was *Far Away in Shanty Town*, with a lyric by poet Christopher Hassall, and the kind of sweeping, exhilarating music that Ivor Novello composed to sustain the mood for his Ruritanian romances. It came from *Glamorous Night,* which opened in May at Drury Lane, with Novello and Mary Ellis sharing the lead. Pat O'Malley sang it for Hylton.

Zing! Went the Strings of My Heart! was a jaunty song by James F. Hanley, whose melody matched its title in exuberance. The big, new Hylton band, 20 strong, gave a bravura

MGM's The Night is Young *co-starred Ramon Novarro and Evelyn Laye, seen here on a Gallaher cigarette card issued in 1935.*

Ivor Novello: When his smash hit Glamorous Night *had to leave Drury Lane for a pre-booked pantomime, he was furious.*

One of the best girl singers around, Eve Becke recorded with many of the top bands.

Vera Lynn: Only 18 in 1935, but heading for stardom. Dame Vera still has a strong, true singing voice, as a television appearance in December, 1988, demonstrated clearly.

performance, using a Billy Ternent arrangement. The singer was again O'Malley.

You're the Top had a clever, sophisticated lyric, and a typically polished Cole Porter tune. O'Malley and Eve Becke duetted. One of the best of the new breed of girl singers, Eve was always in demand for records. This song was revived in 1988, when it became the theme for a television series, *The Charmer*, starring Nigel Havers.

I'll Never Say 'Never Again' Again was reputedly the song which provoked a bandstand row by the Dorsey brothers and Tommy's abrupt departure to form his own band. Written and composed by the ubiquitous Harry Woods, it was sung for Hylton by Brian Lawrance.

This was actually a short-lived band. Hylton had planned to take it to America at the end of 1935, but an embargo by the American Federation of Musicians prevented that. It continued to function under the direction of Sonny Farrar and others until March, 1936, but had broken up before Hylton came home in July.

In August, 1935, Vera Lynn signed-up with Charlie Kunz for his broadcasts, but not to become his regular singer at the Casani Club. Born Vera Margaret Welch at East Ham on March 20, 1917, she was only 18, with a strong, true voice, but virtually unknown to the general public.

She began to record with Kunz in the autumn, among her earliest sides being a waltz, *Sailing Home with the Tide*, by Reg Connelly, Muriel Watson and Jack Denby. Although already quite experienced as an entertainer, her upward climb to stardom really began then. She appeared on a number of Crown records under her own name.

The majority of songs by Rodgers and Hart were created for Broadway or Hollywood, but *Blue Moon* was a notable exception. This evergreen ballad, published in 1934, was recorded early in 1935 by Henry Hall and the BBC Dance Orchestra. The vocalist was Dan Donovan, who had succeeded Les Allen in September, 1934.

Henry Hall and his 'boys' had leading roles in *Music Hath Charms*, an Associated British film made in 1935 at Elstree. At the time it was highly successful; but as shown on Channel 4 in 1986, the zany humour seemed more absurd than hilarious, while the acting by the supporting cast was stilted.

As a museum piece, of course, it was fascinating, giving one an opportunity to see Hall himself, together with sidemen Len Bermon, Bert Read, Burton Gillis and others, as well as

Dan Donovan singing *Honey Coloured Moon*, a very pretty number by Desmond Carter and Mabel Wayne, which he and the band recorded in September.

Sidney Kyte, who had made no records since a brief flirtation with Winner ended in the summer of 1933, began to record for Panachord, a Decca-owned label, in January, 1935. He appeared on Panachord intermittently throughout the year, but was switched to Decca in 1936. Gordon and Revel's *Without a Word of Warning* was waxed for Panachord by Kyte's Piccadilly Hotel Band, the vocalist being Gerry FitzGerald.

On January 23, 1935, the BBC issued an instruction that only the melody of Benjamin Hapgood Burt's amusing song *The Pig Got Up and Slowly Walked Away* could be broadcast, and although the whole point was lost without the lyric, bandleaders had no option but to comply.

This latest example of inspired idiocy had arisen following a recent Music Hall programme in which 'objectionable' words had been used. The BBC decided to tighten up censorship, but why the chill of official displeasure should have embraced such a harmless song baffled its London publishers, Irwin Dash. It had already been recorded for Decca in October, 1934, by Frank Crumit; and would be recorded for Victor in July, 1935, by Rudy Vallee, neither of whom had any use for smut.

The Pig Got Up and Slowly Walked Away was recorded by Bert Ambrose and his Orchestra, with a Sam Browne vocal, and appeared on Decca. The BBC edict kept it off the air, but public curiosity probably increased sales of this inoffensive disc.

In November, 1934, *Revenge with Music* had opened at the New Amsterdam Theatre, with Libby Holman in the cast. It was an unsuccessful venture by Howard Dietz and Arthur Schwartz, who had written a lovely song for it. *You and the Night and the Music* made a delightful Ambrose and Browne recording, to which the unduly sensitive BBC could not possibly object.

Warner's *Gold Diggers of 1935*, starring Dick Powell, Gloria Stuart and Adolphe Menjou, was damned by the faint praise of the critics, but had a superb Busby Berkeley dance spectacular, built around Dubin and Warren's *Lullaby of Broadway,* which Winifred Shaw sang. Streets ahead of most contemporary songs, it was another recorded by Ambrose and Browne, aided by Ronnie Hill, Clive Erard and Jack Lorimer, who called themselves the Rhythm Brothers.

Maurice Winnick: Sweet music in the Lombardo manner.

Sam Browne made no records with Ambrose from July, 1935, to October, 1936, his place being taken by Jack Cooper, a Londoner, born on March 21, 1911, among whose earliest recordings was *Nothing Lives Longer Than Love*, a Sam Lewis and Pete Wendling ballad. Donald Stewart, who sang briefly for Ambrose, recorded *The Good Green Acres of Home*, an Irving Kahal and Sammy Fain contribution to Warner's *Sweet Music*, starring Rudy Vallee and Ann Dvorak. Band shows were still very popular, and at the end of July Ambrose began a two-week engagement at the London Palladium.

MGM's *Broadway Melody of 1936,* actually made in 1935, teamed Jack Benny, Robert Taylor and Eleanor Powell. For it, Arthur Freed and Nacio Herb Brown wrote *You are My Lucky Star,* which Cooper recorded with Ambrose late in the year.

Beyond question, the most distinctive style to be adopted by a London bandleader in the Thirties was that of Maurice Winnick who, after years of successful playing without any particular indentifying feature, suddenly emerged as the British counterpart of Guy Lombardo. *The Sweetest Music This Side of Heaven* could thus be heard live this side of the Atlantic, and the Cliff Friend – Carmen Lombardo title song was recorded by Winnick in 1935 for Parlophone, with a vocal by Sam Costa, Judy Shirley and a trio.

Born in Manchester on March 28, 1902, Winnick, as a child, had studied violin in his native city and later in Belgium. At 14 he was a violinist in a Manchester cinema, but eventually led a band on an Atlantic liner. Visits to America enabled him to study the saxophone there, and in 1922 he left the sea to play at home with various bands.

In 1927 he was doubling violin and saxophone in a nineman combo at Manchester's Rivoli Ballroom; the following year he began to direct his own band at the Plaza Dance Hall. London called, and he was soon leading a quintet at the Hammersmith Palais de Danse.

An engagement at the Piccadilly Hotel in 1930 was a major step forward, and he made his first broadcast from there. Two years later he became resident bandleader at the Carlton Hotel, which was bombed out during the war. Constantly changing venues, he went to Ciro's Club in 1933.

Winnick's most significant move occurred in 1934, when he opened at the San Marco Restaurant in Mayfair, for there he decided (with Lombardo's permission) to use the 'Sweet Music' style for which he is best remembered. He stayed at the San Marco until October, 1936, and it was there, at the start of the previous year, he engaged Sam Costa as pianist and singer, although Costa subsequently concentrated on singing, giving up the piano stool to fellow singer Ronnie O'Dell.

Winnick's later career was equally impressive. He played for a time at the May Fair Hotel, and in 1939 went to the Dorchester, after which he toured. He disbanded in 1950, became a famous impresario, and died on May 29, 1962.

In complete contrast, Carroll Gibbons was perfectly content to direct his Savoy Hotel Orpheans in a style that changed very little over the years. Lewis Ilda and Sam Coslow's *Some Other Time* and Jimmy Kennedy's *On the Other Side of the Hill* were among his 1935 recordings, each with a Brian Lawrance vocal, featuring some tasteful piano in Gibbons' individual manner.

Carroll Gibbons and his Boy Friends, a smaller group, provided accompaniment for a Hildegarde recording, made for Columbia. *Darling, Je Vous Aime Beaucoup* had been written for 'The Irresistible Singer' by Anna Sosenko, and the public liked its ridiculous mixture of English and French. Hildegarde, an internationally famous French cabaret star, also recorded *I'm in the Mood for Love,* a languorous love song by Dorothy Fields and Jimmy McHugh, which suited her rather caressing style.

Hildegarde: Irresistible 'Hildie' made a lot of records for Columbia in the second half of the Thirties, followed by some for Decca.

MGM's *Reckless* starred Jean Harlow, William Powell and tenor Allan Jones, making his screen debut. It had two good songs, the title ballad, created by Oscar Hammerstein II and Jerome Kern, and *Everything's Been Done Before*, the work of Harold Adamson, Edwin H. Knopf and Jack King. As fox-trots, both were recorded for Victor by Richard Himber and his Ritz-Carlton Orchestra, with vocalists Stuart Allen and Joey Nash respectively.

Harold Adamson was born in Greenville, New Jersey, on December 10, 1906. He collaborated with many song composers, Jimmy McHugh, Hoagy Carmichael, Walter Donaldson and Vincent Youmans among them.

Top Hat, an RKO film co-starring Fred Astaire and Ginger Rogers, demonstrated conclusively that Irving Berlin's songwriting genius was in high gear again. Eddy Duchin and his Orchestra recorded *Cheek to Cheek* for Victor, with vocalist Lew Sherwood, while *Isn't This a Lovely Day?* appeared here on Rex, recorded by Archie Bleyer and his Orchestra, with Chick Bullock.

A violinist and gifted arranger, Bleyer had a 'house' band typifying the sweet style now going out of favour. The brass section included trombonist Russ Morgan, who formed a very 'Mickey Mouse' super-sweet band and, with his Music in the Russ Morgan Manner, successfully resisted the onslaught of swing. His 1949 recording of *So Tired*, with its wailing, muted trombone and his own vocal, was a best-seller here on Brunswick.

Fare Thee Well, Annabelle, a light-hearted ditty by Mort Dixon and Allie Wrubel, was featured in Warner's *Sweet Music*, which illustrated all too clearly Rudy Vallee's acting limitations at this time. His co-star was Ann Dvorak; and Helen Morgan was among a strong supporting cast.

The song was given an ebullient performance by Chick Bullock, backed by an equally lively pick-up band. Made in New York for A.R.C., it appeared here on Rex, backed by the 'house' band of Will Osborne, who took his own vocal on Harry Woods' *I'll Never Say 'Never Again' Again*.

Of English parentage, Charles 'Chick' Bullock was born in Butte, Montana, on September 16, 1900, and for a time acted with a repertory company in Denver, Colorado. Later he went to Hollywood, appearing in a number of silent films. It was his wife, Mary Newton, an operetta star, who suggested New York might offer him greater opportunities, and there he was signed up by the American Record Corporation, for whom he made more than a thousand sides from 1930 to 1941, under his own name, or with bands also under contract to A.R.C.

In addition, he made Victor records with such noted bandleaders as Don Azpiazu, Duke Ellington, Johnny Hamp, Luis Russell and Fred Waring. His last recording, *There'll be Some Changes Made*, a song by Billy Higgins and W. B.Overstreet first heard in 1929, was waxed for Okeh in February, 1941.

Returning to Hollywood, where Mary was appearing on radio and later on television, Chick went into the real estate business for a time, but by the early Sixties was in retirement. He died in Los Angeles on September 15, 1981.

Having taken his angry leave of the Dorsey Brothers' Dance Band, Tommy Dorsey wasted no time forming one of his own, which began to record for Victor in September, 1935. It typified the forceful, clean-sounding swing bands which began to set the pace for future dance music in America. A smaller band-within-a-band, the Clambake Seven, played a more jazzy style of music.

Alone, a stylish love song by Arthur Freed and Nacio Herb Brown, was sung by Allan Jones in MGM's *A Night at the Opera*, a classic Marx Brothers comedy. It made an early recording for Tommy Dorsey and his Orchestra, with vocalist Cliff Weston.

Born into an Irish-American family in Shenandoah, Pennsylvania, on November 19, 1905, Tommy Dorsey received a thorough early training on both trumpet and trombone from his father. His instantly recognisable trombone solos graced scores of session recordings, but he also worked with such important bandleaders as Paul Whiteman and Jean Goldkette.

The estrangement with his elder brother Jimmy, a much more tractable individual, lasted for 18 years, although they did come together (with Whiteman) in 1947 to star in United Artists' biopic *The Fabulous Dorseys*. Reconciled in 1953, they began to co-direct a band which recorded for CBS, but Tommy died in Greenwich, Connecticut, on November 26, 1956, to be mourned as a superlative musician, not unkindly despite his explosive temper.

'One of the most tasteful, versatile and musicianly outfits of all time,' was how George T. Simon, editor of Metronome Magazine, and a former drummer, once described Ray Noble's first American band, and he was not one to hand out valueless compliments. Indeed, radio transcripts and Victor records support that assessment. It was an immaculate band which began inauspiciously and ended disastrously.

The Rockwell-O'Keefe Agency had lured Noble, Bowlly and Harty to New York, and it was the agency which unwittingly sowed the seeds of inevitable discord by introducing Noble to Glenn Miller, late of the Dorsey Brother's band, an abrasive, ambitious individual as obstinate in his way as the more reserved Englishman. He was, however, a greatly respected trombonist and a capable arranger. Moreover, he knew where to find the kind of quality players that Noble needed.

Things might have gone smoothly had Noble formed his own band, but he experienced delay in getting an AFM membership card and, putting things in Miller's hands, went to Hollywood, where he wrote music for *The Big Broadcast of 1936.* When he got back to New York, a well-rehearsed band, with an incredibly starry line-up awaited him, but the players understandably looked to Miller for direction, rather than to the elegant, soft-spoken stranger.

Nevertheless, the band prospered for a time. It cut its first Victor sides in February, among them *Down by the River*, a gentle Rodgers and Hart ballad from the film *Mississippi*. The vocal was by Al Bowlly, who never sounded better than when he was in the States.

In April the band opened at the Rainbow Room, high up in the RCA Building, in Manhattan. At that plushy Society venue it was required to play from 9pm to 3am every night of the week. Two months later, the band recorded Irving Berlin's *Top Hat, White Tie and Tails*, another song from the film *Top Hat*, for which Bowlly was joined by the Freshmen, an exuberant, all-male vocal group.

With smoothly orchestrated arrangements by Noble, brassier, up-tempo ones by Miller, an almost all-star line-up and an enviable location, recording and broadcasting frequently, the band seemed to have embarked on a fair-weather voyage. So buoyant was the early mood that nobody saw the breakers lying ahead.

Chapter Fourteen

1936–37

'Love Is A Dancing Thing'

At the start of 1936, Jack Hylton had two bands, that under his personal direction in Chicago, which established itself at the Drake Hotel and began to broadcast, and the British one he had been forced to leave behind. Under Billy Ternent's direction, the latter made a most unusual record in January. For *Moanin' Minnie*, a blues-influenced opus by Sigler, Goodhart and Hoffman, the vocal was belted out with incredible assurance by a deep-voiced 12-year-old named Pat Sibley, later to become famous as Anne Shelton.

Hylton's short-lived American band cut some sides at Victor's Chicago studio in January. It included trombonist Murray McEachern, who joined Benny Goodman that year, and famous drummer George Wettling. Vocalists not being under the same union restrictions as musicians, Pat O'Malley had his first chance to sing with an American ensemble.

He had the vocal spot for *Lights Out*, a sentimental ballad by Billy Hill which was not a great success in the States. Bland as ever, O'Malley would probably have made a good substitute for Ray Eberle with the Miller band. As far as I know, however, he never did sing for an American bandleader after he left Hylton.

Edgar Leslie and Joe Burke's *A Little Bit Independent* was too lively to suit O'Malley's style and handed to the Merry Macs, a quartet, who swung it joyfully. There was nothing about Hylton's Drake Hotel Orchestra, on records at least, to suggest it was in any way superior to the one he had led at home.

On his return to Britain in July, Hylton quickly assembled a 25-piece showband which began to record in August but was broken up at the end of the year. With five brass, five reeds, two flutes, six violins, two harps (one played by Sidonie Goossens), and five rhythm, it was the biggest and most sophisticated concert band ever seen in this country. Paul Whiteman's star might be waning, but his mantle had fallen on his sincerest admirer.

The rich, full sound of this magnificent band was effectively demonstrated when it recorded *Midnight Blue*, a gorgeous torch song by Edgar Leslie and Joe Burke, dramatically rendered by Jewel Faye, a member of the mixed-voice Swingtette, brought over by Hylton from America. This superb singer remained with Hylton until the spring of 1937 when, presumably, most of the Swingtette went home.

Frances McCarty certainly remained behind. In the autumn of 1938 she was part of a vocal quartet appearing with Hugo

Opposite – Pre-recorded commercial radio shows attracted a lot of listeners. These are all from the late Thirties.

TO ENTERTAIN YOU WITH THE MOST THRILLING
MUSIC, THE FUNNIEST BACKCHAT ON THE RADIO

The New
Rinso Radio Revue

SUNDAYS AT 6.30
LUXEMBOURG — NORMANDY
(Transmission for Normandy arranged through the
International Broadcasting Company Limited.)

December 26th

JACK HYLTON
AND HIS BAND

WITH THE ONE AND ONLY
LESLIE HENSON

"HUTCH"
(LESLIE A. HUTCHINSON)

ALICE MANN
(THE PERSONALITY GIRL)

DICK MURPHY
(THE SINGING STAR)

PEGGY DELL
(THE IRISH SINGER)

THE HENDERSON TWINS
(BRIGHT—FRESH—and just 16!)

EDDIE POLA
(COMPÈRE EXTRAORDINARY)

GOLDEN VOICE

Listen to the
All-Star Show!

COOKEEN
COOKING FAT

RADIO PROGRAMME

A dazzling pot-pourri of
SONG - RHYTHM - LAUGHTER
with

CARROLL GIBBONS
and his boys

and favourite guest artists

RADIO LUXEMBOURG : MONDAYS 10–10.30 a.m.
RADIO NORMANDY : SATURDAYS 10–10.30 a.m.

DON'T FORGET THE SUNDAY PROGRAMMES
COOKEEN CABARET
Sundays: LUXEMBOURG   NORMANDY
11.30–11.45 a.m.   9–9.15 a.m.
Radio Normandy transmission arranged through I.B.C. Ltd.

RADIO'S
PICK OF THE WEEK

GRACIE **FIELDS**

and not just once a week,
but twice a week comes our
own inimitable Gracie Fields.
A song, a joke   an entertainment you must never miss.

FAIRY SOAP
PROGRAMMES

LUXEMBOURG
Sundays   2.45–3.00 p.m.

NORMANDY
Wednesdays - 3.15–3.30 p.m.

*Transmissions from Radio
Normandy arranged through
International Broadcasting
Co. Ltd.

Alice Mann had a good voice, but husband Billy Bissett hogged the vocals on the eight sides he made for HMV in 1937.

Bert Yarlett, a Canadian who sang for Jack Hylton and Henry Hall.

Rignold and his Orchestra. She had married Bruce Campbell, who was a trombonist with the band.

20th Century-Fox's *Sing, Baby, Sing*, starring Alice Faye, Tony Martin and Adolphe Menjou, had a brace of good songs to help it along, both being recorded by Hylton's new band. Sidney Mitchell and Louis Alter's *You Turned the Tables on Me* was blithely carolled by the Swingtette, while Jack Yellen and Lew Pollack's title song featured the fine voice of Alice Mann. Married to Billy Bissett, a Canadian, she could be heard on his HMV records in 1937 when he was resident bandleader at the May Fair Hotel.

Hylton's remarkable showband also recorded a new composition by Vivian Ellis, *Drop In, Next Time You're Passing*. The vocal was by Bert Yarlett, a Canadian who made a few records with the BBC Dance Orchestra that year.

Early in 1936, Jack Payne disbanded, but by August had a new, 17-man ensemble, with which he resumed his Rex contract. After about three months he broke up that band too, making no more records for three years. Among his last sides for Rex was *Until the Real Thing Comes Along*, by Sammy Cahn, Saul Chaplin and L. E. Freeman, sung by Billy Scott-Coomber.

Sidney Kyte also dropped out of the record supplements. On June 22 he left the Piccadilly Hotel to begin his variety tour. Eight days later he made four sides for Decca, one being Irving Berlin's *A Pretty Girl is Like a Melody*. Apart from two tunes recorded for Rex, almost three years later, he ceased to record.

Little Harry Roy had become immensely popular, but his ebullient personality, raucous singing voice, shrill clarinet and uninhibited band must have profoundly shaken the sedate May Fair Hotel. His departure at the end of June probably came as a great relief to those who longed for the return of Ambrose and his more subdued style. They had only three months to wait, although this time Ambrose did not stay very long. After that they got Maurice Winnick, whose heavenly harmonies must have been equally welcome.

Goody! Goody! a 'serves you right!' novelty by Johnny Mercer and Matty Malneck (who was in the reed section of Bob Crosby's band), and *Is It True What They Say About Dixie?* an Irving Caesar, Sammy Lerner and Gerald Marks effusion, sentimentalising over the Deep South, were recorded while Roy was still at the May Fair; *Pick Yourself Up* and *A Fine Romance*, both by Dorothy Fields and Jerome Kern, four months after he had left. All had vocals by Roy himself.

A Fine Romance came from RKO's *Swing Time*, co-starring Fred Astaire and Ginger Rogers, and featuring George Metaxa. The film's Musical Director was Nathaniel Shilkret.

The prettiest song in *Swing Time* was *The Way You Look Tonight*, a triumph equally for Fields and Kern. It won an Oscar for the best film song of 1936. It was recorded by Roy Fox and his Band, with Denny Dennis, as was *Serenade in the Night*, an Italian hit by C. A. Bixio and B. Cherubini, given an English lyric by Jimmy Kennedy. For the latter, Dennis sang the entire song and not just the chorus, which was quite unusual in those days.

This'll Make You Whistle opened at the Palace Theatre in September, with Jack Buchanan in the lead. It had lyrics and music by Sigler, Goodhart and Hoffman, including *I'm in a Dancing Mood*, which was recorded as a fox-trot by Carroll Gibbons and his Savoy Hotel Orpheans, with Anne Lenner.

Gibbons also recorded *These Foolish Things*, an evocative, late-night ballad by Holt Marvell, Harry Link and Jack Strachey with a vocal by Brian Lawrance, while George Melachrino stepped out of the reed section to sing Fields and Kern's *Never Gonna Dance*, another hit from *Swing Time*. Of Greek parentage, he was born in London on May 1, 1909, and joined Gibbons in 1932, playing with the band for seven years.

After the war, Melachrino became famous for his big concert orchestra, rivalling that of Mantovani. Its treatment of delicate melodies was sometimes insensitive, but it did make some attractive records for HMV, *La Golondrina* (1948), and *The Legend of the Glass Mountain* (1949), among them. George Melachrino died on June 18, 1965.

Composer Jack Strachey, born in Chelsea on September 25, 1894, went to Marlborough and University College, Oxford. His career in show business started in 1919 when he joined the Quaints, a concert party, as pianist. After a thorough grounding in such entertainment he turned to the West End, composing the music for *Dear Little Billie* (1925), and *Lady Luck* (1927), both with H. B. Hedley, as well as for André Charlot revues. Throughout the war years he wrote music for ENSA productions.

Fritz Kreisler, although world renowned as a violinist, never disdained popular music, recording many tunes as violin solos for Victor. He is believed to have donated his royalties from such records to his favourite charities. Dorothy Fields wrote a lyric for his waltz *Stars in My Eyes*, which

Maurice Winnick and his Sweet Music recorded, with a vocal by Joe Leigh.

Like *Hit the Deck*, RKO's *Follow the Fleet* was based on Hubert Osborne's play *Shore Leave*. It starred Fred Astaire, Ginger Rogers and Randolph Scott; with Lucille Ball, Betty Grable and Tony Martin lending support. Irving Berlin's *We Saw the Sea* and *Let's Face the Music and Dance* were written for this movie. Both were recorded by Billy Cotton and his Band, with Alan Breeze.

Quiet and unassuming Charlie Kunz chose from the best available to sing for the Casani Club Orchestra. Among them was George Barclay, who appeared with Mantovani in his pre-concert orchestra days, and later with Felix Mendelssohn's Hawaiian Serenaders. Two of his records with Kunz were *Love is a Dancing Thing*, by Howard Dietz and Arthur Schwartz, and *The White Cliffs of Dover*, a pretty song by Harry Leon and Leo Towers, not to be confused with Vera Lynn's later hit, which had bluebirds flying over them.

Vocalists were still anonymous on Rex labels, but they made an exception sometimes of Vera Lynn; a delicate compliment. Her early recordings with the Casani Club Orchestra were charming, and it was obvious a star had been born. *Have You Forgotten So Soon?* was a routine ballad by Joe Gilbert and Horatio Nicholls, but it had a little extra something when sung by Vera Lynn.

Cyril Grantham, who played alto saxophone and clarinet for Geraldo, among others, was a highly regarded vocalist who has only in recent years become of interest to dance music enthusiasts. Geraldo knew his worth, featuring him on Erell Reaves and Tolchard Evans' *Whistling Waltz*.

Cyril Grantham: In 1950 he returned to Geraldo.

Born in Manchester on June 16, 1910, Grantham could be heard on a number of recordings made by the Casani Club Orchestra that year, but he had been playing for Geraldo since 1933, and was still Geraldo's vocalist and sideman when the Thirties ended. Eventually he moved on, but rejoined his old leader in the summer of 1950.

The singing cowboy still rode the range in 1936, and Billy Hill's mournful *Empty Saddles* sold a lot of records. Bert Ambrose recorded it with Jack Cooper, together with Johnny Mercer's *I'm an Old Cowhand from the Rio Grande*, which poked a little gentle fun at Western songs. It was sung by Bing Crosby in Paramount's *Rhythm on the Range*.

Half-way through September, Ambrose returned to the May Fair Hotel, and in October Sam Browne replaced Jack

Cooper, being the vocalist for Cole Porter's *Easy to Love* and *I've Got You Under My Skin*, two memorable songs from MGM's *Born to Dance*, teaming Eleanor Powell, James Stewart and Virginia Bruce.

In the spring, the famous black bandleader, multi-instrumentalist and arranger Benny Carter came to London. While here he provided Henry Hall with some very modern arrangements of current songs, such as *I'm Putting All My Eggs in One Basket*, another Berlin song from *Follow the Fleet*. It was recorded in April, with a Dan Donovan vocal.

Late in May, Hall handed over his baton to Bert Read, his pianist and staff arranger (who died in 1985), so that he could cross the Atlantic on the R.M.S. Queen Mary's maiden voyage. A few weeks earlier, the BBC Dance Orchestra had recorded Hall's *Somewhere at Sea*, also with a Donovan vocal. The song became the great liner's official signature tune.

During Hall's absence the band continued to record, Columbia perpetrating an earlier BBC deception by labelling such sides as being under Hall's direction. One such was Sam Coslow's *Got to Dance My Way to Heaven in Your Arms*, a routine song, well handled by Donovan.

Rusty Brown was a little boy with the reddest head of hair, and Dusty (his dog) was the colour of a teddy bear, Jimmy Kennedy and Michael Carr informed us in a cheerful song called *Rusty and Dusty*, which delighted the much less sophisticated children of 1936. It sounds quaint today; and the vocal by the Three Sisters – we know them only as Marie, Mary and Molly – comes over rather stilted, with impeccable, cut-glass accents. Hall was back in charge when this was recorded.

Ay, Ay, Ay! a lament for unrequited love, had first appeared in 1927. With a lyric by Max Gartman and a lively Spanish melody by Osman Perez Freire, it was quite a hit when revived nine years later. Troise and his Mandoliers recorded it for Rex, with a concert tenor vocal by Birrell O'Malley, as Don Carlos.

The 'house' bands assembled for Crown by Jay Wilbur often had a strong flavour of swing. The Rhythm Rascals recorded *The Music Goes 'Round and Around*, a nonsensical ditty by Red Hodgson, Edward Farley and Michael Riley, which provided an excuse for some good, hot solos. Billy Farrell (trumpet), Freddy Gardner (doubling alto saxophone and clarinet), Ted Heath (trombone), and Max Abrams

Freddy Gardner: Played hot for Jay Wilbur and sweet for Peter Yorke.

(drums), helped to ensure that things really did go with a swing. The vocalist was Gerry FitzGerald.

For two sides waxed by the Swing Rhythm Boys in September, Wilbur chose good old tunes, well suited for a hotter session band. Shelton Brooks' *Some of these Days* (1910), and Leo Wood's *Somebody Stole My Gal* (1922), were performed by men capable of giving a good account of themselves in up-tempo numbers, aided by Jack Cooper's vocals.

A fine example of loose-knit, gently swinging music was provided by the Radio Serenaders, yet another Crown 'house' combo. *Moon Over Miami* was the perfect romantic ballad, written by Edgar Leslie and composed by Joe Burke. Wilbur's session men, Gardner, Heath and Max Abrams among them, showed that swing music could sound relaxed and mellow, preserving the melody. Sam Costa's vocal fitted in well.

Costa was a Londoner, born in 1910. During his war service he met Kenneth Horne and Richard 'Stinker' Murdoch, becoming a key figure in the BBC's *Much Binding in the Marsh* (a humorous allusion to R.A.F. Moreton-in-Marsh), which remained popular in the early post-war period. From 1976 to June, 1981, he presented *Glamorous Nights* weekly over Radio 2. Kindly and well-liked, he died on September 23, 1981.

Sam was the singer on a Primo Scala recording of *When the Poppies Bloom Again*, a British hit by Leo Towers, Morton Morrow and Don Pelosi. He always gave the impression of being very relaxed. In all probability he would have become a singing star, had the war not turned him into a radio comedian instead.

Although Jimmy Kennedy had begun a profitable association with Michael Carr, he still wrote lyrics for Will Grosz, whose *Bird on the Wing* had a typically lilting melody. It was recorded for HMV by the baritone Robert Ashley who, in 1939, began to sing for Jack Payne.

Having played and sung for British bandleaders for ten years, Les Allen had bade Henry Hall an amicable farewell in the summer of 1934 to try his luck in Variety. His Canadian Bachelors became popular and began to record for Columbia, being featured on the magenta label, launched in 1935 at 1s 6d (7½p) each.

A Melody from the Sky was typical of the Canadian Bachelors' breezy style. A ballad by Sidney Mitchell and Louis Alter, it came from Paramount's *The Trail of the Lonesome Pine*, in which Sylvia Sidney, Fred MacMurray (a

Robert Ashley made a few solo records for HMV before joining Jack Payne in 1939.

former dance band saxophonist) and Henry Fonda appeared in decidedly unnatural hues of Technicolor.

In 1936, the constant friction between Glenn Miller and Ray Noble came to a head, and the former departed; unfortunately, so did Charlie Spivak, Will Bradley, Bud Freeman and Claude Thornhill, leaving Noble without a single star player. He found replacements, but much of the magic had gone.

Worse was to follow. Perhaps grown weary of the feuding, Al Bowlly left for London in December, after which there was no magic at all. The band lost its great following, and the Rainbow Room decided they could do without it. 1937 would begin as a very bleak year for the disillusioned Englishman whose magnificent band was falling apart.

Nevertheless, recordings made in 1936 still sounded very stylish and relaxed. *The Touch of Your Lips*, a charming serenade by Noble, had an impeccable vocal by Bowlly; Andy Razaf and Fernando Arbelo's *Big Chief de Sota* had a

Al Bowlly, seen here singing at the Rainbow Room with Ray Noble's lovely but ill-fated band, probably in 1936.

humorous vocal duet by Bowlly and trumpeter Sterling Bose, brought in to replace Spivak; and *Where the Lazy River Goes By*, a soothing little ditty by Harold Adamson and Jimmy McHugh, brought out the best in Bowlly's silken voice.

The last of these songs had been featured in 20th Century-Fox's *Banjo on My Knee*, starring Barbara Stanwyck, Joel McCrea and Walter Brennan, sung by Miss Stanwyck herself.

No band better deserved the unwelcome 'Mickey Mouse' soubriquet than Shep Fields and his Rippling Rhythm. To dip a straw in water and bubble it before the commencement of a broadcast was surely the ultimate in ludicrous gimmickry. Apart from that, the band was pleasant but undistinguished. Its recording of Robin and Rainger's *A Rendezvous with a Dream*, made at Victor's New York studios, appeared here on Regal-Zonophone, the vocalist being Charles Chester.

Billy Mayhew's *It's a Sin to Tell a Lie* was a curiously old-fashioned song and his only best-seller. It was recorded for Victor in New York by George Hall and his Hotel Taft Orchestra, with a vocal by Dolly Dawn. This too was issued by Regal-Zonophone.

Hall's band, which used to broadcast from the Taft's Grill Room, had no special qualities, but at least its leader eschewed gimmickry. When he retired in July, 1941, Hall made a present of the band to Dolly Dawn.

Johnny Johnson was another bandleader happy to play sweet music in a pedestrian manner. His records for the A.R.C. Group – it included Banner, Melotone, Oriole and Perfect – were distributed here by Rex. Among them were *Let's Sing Again*, an unexceptional fox-trot by Gus Kahn and Jimmy McHugh, and *South Sea Island Magic*, by Lysle Tomerlin and Andy Iona Long, a song which deserved a more stylish performance.

Saddle Your Blues to a Wild Mustang was not so much a cowboy song as an antidote for the megrims. George Whiting and Buddy Bernier wrote the lyric; Billy Haid the swingy tune. It was fine for Paul Whiteman, who recorded it for Victor in New York with Bob Lawrence and the King's Men, but hardly suitable for Peter Dawson, who waxed it for HMV.

But by 1936, few new concert ballads were appearing (although Dawson composed a few himself around that time), and the Australian bass-baritone must have been hard-pressed to find fresh songs worthy of his magnificent voice.

* * *

In 1937, British Lion announced that they were to make a film called *Song Writers on Parade* at their Beaconsfield studios. They were hoping to feature, among others, Jimmy Kennedy, Michael Carr, Elton Box, Sonny Cox, Paddy Roberts, Horatio Nicholls, Annette Mills, Ralph Butler, Harry Carlton and Arthur Le Clerq.

The last-named, a prolific songwriter, was responsible for such shafts of musical wit as *Is Izzy Azzy Wozz? Nobody Loves a Fairy When She's Forty* and *He Played his Ukulele as the Ship Went Down*. It took all sorts, especially in the diverse world of popular songs, and Le Clerq made quite a name for himself. He was born at Brixton in 1893.

It would be of great interest to know whether the film was released, and if a print still exists. The majority of British songwriters rarely courted personal publicity, and the historic value of such a movie would be inestimable.

Charlie Kunz took his Casani Club Orchestra to the Rex studios for the last time in March before disbanding. Mack Gordon and Harry Revel's *Goodnight, My Love*, sung by Vera Lynn, was one of the four songs recorded.

Brian Lawrance, still resident at Lansdowne House, recorded throughout 1937 for Rex with his Sextet or Orchestra. In May he recorded *September in the Rain*, that perfect expression of a melancholy, early-autumn mood by Dubin and Warren.

September in the Rain began in 1935 purely as a background melody in Warner's *Stars Over Broadway*, and came into its own two years later in another Warner movie, *Melody for Two*, starring James Melton and Patricia Ellis.

Billy Cotton was not only a consummate showman but a highly skilled racing motorist. In March he won the Easter Short Handicap at Brooklands, reaching 111 m.p.h. His band made some lovely records in 1937, sensitive in both arrangement and performance.

Two which come readily to mind are Irving Kahal and John Jacob Loeb's *You're Here, You're There*, and Jack Sharpe and Jerry Herst's *So Rare*, the latter a runaway hit for Jimmy Dorsey some years later. Each had an Alan Breeze vocal.

Breeze and Cotton also recorded *At the Balalaika*, by Eric Maschwitz and George Posford. It came from Maschwitz's musical play *Balalaika*, which had music by Posford and the Viennese composer Bernard Grün. It had opened at the Adelphi in December, 1936, with Clifford Mollison and Betty Warren sharing the lead.

Primo Scala's Accordion Band helped to keep Rex profitable, which probably saved the label when Decca purchased Crystalate in March. Crown was less fortunate, and that meant curtains for Harry Bidgood's equally popular venture as 'Rossini'.

Primo Scala recorded Jimmy Kennedy and Michael Carr's *Hometown*, a hit from the Palladium revue *London Rhapsody*, which began in September. The nostalgic, slightly Americanised lyric and cheerfully catchy tune made the song ideal for a piano-accordion rendition, and for the kind of vocal that the Three Ginx always handled well.

The demise of Crown more or less put an end to the recording activities of Billy Merrin and his Commanders. Their last Crown session took place in March, the month in which the label was phased out. It included Rodgers and Hart's title song from *On Your Toes*, a revue which had opened at New York's Imperial Theatre in April, 1936. Save for four sides made for Rex in November, Merrin left the record catalogues.

On the other hand, a new band cut a handful of sides for HMV in March and June, after which it made no more. Billy Bissett had become resident at the May Fair Hotel, directing his band from the piano. According to a *News Chronicle* report, he made his first broadcast from there in May. Most of the records had his own vocals, but Alice Mann was heard on *There's a Lull in My Life*, by the prolific partnership of Gordon and Revel.

There's a Small Hotel had that touch of distinction which turned so many Rodgers and Hart ballads into standards. It was another contribution to *On Your Toes*. Nobody could have sung it better than Jewel Faye, again helping to make a Jack Hylton recording something special.

This was waxed in January by another of his big bands, which only survived until the end of spring. At the same session, Hylton's new vocalist, Tom Wareing, sang *Pennies from Heaven*, Arthur Johnston and John Burke's title song from a Columbia film starring Bing Crosby. Hylton's make and break policy took a rest after he disposed of this band. His next was not assembled until the autumn of 1938, thus creating a recording gap of 15 months.

Billy Hill, still a very active songwriter, was inclined to follow one successful song with another rather too similar in theme. *In the Chapel in the Moonlight* and *In the Mission by the Sea*, the latter a collaboration with Peter de Rose, provide good examples of a somewhat unimaginative trend, pleasant though they both were.

Billy Bissett, Canadian pianist who directed a band at the May Fair Hotel in 1937.

Joe Loss recorded the first song for Regal-Zonophone, with Chick Henderson, having joined that label in November, 1936, after appearing for the previous 12 months on HMV, while Maurice Winnick offered a Sweet Music version of the second number on Decca, among his first recordings for them, following his departure from Parlophone. Winnick's singer was Sam Costa.

Cowboy songs were still money-spinners sometimes. Charles and Nick Kenny's *There's a Gold Mine in the Sky* certainly caught the public fancy. Winnick recorded it just after Christmas, his vocalist being Al Bowlly, now comfortably re-established in London. Winnick also recorded Harry Woods' *So Many Memories* in December, and was joined on this occasion by Vera Lynn, just two days before her twentieth birthday.

Vera Lynn, although making records for others, like most vocalists, went on Ambrose's payroll in the spring, much to the displeasure of American singer Evelyn Dall, who wanted no younger rival. *Moonlight on the Waterfall*, by Jimmy Kennedy and Will Grosz (as Hugh Williams), was recorded by Vera in the autumn, but she missed out on *Harbour Lights*, which would have been ideal for her. That smash hit by the same team, which also did very well in America, arrived very early in the year and was allocated to Sam Browne.

There is evidence to suggest that initially Ambrose failed to appreciate the potential of his latest acquisition, just as Henry Hall had turned her down after an audition. But the former's early reservations were soon dispelled. Before long, Vera Lynn's crystal clear voice was gracing many an Ambrose recording, although he retained Miss Dall's services too, for she was an excellent singer.

Paramount's *Waikiki Wedding* gave Bing Crosby a beautiful hit with *Sweet Leilani*. In fact the song had been written and composed in Hawaii about two years earlier by Harry Owens, a native of the Islands. It was dedicated to Leilani, his little daughter, whose name meant 'Heavenly Flower', and justifiably won the Motion Picture Academy award as the best film song of 1937. Sam Browne recorded it with the Ambrose band.

Blue Hawaii, a contribution by Leo Robin and Ralph Rainger to *Waikiki Wedding*, also became popular. Denny Dennis recorded it with Roy Fox, enabling people to make comparisons with Bing Crosby, if they wished. The publicity which sought to equate Dennis with the American singer probably did Dennis more harm than good. He was no copyist; and his voice was only suggestive of the Old Groaner's.

George Gershwin was at the peak of his creative powers when he died in 1937 while composing songs for *The Goldwyn Follies*. *They Can't Take That Away From Me* (with a lyric by brother Ira), is proof enough that he was still a superb songwriter. It appeared in RKO's *Shall We Dance?* starring Fred Astaire and Ginger Rogers, being sung by the former. This too was recorded by Dennis with the Fox band.

High, Wide and Handsome, a Western musical by Oscar Hammerstein II and Jerome Kern, was lavishly screened by Paramount and starred Irene Dunne, Dorothy Lamour and Randolph Scott. Its two outstanding songs, *Can I Forget You?* and *The Folks Who Live on the Hill*, were recorded by Barry Gray and Denny Dennis respectively; but, of course, everyone thinks of Crosby's classic recording of the second number.

Roy Fox had engaged Barry Gray towards the end of 1936, but used his vocal talents rather sparingly on records. He gave Gray another fine song, though, *The Night is Young and You're So Beautiful*, a lingering serenade, written by Billy Rose and Irving Kahal, for which Dana Suesse composed one of her prettiest melodies.

Barry Gray, who was also the Fox band's bass player, was in reality Eric Pountain, Denny Dennis's younger brother. He had a lighter, higher voice. Sadly, he was killed on active service when the Second World War came along.

HMV 'house' bands were never quite the same after Ray Noble crossed the Atlantic. As the Thirties moved towards their unhappy close – the Depression was over but war drums were beating softly – various men directed the New Mayfair Dance Orchestra. Harry Leader, a well-known bandleader, Philip Green, a gifted arranger, and Ronnie Munro did their best, but the old excitement was noticeably absent.

Munro also directed an HMV studio band under his own name, and on one occasion turned to *Hide and Seek*, the musical play at the Hippodrome which had lured Cicely Courtneidge away from films. She was partnered by Bobby Howes, who sang Vivian Ellis' *She's My Lovely*. It was recorded by Ronnie Munro and his Orchestra, with a vocal by Jack Cooper.

After a four-year absence from any recording studio, Jack Harris signed up with Decca in the spring of 1936, but bowed out in October. For nine months he made no more records, then in July, 1937, began to direct a new band which appeared on HMV until the Thirties were almost done.

Harris' first side for HMV was a big hit by Edgar Leslie and Joe Burke, *It Looks Like Rain in Cherry Blossom Lane*, a sort of Tin Pan Alley local weather forecast. The new Harris band had Alfie Noakes as lead trumpeter and Lew Davis as lead trombonist. The three violinists included Harris himself and Max Jaffa, who had played in earlier years for Maurice Winnick at Ciro's. Later, he became famous for his 'Palm Court' light orchestral music. On this occasion, Jack Cooper was Harris' vocalist.

Geraldo still had his Gaucho Tango Orchestra in 1937, but its days were numbered. He had become much more interested in lushly orchestrated music, using big bands. He instinctively understood how to present a singer to best advantage, and over the years used many of the finest.

He had become one of the biggest names in the business, and would remain so, among the few whose careers extended well into the post-war era. By then, however, his broadcasts and records were usually little more than a series of long vocals, with the band as accompanist.

Gerry was still on Decca in 1937, and just before Christmas, with Cyril Grantham, recorded the Gershwins' *A Foggy Day in London* and *Nice Work if You can Get It*, both from RKO's *A Damsel in Distress*, in which Joan Fontaine starred with Fred Astaire.

On September 25, the BBC Dance Orchestra went on the air for the last time, its director having decided to end his long and amicable association with Broadcasting House. As Henry Hall and his Orchestra, recording continued only until May, 1939, although he did not disband until 1949. He then went into managemant and production, being awarded the C.B.E. in 1970. He died at Eastbourne on October 28, 1989. The BBC never bothered with another 'house' dance band.

After bidding the BBC adieu, Hall took a slightly altered band on an Empire Theatre tour. Allie Wrubel and Nat Shilkret's *The First Time I Saw You* was recorded with singer Bob Mallin at Liverpool in October; *Little Old Lady*, an old-fashioned but endearing song by Stanley Adams and Hoagy Carmichael, at Edinburgh the following month, both in the theatres. The latter had a vocal by Leslie Douglas, who in 1934 had sung for Bertini and Teddy Joyce, as well as making records for Plaza as Percy Watts.

Allie Wrubel, born in January, 1905, at Middletown, Connecticut, really began to make his mark as a songwriter when he turned to Hollywood in 1934. He was still doing well

Frances Farmer: Adverse publicity wrecked her Hollywood career.

there ten years later. *The First Time I Saw You* was written for RKO's *The Toast of New York*, starring Edward Arnold, Cary Grant and Frances Farmer.

Carroll Gibbons, surely the least restless of all band-leaders, still recorded for Columbia at frequent intervals with his Savoy Hotel Orpheans. Would the original Orpheans have quit the Savoy, one wonders, had he controlled their destiny and not de Mornys? In 1937, with Anne Lenner, he recorded *That Old Feeling*, a fox-trot by Lew Brown and Sammy Fain from MGM's *The Great Ziegfeld*, a ponderous biopic starring William Powell, Luise Rainer and Myrna Loy.

In 1935, Mantovani and his Tipica Orchestra had been recording dance music for Regal-Zonophone, but the following year he dropped the 'tipica', without changing his style, and moved to Columbia, with whom he remained for the rest of the Thirties.

George Barclay seems to have been his principal vocalist, on records anyway, in 1937. He could be heard on *All Alone in Vienna*, by Leo Towers, Morton Morrow and Lewis Ilda, and another British hit, *Ten Pretty Girls*, a novelty by Jimmy Kennedy and Will Grosz. However, a minor American success, Nat Madison and Al Frazzini's *My Cabin of Dreams*, had a Ken Crossley vocal.

Annunzio Paolo Mantovani will always be remembered for his superb concert orchestras, with their soaring strings, but they began during the post-war period and made him internationally famous. Throughout the Thirties he dispensed entertainment on a less grandiose scale.

He was born at Venice on November 15, 1905, the son of Benedetto Mantovani, a violist and violinist who, in Italy, had played under the batons of Arturo Toscanini and Pietro Mascagni. Brought to England as a child, the younger Mantovani studied piano and violin under his father's tuition.

His early years brought him little fame. As Leonelli Gandino he recorded violin solos for Imperial at the start of the Thirties, together with light orchestral pieces as Gandino and his Orchestra. Harry Hudson employed him as an anonymous session violinist for his Radio dance bands.

Mantovani's upward climb really began when he formed his Tipica Orchestra and secured a lengthy engagement at the Monseigneur Restaurant while Lew Stone was there. His lunch-time broadcasts made him better known. Later he appeared at the Cafe de Paris and the San Marco Restaurant. His father was a member of the Tipica Orchestra in its early days.

Mantovani's style of dance music for Regal-Zonophone and Columbia revealed a Continental influence, but in 1940 he signed a Decca contract, and gradually light orchestral music began to take over. It was the 'Champagne Orchestra', with its 'cascading strings', which brought him world renown, aided by a best-selling record of *Diane* and *Charmaine*, made in 1951.

For that tremendous surge in popularity he owed much to his long-time arranger and piano-accordionist, Derby-born Ronald Binge, later to compose the exquisite *Elizabethan Serenade*. Without him, Mantovani might never have achieved the stature he did. After a period of illness, Mantovani died in a Tunbridge Wells nursing home on March 30, 1980.

20th Century-Fox's *On the Avenue* starred Dick Powell, Madeleine Carroll and Alice Faye. For it, Irving Berlin gave of his best with *This Year's Kisses* and *I've Got My Love to Keep Me Warm*. Both were recorded for Columbia by Hildegarde but, despite accompaniment by Carroll Gibbons and his Boy Friends, she dragged at the melodies with a laboured insensitivity quite surprising for such an experienced entertainer.

Mantovani: From session band violinist on records for Woolworth's to international fame on Decca. It took more than twenty years.

Ray Noble's demoralised band finally fell apart in February, apparently because of violent disagreement between leader and players. One of its last records, made in January, was *Slumming on Park Avenue*, another Berlin song from *On the Avenue*. The Merry Macs' vocal was supplemented by a little humour from Noble himself.

He turned his back on New York and went off to Hollywood, taking Bill Harty with him. He formed a new band on the West Coast, for which Tony Martin sang. It had nothing like the sparkle of his ill-fated Rainbow Room orchestra.

Just what provoked that last explosion has never been revealed; nor does it really matter. Ray Noble's reputation rests securely on his lovely songs and skilful arrangements, as well as his HMV 'house' records and those he made in New York. The rest of his career was simply anticlimax.

There was no combo in England to compare with Tommy Dorsey's Clambake Seven, which could pound the daylights out of a tune in the most delightful way. Its Dixie-beat was ideal for Rodgers and Hart's *The Lady is a Tramp*, from *Babes in Arms*, a Shubert Theatre production which opened in April. Hart's ironic lyric was handled by Edythe Wright.

Neither *The Lady is a Tramp* nor *My Funny Valentine* from

Edythe Wright made her first Victor record with Tommy Dorsey's band in September, 1935. She also appeared with his Clambake Seven.

the same show was recorded at the time by a British band, but then *Babes in Arms* never reached London, and its fine songs had to wait for other bands and singers here at a later date.

It was perhaps poetic justice that Glenn Miller's first venture as a bandleader should end disastrously. Formed in January, 1937, its line-up included trumpeters Charlie Spivak and Sterling Bose, and pianist Howard Smith, all former Noble alumni; Hal McIntyre, doubling clarinet and alto saxophone, who stayed with Miller for years but eventually led his own band; and drummer George Simon, better known as *Metronome's* editor and as an author. The vocalist was Doris Kerr.

The band swung loosely, with no identifying style, and achieved nothing better than one-night stands. It appears to have been an unhappy one too, for which Miller's driving, abrasive and humourless personality may have been partly responsible.

A big band cost a lot of money to run, and this one ran at a loss right from the start. In March it cut six rather odd sides for Decca (issued here on Brunswick), including *Moonlight Bay* (1912), and *Peg o' My Heart* (1913), which illustrate Miller's paucity of ideas at that time. He still had much to learn, but he knew when to cut his losses. At the end of 1937 he broke the band up.

Chapter Fifteen

1938–39

'I Let A Song Go Out Of My Heart'

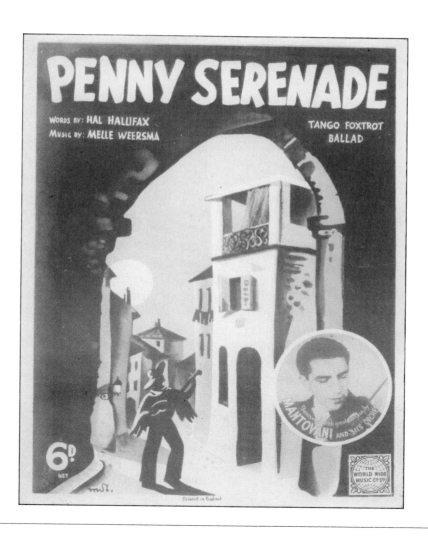

The American sweet bands were facing a bleak future, with a few notable exceptions. Paul Whiteman was shrewd enough to accept that swing had come to stay, but his belated attempt to embrace the new style was none too successful. Most of the famous leaders of the Twenties and early Thirties were already half-forgotten. Even Ben Selvin, one of the most enduring, had disbanded four years previously. Quite logically, it was younger men, black and white, who swung into the Forties, adding a vital new chapter to the annals of popular music.

By 1938 the so-called 'golden age' was virtually over in Britain. Few exciting new bands would emerge in the following decade, and many leaders here too had disbanded or ceased to record. Dance music was no longer the big seller it had been in palmier days, and the recorded output of most bands had dropped sharply. As the sweet band went into decline, so the age of the vocalist began.

The down-turn of interest in British dance music is dramatically revealed by the recording ledgers of leading manufacturers. In 1932, Carroll Gibbons and the Savoy Hotel Orpheans had recorded 122 sides for Columbia in their first full year as a band; in 1938 it was as little as 38. Harry Roy was kept busy by Parlophone in 1933, notching up 100 sides; in only five years it was down to 32. Lew Stone, recording first for Decca and then Regal-Zonophone in 1934, waxed 78 tunes; but Decca only needed 36 in 1938.

Swing music was never played as much here as in the U.S.A. By the late Thirties some of our more progressive players had become aware of its exciting possibilities, of course. Nat Gonella and his Georgians were helping to spread the word; Freddy Gardner had directed some very hot sessions. But we had no torch-bearers like Benny Goodman, Tommy Dorsey, Artie Shaw, Charlie Barnet, Woody Herman, Duke Ellington, Jimmy Lunceford, Don Redman and Count Basie, and we never would have, although Ted Heath, Vic Lewis and Johnny Dankworth later directed bands of great interest, and the Squadronaires swung superbly.

In fact, most British bandleaders had become set in their ways and (disregarding Forces bands) no dramatic changes would occur before the late Forties. In 1938, Germany and Austria formed the Anschluss, in defiance of the Treaty of Versailles, and perceptive minds now saw war as inevitable. When it came, bands would be depleted as younger men were called up; inevitably, the musical standard dropped.

Roy Fox made his last recordings for HMV in early August and disbanded shortly afterwards. His last side was Duke Ellington's *I Let a Song Go Out of My Heart*, with a lyric by Irving Mills and Henry Nemo. The vocalist was Denny Dennis. For Fox, never again to direct a famous band, the title was indeed symbolic.

MGM's *Rosalie*, starring Nelson Eddy and Eleanor Powell, had a lovely song by Cole Porter, who forsook brittle sophistication for graceful romanticism. *In the Still of the Night* was recorded by Maurice Winnick and his Sweet Music, with a fine vocal by Al Bowlly.

Although Winnick continued to direct bands until the early Fifties, he made his Decca last sides in June, 1938. Al Bowlly was on hand then to sing *When the Organ Played 'O Promise Me'*, an overdose of sentiment by Jack Meskill, Al Sherman and Abner Silver; and the Trio dealt with Terry Shand and Jimmy Eaton's *Cry, Baby, Cry*. Winnick's only later recordings were a handful made for HMV at two sessions in March, 1940.

Bowlly found himself in constant demand at recording studios now that he had settled down again in London. He sounded particularly at home with Geraldo, who cushioned his voice with singularly rich orchestrations. Among Bowlly's most appealing records that year were *Penny Serenade*, by Hal Hallifax and the Dutch composer and arranger Melle Weersma, and two Frank Loesser and Hoagy Carmichael collaborations, *Heart and Soul* and *Two Sleepy People*.

Born in New York on June 29, 1910, Loesser had long been recognised as an able lyricist before he turned to composition in the Forties. He wrote much for Hollywood, but also helped to create two Broadway hits, *Guys and Dolls* (1950), and *The Most Happy Fella* (1956), both of which came later to London. He died in New York on July 28, 1969.

Bowlly put the clock back four years in 1938 by making records again with Lew Stone and his Band. One was a charming waltz, *The Girl in the Alice Blue Gown*, by a new song writing partnership, that of Hughie Charles and Ross Parker.

Two months after the Fox band broke up, Denny Dennis joined Ambrose, with whom he recorded until the summer of 1939. Their first recording together was *Love Walked In*, one of the few songs the Gershwins had written together for *The Goldwyn Follies*. Samuel Goldwyn's movie went on release in 1939, starring singer Kenny Baker, with Ella Logan in a supporting role.

Ambrose had been away from the Decca studios for

Max Bacon: Powering the Ambrose rhythm section since 1928.

Born on December 24, 1912, Anne Lenner was singing with a band at Murray's Club in 1934 when Carroll Gibbons signed her up, but she made her radio debut with Charlie Kunz.

exactly a year, and the band which began to record in October was much revised. Max Goldberg, Tommy McQuater and George Chisholm were among the brass; Joe Crossman and Billy Amstell in the reeds; while the rhythm section comprised Bert Read, Ivor Mairants, Tiny Winters, Max Bacon and (late of Charlie Kunz) Jimmy Blades. Bert Ambrose was still picking the best.

At a time when there was a marked decrease in the number of good new songs coming along, Leo Robin and Ralph Rainger wrote a little gem, *Thanks for the Memory*, with its pungent lyric and ironically sweet melody. It was heard in Paramount's *The Big Broadcast of 1938*, in which Bob Hope made his screen debut. Shep Fields and his Rippling Rhythm were in this movie too. *Thanks for the Memory* won an Oscar for the best film song of the year. It was recorded by Billy Cotton and his Band, with Alan Breeze.

Another treasurable ballad was *Once in a While*, a love song in exquisite taste by Michael Edwards and Bud Green. Sam Browne recorded it with Jack Harris and his Band, as well as *The Pretty Little Patchwork Quilt*, a novelty by Elton Box, Sonny Cox, Paddy Roberts and Ralph Butler, though why such an engaging trifle should have required four experienced songwriters is beyond comprehension.

Music, Maestro, Please! was a sad but successful effort by Herb Magidson and Allie Wrubel. Its self-pitying sentiments were handled supremely well by Anne Lenner, one of the best girl singers around. She recorded it with Carroll Gibbons and the Savoy Hotel Orpheans.

The Lenner sisters from Leicester were very talented young ladies. Shirley Lenner sang with George Elrick and his Swing Music Makers; Judy Shirley (born February 25, 1907), with Maurice Winnick. Rosa Lenner was vocalist for a time with Jack White and his Collegians, while Ida Lenner was on the Halls. There was yet another sister, Maidie, who may not have turned professional.

Jimmy Eaton and Terry Shand had a few hits towards the close of the Thirties, in particular *I'm Gonna Lock My Heart and Throw Away the Key*, which Joe Loss and his Band recorded, with singer Clem Stevens. Loss was one of the few bandleaders actually turning out more records. He made 74 sides for Regal-Zonophone in 1938 and 97 in 1939, sticking to an uncompromisingly commercial style and employing good singers. Indeed, the majority of his recordings were almost entirely given over to the vocal.

Hawaii had been neglected by the tunesmiths once the singing cowboy took over, but a South Seas charmer made its debut in 1938 when Frank Loesser joined Alfred Newman to create *The Moon of Manakoora*, destined to become a classic of its kind. It received an initial boost from glamorous Dorothy Lamour, who sang it in Samuel Goldwyn's *The Hurricane*, her co-star being Jon Hall.

This enchanting song was recorded by Oscar Rabin and his Romany Band, with singer Beryl Davis, at their first session for Rex, following an absence from any studio of well over two years. Never prolific, Rabin made only 12 sides in 1938 and exactly double that number in 1939. Still the ideal palais bandleader, he would go on well into the post-war period, shedding the Romany tag, and occasionally forgetting himself by cutting loose with some quite creditable swing.

Victor Schertzinger's *Something to Sing About* made a pleasant recording on Columbia for Mantovani's little dance orchestra, one of several with vocals by Al Bowlly. Mantovani also recorded *The Humming Waltz*, a new Tolchard Evans number, with a Stanley Damerell lyric. The vocalist was Jack Plant.

Jack Hylton's latest band did not start to record until September, little of interest being waxed. Sam Browne was back, and would stay until Hylton ceased to be a bandleader; Peggy Dell and June Malo added a touch of glamour, as well as some stylish vocals.

Now It Can Be Told was sub-standard Irving Berlin, but Peggy Dell's rendition gave it an undeserved lustre. In contrast, June Malo had a very lively song by Eaton and Shand, *Why Doesn't Someone Tell Me These Things?* and she handled it exuberantly.

Beryl Davis: Harry, her father, made all the announcements for the Oscar Rabin band. Born in Plymouth on March 16, 1924, she became a band singer at 14!

June Malo: She swung the hits exuberantly for Jack Hylton's big showband.

Leslie Douglas had the vocal spot on Henry Hall's last record, made at the Birmingham Hippodrome on May 25, 1939.

Blue Skies are 'Round the Corner, Hughie Charles and Ross Parker informed us, at a time when war clouds were darkening ominously; and *Don't Let That Moon Get Away!* pleaded Joe Burke and James Monaco. Both were recorded by Henry Hall and his Orchestra, with vocals by Bob Mallin and Leslie Douglas respectively.

Undeterred by his previous failure, Glenn Miller formed a new band, the personnel of which would alter frequently until it settled down. In September it began to record for Bluebird, a cheaper label owned by Victor. Miller was still attracted to curious material, his maiden recording venture being a two-part, non-vocal arrangement of Thurlow Lieurance's *By the Waters of Minnetonka*, with his own trombone solo. As a concert ballad, with verse by J. M. Cavanass, it had been first heard in 1921.

But it was the rather odd acorn from which a mighty musical oak would grow all too swiftly; and when his clarinet-over-saxes 'Miller sound' caught on, his music would sweep all other sweet styles away. All? Well, not quite! Nobody ever changed Guy Lombardo's style, and it would still be heard when other bands were only melodious memories.

* * *

Dr Sigmund Spaeth believed that wars do not inspire good songs. Neither, I would venture to suggest, does an immediate pre-war period. Certainly, 1939 was a particularly barren year in that respect. The world was holding its breath, for it had become obvious, even to the most obtuse politician, that the uneasy peace of the past two decades could not last much longer. The only remaining question was when would it end; and Hitler answered that unequivocally on September 1 by sending his jack-booted hordes into Poland. Two days later, Britain and France declared war on Germany.

Jack Harris would disband in April, 1940, and go back home, prevented from returning here by the war. In 1939 he made records for HMV every month from January to September, with the exception of August, but like those of other leaders, few were of interest.

In April, the Harris band recorded *Heaven Can Wait*, with a lyric by bandleader Eddie de Lange and a tune by Jimmy van Heusen, whose real name was Edward Chester Babcock. Born at Syracuse, New York, on January 26, 1913, he had a struggle to make headway as a song composer, but from the late Thirties until well into the Fifties had a string of hits. He died in California in February 1990.

Harris' last recording session took place on the day that Hitler invaded Poland. Irving Berlin's *I'm Sorry for Myself*, not one of his best songs, was recorded on that grim day, with girl singer Pat Taylor.

So highly did Geraldo esteem Mitchell Parish and Peter de Rose's *Deep Purple*, he actually made a concert recording of it, occupying two sides of an HMV record. It had a lovely vocal by Eve Becke, otherwise the Countess di Rivarolo, who in previous years had sung for Roy Fox, Teddy Joyce, Louis Levy and Oscar Rabin. *Deep Purple* began as a piano piece, composed by de Rose in 1935, and waited four years for its lyric.

Paramount's *Paris Honeymoon* starred Bing Crosby as a wealthy cowboy, and gave him *The Funny Old Hills* to sing. An unusual, quite unforgettable novelty by Leo Robin and Ralph Rainger, it was waxed in May by Oscar Rabin and his

Romany Band, with vocalist Garry Gowan, who was born in Fulham on April 2, 1916.

In the spring, Jaromir Vejvoda's *Skoda Lasky* came here from Czechoslovakia by way of the United States, where Lew Brown had transformed it into *The Beer Barrel Polka*. Everyone loved to 'roll out the barrel', and this cheery song became one of the biggest hits of the year. George Scott-Wood recorded it for Regal-Zonophone with his London Piano-Accordion Band, which seems to have been phased out by the end of 1940.

So superb were several of the records made by Jack Hylton in 1939 it is sad to think our greatest British bandleader soon discarded the baton for the impresario's office. Some of the tunes he recorded had been waxed a little earlier by Glenn Miller, a pointer to the way things would go, but at least Hylton's arrangements were never imitative.

Gotta Get Some Shut-Eye was an early hit for Miller; a bouncy number by Johnny Mercer and Walter Donaldson, with a vocal by vivacious Marion Hutton, sister of tempestuous Betty, who ruined her film career by throwing one tantrum too many. Hylton recorded the song one month after Miller, with June Malo giving an equally lively rendition.

Dolly Elsie: Clear-voiced sister of Jack Hylton who later had her own radio show with organist Charles Smart.

During the last three months of 1939, Hylton's sister Dolly Elsie made some records with the band. Her clear voice and faultless diction put one in mind of Vera Lynn. Born at Stalybridge, she became a pantomime principal boy when she was 17. After leaving her brother's band, Dolly Elsie sang with Billy Cotton for four years, but also had her own morning radio programme, accompanied by organist Charles D. Smart.

She sang with tremendous verve, enlivening Hylton's recordings of *Get Out of Town*, a distinctive song by Cole Porter, and *Why Does My Heart Go Boom?* composed by the famous French singer Charles Trenet, with an English lyric by Roma Campbell Hunter.

Joe Burke and James Monaco joined forces to write songs for Universal's *East Side of Heaven*, starring Bing Crosby and Joan Blondell. *Sing a Song of Sunbeams* and *That Sly Old Gentleman from Featherbed Lane* were recorded by Billy Cotton and his Band, with Alan Breeze, but neither had any outstanding qualities.

Wishing Will Make It So was a simple and charming song which Buddy de Sylva wrote unaided. Ambrose recorded it with Denny Dennis. It was typical of American sentimental ballads of the time, but British songwriters had turned to the war for inspiration. *We're Gonna Hang Out the Washing on the Siegfried Line* must have put Jimmy Kennedy and Michael Carr on Adolf Hitler's black list very quickly. It apparently infuriated him. Ambrose handed out the vocal to Jack Cooper, who was back on his payroll.

Quite a few comedy numbers appeared in 1939. Another hit was *Kiss Me Goodnight, Sergeant-Major*, by Art Noel and Don Pelosi. Sounding remarkably like something from World War One, it was sung by Les Carew, one of Ambrose's trombonists.

In very different mood was the carefree cynicism of Cole Porter's *My Heart Belongs to Daddy*, in which a young lady expressed her loyalty to her sugar daddy. Evelyn Dall was Ambrose's choice on that occasion. Somehow, one cannot quite associate such a song with Vera Lynn.

Somewhere in France With You, written and composed by Michael Carr, was more in Vera's style. She recorded it on December 8, a fortnight before Ambrose went back again to the May Fair Hotel. He would continue to make records until 1961, well into the era of the long-playing album.

Hughie Charles and Ross Parker soon turned to war themes of varying quality. *Berlin or Bust* was pure sabre-rattling, but Jack Jackson recorded it in November at his last recording session. However, the war had been over for two years when he finally laid aside his baton.

Joe Loss took his band so frequently to the recording studio it was inevitable a good deal of dross would be waxed. But despite a surfeit of mediocrity, several remarkably good records were made in 1939. *A Violin in Vienna*, by Art Strauss and Bob Dale, was simple and unaffected. With a vocal by Monte Rey, it hearkened back to a time when the name of Austria's capital conjured up all the magic of Viennese music and song, gone, alas, these many years. *We'll Meet Again* was Hughie Charles and Ross Parker in a more sentimental mood, which suited them better. This time the singer was Chick Henderson.

The Western song had almost had its day, but it did not go out with a whimper. On the contrary, *South of the Border* was one of the biggest hits Jimmy Kennedy and Michael Carr wrote together, a sensation in Britain and America. Joe Loss recorded it with Monte Rey, whose virile, romantic voice made him a star. Born on October 5, 1900, his real name was James Montgomery Fyfe. When he was getting on in years he

Top – *Evelyn Dall: She gave Vera Lynn a cool reception.*

Above – *Monte Rey: Romantic Scottish tenor who went 'South of the Border'.*

Bob Mallin: Cowboy songs for Henry Hall on his last recording date. He is seen here in June, 1939, with his fiancée, Yvonne Mageean.

used to talk wistfully of making a come-back but, of course, he never did. He died on August 5, 1982.

South of the Border was also recorded at Birmingham Hippodrome by Henry Hall and his Orchestra, with Bob Mallin, who made some records in his own name for Decca, mostly of cowboy songs. It was Hall's last session. Another famous name would shortly disappear from the catalogues, although as a showman Hall had many good years before him.

In my view, one of the best records Joe Loss ever made was *Begin the Beguine*, that poignant, yearning love song, with its seductive, tropical melody, which Cole Porter wrote in 1935 for *Jubilee*, at New York's Imperial Theatre. Loss, who died on June 6, 1990, devoted the entire record to Chick Henderson, but the band's subtle accompaniment enhanced a superb vocal.

Chick Henderson had been a popular amateur singer in his native town of West Hartlepool before winning a song competition and joining Joe Loss. In 1939 he was 27. He made his last record for Loss on January 10, 1942, and on June 28, 1944, was killed by a bomb.

Jack Payne took a new band to the Decca studios in

October, cutting his first sides for three years. One was a comedy number; the others war songs. The best, beyond question, was Charles and Parker's patriotic *There'll Always be an England*, sung by Robert Ashley. In 1988 the melody was used for a television commercial.

This band was broken up at the end of July, 1940, and may have been Payne's last regular one, although he recorded for HMV from February to November, 1945. In 1941 he married the concert pianist and violinist Peggy Cochrane, and eventually became a BBC disc jockey in the days when music took precedence over vapid chatter. He died at Tunbridge Wells on December 4, 1969.

The wartime black-out inspired Art Strauss, Bob Dale and Sonny Miller's *They Can't Black-out the Moon*. It was recorded by Carroll Gibbons and his Savoy Hotel Orpheans, with a vocal duet by Anne Lenner and Eric Whitley.

The American singer Kenny Baker, who recorded for Victor, should not be confused with the British hot trumpet player who used to broadcast after the war with his 'Dozen'. *On a Little Street in Singapore* was by Billy Hill and Peter de Rose who, having forsaken the Wild West for the Far East, did not seem particularly at home there. Baker did his best to inject some magic into a singularly uninspired potboiler.

Even swing bandleaders had to record commercial songs if they wished to pay their bills, and usually performed them supremely well. Count Basie gave Irving Mills and Henry Nemo's *Blame it on My Last Affair* the kind of treatment expected from a musician of his calibre, waxing it in New York. It was a well above average torch song; and in Helen Humes he had a charming vocalist.

It is only fitting that this all too sketchy review of the popular music of two decades should end with Glenn Miller, who became to the Forties what Paul Whiteman had been to the Twenties. Much that Miller committed to wax was abysmal trash, but he made some beautiful records too, and they have ensured that he will never be forgotten. Self-willed and autocratic, he died needlessly at the early age of 40. Against orders, he took off for France in a night of storm on December 15, 1944, and the small aircraft has never been found. Of such stuff are legends made.

Miller had his 'sound' by 1939, and it was never lovelier than on his recording of *Moonlight Serenade*, a tune he had composed while with the Ray Noble band. Then he had called it *Now I Lay Me Down to Weep*. The title change and Mitchell Parish's lyric came later.

Frankie Carle's *Sunrise Serenade* was recorded by Miller's tightly disciplined band that year too, and so was *And the Angels Sing*, originally a swing number by hot trumpeter Ziggy Elman. Johnny Mercer put words to it, Miller turned it into a so-smooth ballad, and Ray Eberle sang it without a trace of fire. But the age of Glenn Miller extends far beyond the scope of this volume.

Just what, the reader may reasonably enquire, is a 'golden age'? Perhaps it can best be described as the period in which anything reaches and maintains its finest flowering. The great days of American dance bands began in 1920, when Paul Whiteman cut those wonderful first sides for Victor; but they were already over before the Depression came along.

Here in Britain they started a little later and lasted rather longer. Probably our 'golden age' began in 1923 when the fabulous Savoy Orpheans blew their first notes. Once the Thirties had passed the half-way mark it was fading, and by 1938 it was finished.

Such assertions on my part are debatable, of course. What is undeniable is our debt of gratitude to all those skilful recording engineers who enshrined a wealth of popular music in brittle shellac. For years such records were played and put aside, their numbers ever depleted, until perceptive collectors began to recognise their value. In recent times, much has been lovingly transferred onto long-playing albums, such has been the re-awakening of interest in this minor art form.

Too much of our musical heritage has been lost because people cared little about the pre-war gramophone record. Even today, light orchestral music and most of the ballad singers (Dawson and McCormack being notable exceptions) are being neglected. Let us hope that at least the best from the dancing years will now be preserved.

INDEX

(Folios in italic type indicate illustrations)

CREATIVE AND OTHER PERSONNEL

SONGS AND MUSIC

SHOWS — STAGE, SCREEN AND RADIO

RECORD LABELS

BIBLIOGRAPHY

And the Bands Played On, Sid Colin; Elm Tree, 1977

BBC Hand/Year Book; BBC, 1929, 1932, 1933

Big Bands, Peter Gammond and Raymond Horricks; Patrick Stephens, 1981

Blue Amberol Cylinders, Sydney H. Carter; Talking Machine Review, 1978

British Dance Bands 1912-1939, Brian Rust and Edward S. Walker; Storyville, 1973

British Dance Bands on Record 1911-1945, B. Rust and S. Forbes; Gen. Gramo. Pub., 1987

The Dance Band Era, Albert McCarthy; Spring, 1974

Dictionary of Modern Music and Musicians, A. Eaglefield-Hull; J.M. Dent, 1924

Dominion Records, Arthur Badrock; Talking Machine Review, 1986

The Fabulous Phonograph 1877-1977, Roland Gelatt; Cassell, 1977

The Footlights Flickered, W. MacQueen-Pope; Herbert Jenkins, 1959

Gramophone Records of the First World War, Brian Rust; David & Charles, 1976.

A Guide to Popular Music, Peter Gammond and Peter Clayton; Phoenix House, 1960

Halliwell's Film Guide, Leslie Halliwell; Granada, 1977

Here's to the Next Time, Henry Hall; Odhams, 1955

A History of Popular Music in America, Sigmund Spaeth; Phoenix House, 1960

HMV Studio House Bands 1912-1939, Brian Rust; Storyville, 1976

Hollywood, Mayfair and All That Jazz, Roy Fox; Leslie Frewin, 1975

The Hollywood Musical, Clive Hirschhorn; Octopus, 1981

I Did It My Way, Billy Cotton; Harrap, 1970

I'm on a See-Saw, Vivian Ellis; Michael Joseph, 1953

Lew Stone – A Career in Music, Kenith Trodd; Joyce Stone, 1971

Memory Lane 1890-1925, Max Wilk; Studio International, 1973

The MGM Story, John Douglas Eames; Octopus, 1982

Milestones to the Silver Jubilee, H.C. Dent; Halcyon, 1935

Musical Comedy, Raymond Mander and Joe Mitchenson; Peter Davies, 1969

Of Mice and Magic, Leonard Maltin; New American Library, 1980

A Pictorial History of the Silent Screen, Daniel Blum; Spring, 1953

The Picturegoer's Who's Who and Encyclopaedia; Odhams, 1933

Radio – The Great Years, Derek Parker; David & Charles, 1977

Revue, Raymond Mander and Joe Mitchenson; Peter Davies, 1971

Scott Joplin and the Ragtime Era, Peter Gammond; Abacus, 1975

Second Movement, Spike Hughes; Museum Press, 1951

Lawrence Wright: Souvenirs for a Century, Lawrette Wright; Wright, 1988

The Sweet and Twenties, Beverley Nichols; Quality Book Club, 1958

They All Played Ragtime, Rudi Blesh and Harriet Janis; Oak Publications, 1971

This – Is London, Stuart Hibberd; MacDonald & Evans, 1950

Tit-Bits Year Book, Leonard Crocombe and C.H. Dand; George Newnes, 1930

The Twenties, John Montgomery; Geo. Allen & Unwin, 1970

The Victor Master Book 1925-1936, Brian Rust; Rust, 1969

Vocal Refrain, Vera Lynn; W.H. Allen, 1975

The Warner Bros. Story, Clive Hirschhorn; Octopus, 1983

We Danced All Night, Barbara Cartland; Hutchinson, 1971

Who's Who; A. & C. Black, 1933

Who's Who in Music, Sir Landon Ronald; Shaw, 1935

Who's Who in the Theatre, John Parker; Pitman, 1930, 1949

World Film Encyclopaedia, Clarence Winchester; Amalgamated Press, 1933

The World of Big Bands, Arthur Jackson; David & Charles, 1977

Yesterdays – Popular Song in America, Charles Hamm; W.W. Norton, 1979

You Must Remember This, Mark White; Frederick Warne, 1983

Zonophone Studio House Bands 1924-1932, Brian Rust; Storyville, 1976

NEWSPAPERS AND MAGAZINES

Daily Express	*Film Weekly*	*Play Pictorial*
Daily Mail	*Melody Maker*	*Radio Pictorial*
Daily Mirror	*Musical Opinion*	*Radio Times*
Daily Sketch	*Needle Time*	*Sounds Vintage*
The Daily Telegraph	*News Chronicle*	*Sunday Pictorial*
Evening News	*News of the World*	*Theatre World*
Evening Standard	*The People*	*The Times*
Film Pictorial	*Picture Show*	*T.V. Times*

RECORD CATALOGUES AND SUPPLEMENTS

Brunswick	*His Master's Voice*	*Victor*
Columbia	*Imperial*	*Zonophone*
Decca	*Parlophone*	